WALLEYE
WISDOM

WALLEYE
WISDOM

Al Lindner
Dave Csanda
Tony Dean
Ron Lindner
Bob Ripley
Doug Stange

In-Fisherman® Corporate Educational Publications
Book Division

Director *Al Lindner*
Publisher *Ron Lindner*
General Manager *Dan Sura*

Executive Editor *Doug Stange*
Editor *Steve Quinn*
Managing Editor *Joann Phipps*
Production Director *Scott Pederson*

WALLEYE WISDOM

Book Compiled by *Bob Ripley*
Cover Art by *Larry Tople*
Artwork by *Chuck Nelson and Jim Cervin*
Typesetting by *Nordell Graphic Communications*
Printing by *Bang Printing*

ISBN 0-929384-49-0

The In-Fisherman®
"Handbook of Strategies" Book Series

One of the

(F) Fish + (L) Location + (P) Presentation = (S) Success℠

Educational Services

First Edition, 1983	Ninth Printing, 1986	Seventeenth Printing, 1993
Second Printing, 1983	Tenth Printing, 1987	Eighteenth Printing, 1994
Third Printing, 1984	Eleventh Printing, 1988	Nineteenth Printing, 1995
Fourth Printing, 1985	Twelfth Printing, 1988	Twentieth Printing, 1997
Fifth Printing, 1985	Thirteenth Printing, 1989	Twenty-first Printing, 1998
Sixth Printing, 1985	Fourteenth Printing, 1990	Twenty-second Printing, 1999
Seventh Printing, 1985	Fifteenth Printing, 1991	
Eighth Printing, 1986	Sixteenth Printing, 1993	

Library of Congress Catalog
Card Number 82-82692

ACKNOWLEDGEMENT

W hen any book is written there are a number of people who have helped to make it possible. This is particularly true of a book like this one, since no one man could have written it. Over the last two decades, a person here has made a contribution—and then a person there has added to it—and so little by little we learned more and more of the way of the walleye. So, at this time we would like to give a sincere "thanks" to all who, over the years, directly or indirectly contributed to the accumulated knowledge of WALLEYE WISDOM. Men like the legendary Bill Binkelman who helped devise the Calendar Periods, Ron Lindner who developed the body of water classification system, Dr. Dwight Burkhardt who did research on walleye vision, biologist Dick Sternberg who helped explain the predator/prey relationship, Carl Lowrance who offered the technology of the depth finder, and anglers like Gary Roach who worked on the fishing systems themselves. The list of greats, near-greats and little-knowns could go on and on.

Beyond this kind of background material, each of the authors themselves have shared in breakthroughs of major importance. Through their on-the-water experience, both individually and with great walleye fishermen from all across the North American continent, many secrets, tricks and tips are able to be passed on to you in this original edition of WALLEYE WISDOM—for indeed, that is what it is—*wisdom*.

IN-FISHERMAN MASTERPIECE SERIES

- **WALLEYE WISDOM:** A Handbook of Strategies
- **PIKE:** A Handbook of Strategies
- **SMALLMOUTH BASS:** A Handbook of Strategies
- **CRAPPIE WISDOM:** A Handbook of Strategies
- **CHANNEL CATFISH FEVER:** A Handbook of Strategies
- **LARGEMOUTH BASS IN THE 90s:** A Handbook of Strategies
- **BIG BASS MAGIC**
- **FISHING FUNDAMENTALS**
- **ICE FISHING SECRETS**

Each masterpiece book represents the collaborative effort of fishing experts. The books don't represent a regional perspective or the opinions of one good angler. Each masterpiece book teems with information applicable to all areas of the country and to any fishing situation.

In-Fisherman Inc., Two In-Fisherman Drive, Brainerd, MN 56425, 218/829-1648

TABLE OF CONTENTS

ACKNOWLEDGEMENTS
INTRODUCTION
I WALLEYE WISDOM BASIC KNOWLEDGE

INTRODUCTION

A long-time favorite of "northwoods" fishermen, the walleye today, through stocking efforts, is now available in more and more diverse regions of the country. Anglers in such far-flung corners as the Columbia River in Washington, Rye Patch Reservoir in Nevada, Lake Meredith in Texas, Wilson Reservoir in Kansas and the Missouri River in Montana now have something in common with anglers in the Dakotas, Minnesota, Wisconsin, on Lake Erie and in Ontario, Canada. In fact, recent studies indicate that walleye fishing, in terms of popularity, is the fastest-growing segment of the angling world. Today, walleyes are in reach of anglers almost everywhere.

More and more fishery agencies across the nation are setting aside portions of their fishing programs to include walleyes. Why? Well, the answer's simple: The walleye not only is one of the finest eating fish—but it fights well, schools up, bites readily at times—and can be caught by novice as well as expert anglers. With a recommendation like this, it is little wonder there is such a growing interest.

In the last decade there have been a number of major advancements in walleye fishing—not the least of which were the use of the depth finder, and the innovation of backtrolling and deep water fishing systems popularized by Ron and Al Lindner. However, walleye fishing is more than live bait and structure fishing. Through modern technology, we have been able (by way of research like electronic tagging studies) to learn how walleyes adapt to various kinds of environments. We now know that walleyes will use weeds as cover in certain classes of lakes, and in other types they won't. We've learned that there are predictable movements in certain categories of rivers, and have documented them. We've also determined that walleyes might use timber as cover in some types of reservoirs—but in other kinds of reservoirs, avoid it. More than this, we are aware that the predator/prey relationship (what kind of walleye food is available) affects not only how healthy a walleye fishery will be—but where the fish will be and how they will act and react in that body of water. Then, too, we have cracked the seasonal code of how walleyes will most probably respond in spring, summer, fall and winter. And we even know that they will react season by season differently in a lake, a river or a reservoir. Until now no one has put together a book on all these modern aspects of walleye fishing.

Over the years, the publishers, editors and contributors of the *IN-FISHER-MAN* Magazine have pioneered the art of walleye angling. Most major breakthroughs were either published first in the magazine or spearheaded by one of its people. Therefore, probably no one was more qualified to compile a complete book of *WALLEYE WISDOM* than these folks. Because the subject is so broad—and spans such diverse regions of North America—no one person would have done justice to such an undertaking. Therefore, six authors combined their experience, contacts and know-how to produce this comprehensive book.

Throughout the book we make use of the *IN-FISHERMAN* classification system of lakes, rivers, and reservoirs, and our Calendar Period format, to *exactly* explain specific circumstances—in terms of when (what season, what time of day, etc.), and where (the exact structural locale). In this way, when we explain "presentation" (how to go about catching the walleye), the reader will be able to visualize exactly under what circumstances to apply that specific method. No guesswork here!

WALLEYE WISDOM is at once a reference guide and a handbook. It is meant to be read for background material and to act as a tutor for practical applications on the water. The book is written in a "result-oriented" manner. After reading the book, you can weigh its worth by the fish you catch and your ever-increasing ability to adapt to different walleye waters and different seasons of the year.

Chapter 1

THE WAY OF THE WALLEYE

S *tizostedion vitreum.* The walleye! Whether called dore, jacksalmon, grass
pike, gum pike, yellow pickerel or just plain ol' marble eyes, the walleye is
without question one of North America's most sought after fish.

Adored by gourmets for its superb table qualities and by sport fishermen for
its crafty ways and stubborn fight, the walleye derives its name from its most
prominent feature—bulging, glossy eyes.

The eyes, indeed! Always crystal-clear and glistening, these magnificent
organs deserve more than mere mention-in-passing. It's the eyes that help fit
the fish into its unique niche, and determine so much of how the fish reacts.
Their unusual construction allows walleyes to see well during low-light
periods. Even though walleyes can feed very effectively in the dead of night or
in the light of day, they feed most efficiently at twilight, when prey is still active but their ability to see is diminishing rapidly. The walleye is often considered primarily a "twilight feeder."

Besides the eyes, other prominent walleye features include its torpedo-shaped body, usually some five times longer than deep; two distinct spined dorsal fins; and a broad, forked tail with a pronounced white spot on the lower tip. Color, however, can vary widely and is not a reliable guide to identification. Depending on the water, dark-backed walleyes may range from olive drab or dark olive along the sides and white or gold underneath, to slate gray, gold, or even blue along the sides and white or pale yellow below.

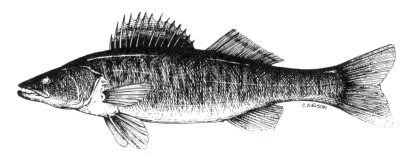

Interestingly, even though walleyes are commonly termed "walleyed pike, " they are not part of the pike family. Actually, the walleye is the largest North American member of the family Percidae, or just plain perch.

Walleyes and their close cousins the sauger, yellow perch, log perch, and so many of the darters, do best in waters which are neither extremely cold, clear and infertile (termed oligotrophic), or at the other extreme, warm, turbid and very fertile (termed eutrophic). Walleyes do best in moderately fertile and clear lakes (termed mesotrophic). Scientists call them "cool water" fish, as opposed to the largemouth bass, a warm water species, or the cold water lake trout. That's not to say walleyes can't tolerate a wide range of water conditions. They can survive in other water types, but they flourish in mesotrophic, cool water environments.

Most experts believe walleyes were originally a fish of rivers. Obviously, they have adapted to life in the type of closed environments provided by lakes and reservoirs. True to their heritage, however, walleyes favor rivers or streams as spawning sites when they are available. They may even travel hundreds of miles to accomplish this reproductive imperative in a native stream. But walleyes do spawn very successfully on windswept, shallow lake or reservoir shoals providing proper bottom content—rock-rubble—is available.

The walleye's present range is shown on our walleye range map. But never forget that walleyes function in many different kinds of waters. Cold, cool and warm water environments can all support walleyes, although they do best in cool, mesotrophic waters. Sparkling Canadian lakes can hold tremendous walleye populations. They are also found in many adult, mature and middle-aged rivers. And the fish are not uncommon to highland, hill-land and plateau reservoirs—especially if they were native to the rivers feeding these impoundments. Within these diverse habitats, they can adapt to life in or around timber, weeds, brush, rocks, or even open water, and will utilize a variety of prey species as food. The walleye is an adaptable critter!

Certainly, stocking has expanded the walleye's availability to anglers. Until

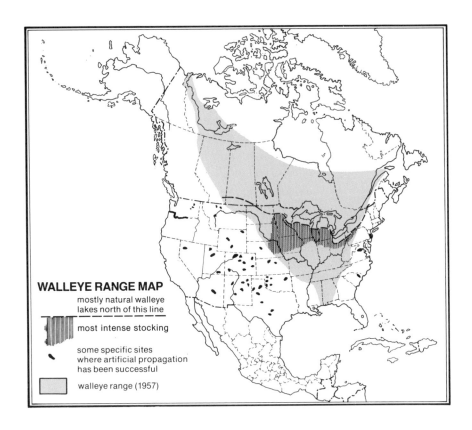

WALLEYE RANGE MAP

mostly natural walleye
lakes north of this line

most intense stocking

some specific sites
where artificial propagation
has been successful

walleye range (1957)

recently, this expansion was generally accomplished within its original native range. Only in the last two or three decades has the walleye been successfully transplanted outside its native range. While records detailing the introduction of many species are well documented, this isn't so for the walleye. Reliable records date back only 20 or 30 years.

In the great walleye states of Minnesota and Wisconsin, most early plantings were of the "wildcat" variety. Pioneer fish culturists and game wardens simply filled a metal milk container full of fry and dumped them at will. Today it is difficult to know if a lake originally had walleyes and lost them as the lake aged, or if the lake never had them in the first place. The few existing walleyes in a lake may be the product of haphazard stocking, or the result of habitat deterioration and/or a steadily aging ecosystem. Our point, though, is that walleyes were not native to many lakes!

You must realize that walleye populations will vary considerably from one body of water to the next. Just because someone catches a ten pound walleye in the spring doesn't mean the water has an excellent walleye population. Inquiries at local bait shops or your fisheries department should garner information about your area walleye populations. If the population is marginal, fish it only if the fish are large or if you have few other choices. Obviously, it's always smart to play the percentages and fish waters that have good walleye populations. One of our primary objectives in *WALLEYE WISDOM* is to teach you how to recognize—and, of course, fish—a good walleye fishery.

It's been said that a walleye is a walleye wherever it swims. Yes, the fish does have a basic nature it conforms to. But each fish, and especially the adaptable walleye, also makes certain adaptations based on environmental factors. There is no major difference between walleyes in timbered reservoirs or natural lakes, but because the environments are different, the fish in each area react somewhat differently. Thus, while walleyes will spawn in the 43-49°F temperature range, natural lake spawning may occur on rock-rubble shoals, and reservoir spawning on rip-rap at the face of the dam. It's the same basic fish, but the environment's different, so the fish adapts and uses what's available.

It's also important to bring up this point: In any body of water, walleyes will not all be doing the same thing at the same time. In a natural lake, it isn't unusual to find fish using weed edges, deep rocks, gravel humps and feeder creek areas, *all at the same time.* Walleye location is an interesting challenge. Taking walleyes consistently takes some thinking!

Walleyes are also well-known "wanderers." They will set up "activity centers" for short periods, only to move again when the period ends. In shallow, soup-bowl-shaped lakes, the walleyes often roam for the entire year, rarely stopping in any area for more than a week. Like cattle grazing on the open prairie, they move on and on.

That's not to say that your approach to finding walleyes in these lakes is haphazard. The fish will often move out to a hard bottom edge during the day and move towards shore during the evening. During certain periods the fish may also suspend in open water. The point is, experience has shown where you should spend time fishing during certain yearly periods, on certain water types. Somewhere in this book, we'll cover the type of water you personally fish.

There are simply no ironclad patterns you can rely on, such as walleyes always liking drop-offs, or always relating to deep, rock-capped sunken islands. They may relate to such structural configurations, but only if conditions allow.

Time and time again, you'll find that walleye location depends on a host of interrelated factors that can vary considerably from one body of water to another. One factor remains constant, however. The walleye needs to eat! Except during the spawning period, the fish always relates to forage of some sort.

Thus, we often talk of prey/predator relationships and their effect on walleye location. This, too, can be a complex topic, in part because it means we have to study the movement of prey species as much as we do the movement of walleyes. The two are interrelated.

It's obvious that a 12 inch walleye can't forage successfully on a seven inch perch. Therefore, not only is general prey location important, but the size of prey using an area will tend to determine what size walleyes will be there.

The fact that walleyes school or group is no secret. This schooling tendency is one sign of a complex social life. Three things are imperative in the walleye's life: reproduction, suitable habitat and food. As with other fish, schooling

Generally speaking, fish tend to grow faster in more southerly latitudes because of a longer growing season. Since they are cold-blooded, their metabolic rate is considerably faster at higher temperatures (within limits of temperature acclimation). However, since growth is mainly a function of density and food supply (the amount of food available per individual fish), fish from well-balanced, less dense populations in the North may well grow at a faster rate than fish from overcrowded populations in the South. To further complicate the picture, slower-growing fish from colder, more northerly latitudes enjoy greater longevity than their more southerly counterparts, and thus may reach similar or greater ultimate size even though growing at a slower rate.

Like the muskellunge, the walleye also appears to be a fish that had its origins in rivers. Today, the species is found in more than 1,000 Wisconsin lakes and all major rivers, but that was not originally the case. A glance at the original range of the walleye (below) in that state shows that is was quite restricted. At that time, most waters were basically largemouth bass waters with northern pike as a secondary predator.

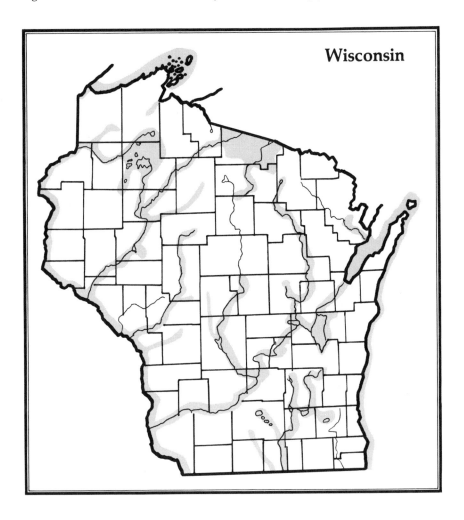

Wisconsin

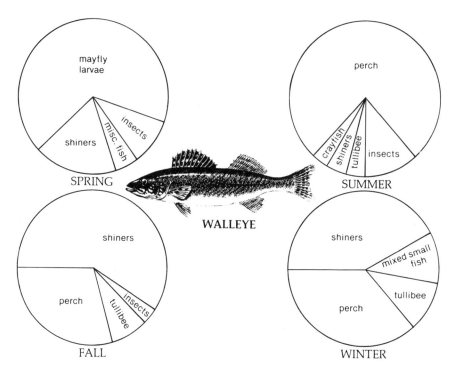

SPRING — mayfly larvae, shiners, misc. fish, insects

SUMMER — perch, crayfish, shiners, tullibee, insects

FALL — shiners, perch, tullibee, insects

WINTER — shiners, mixed small fish, tullibee, perch

WALLEYE

SEASONAL FOOD TARGETS OF WALLEYES

At different times of the year certain kinds of aquatic foods are more abundant than others.

For fish to survive and thrive, food must be available to a fish within its niche. The accompanying charts show how walleyes make use of the different foods they find in their environments. It was assembled from a study of stomach samples of fish in an early meso lake in Wisconsin.

In meso lakes, when mayfly larvae are abundant in spring, the young-of-the-year perch are not big enough for efficient predation by adult fish. So the larvae are heavily preyed upon and make up a significant portion of the walleye's diet. But, by mid-to-late summer the small perch grow to a proper size and the walleyes switch targets. Then, as the perch population begins to dwindle in fall, the shiner minnows that have spent the summer running open water tend to move shoreward. The walleyes (under certain circumstances), then begin to feed on the larger minnows. In winter, ciscoes and other mixed small fish become food targets, along with perch and shiners. This occurs because the entire food population is reduced and protein is at a premium.

It's obvious that knowing the seasonal location of mayfly larvae, perch, shiners, or ciscoes will make it easier to find walleyes.

or grouping helps to satisfy these needs.

The response of a school of perch, ciscoes or shiner minnows is synchronized. A "cloud" of baitfish may seem disoriented, but once a predator approaches, they dart away in unison like a single living organism. Even when they change direction, they tend to maintain the same distance between themselves. If a fish slashes into the group, it immediately disperses, but still with some organization.

For the walleye, schooling (grouping) is an aid in the hunt. Packs of walleyes herding or ambushing prey are simply more efficient at feeding.

Although we refer to "schools" of adult walleye, strictly speaking, a school of fish acts in perfect unison. Walleyes don't do this. Thus, technically speaking, if a number of walleyes are working together, "aggregation" is more descriptive than school. Yet "school" is used universally, and we'll use it throughout this book.

The ability to recognize how walleyes adapt and respond to different environments is the key to consistent fishing. The following two studies vividly demonstrate how walleyes make seasonal adaptations within different bodies of water.

APPROXIMATE WEIGHT OF WALLEYES BY LENGTH

LENGTH	WEIGHT
12"	10 oz.
13"	13 oz.
14"	1 lb.
15"	1¼ lbs.
16"	1½ lbs.
17"	1¾ lbs.
18"	2¼ lbs.
19"	2½ lbs.
20"	3 lbs.
21"	3½ lbs.
22"	4 lbs.
24"	5 lbs.
26"	7 lbs.
28"	8¾ lbs.
30"	11 lbs.
32"	14 lbs.

Note: These are estimated averages.

WALLEYE MOVEMENTS IN RIVERS

Studies of walleye behavior in rivers are not scarce, but they are little publicized! Perhaps one reason is that rivers often play second fiddle to the more glamorous lake scene in prime areas of the walleye range.

Dave Bahr studied walleye movements on the Mississippi River as part of his Master's Degree requirements at the University of Wisconsin, LaCrosse. His study was conducted on a big river environment; one with large navigational dams, backwater areas and various structural elements.

Dave tagged a total of 12 female walleyes with radio transmitters. All of the fish were four or five years old and weighed about three-to-five pounds.

Between March 13 and May 4, 1979, Dave spent nearly 1,000 hours tracking these walleyes. Sometimes, the fish were observed 'round-the-clock', while at other times they were followed for shorter periods. Dave found that walleye behavior and mood changes in different types of current. This, of course, is important because it affects your location as well as your choice of presentation.

In slack water areas, the fish swam three times farther between stops than they did in areas where there was current. It was postulated that reduced current flow forced the fish to move about more to find food. On the other hand, the flow in an eddy directs food right to the fish in a concentrated area.

Dave observed two types of swimming patterns. He labeled them "random" or "directional." Random swimming is movement having no specific direction of travel and is characterized by a slow rate of travel over short distances (30 to 1,000 feet per hour). Directional swimming was characterized by rapid movement (1,000 to 4,000 feet per hour) between areas, usually in relatively straight lines and over longer distances.

Interestingly, the fish swam the fastest (3,000 feet per hour) and covered the greatest average distance (about 2,200 feet) when they swam at right angles to the current. Whether the fish were swimming with or against the current, their speed was nearly identical. Apparently, current had little or no effect on swimming speed. However, when swimming against current they swam for shorter periods and covered less distance.

HOW DEEP DID THE FISH GO?

Dave's walleyes preferred depths less than 16 feet during most of the tracking period. The fish spent 95% of their time in slack water, and 67% in the slack water of eddies. In the eddies, there was a definite preference for three-to-six foot depths. In all slack water areas, the fish usually used water from five-to-ten feet deep.

DAILY MOVEMENTS

Between 9:00 P.M. and 3:00 A.M., the walleyes were usually resting in slack water. At about 3:00 A.M., the walleyes started to move. Some of the fish moved out of the slack water and began to cruise randomly.

Eventually, about 9:00 A.M., the walleyes would take up positions in the eddy areas and would stay there for most of the day. Eddy activity usually peaked at about noon. There was an increase in random movement at 3:00 P.M., and this movement lasted until about 8:00 P.M., when the fish would again position themselves in slack water.

AREAS OF USE
EDDIES AND SLACK WATER AREAS

In the tailwater area immediately below the dam, the fish established 15 areas where they spent at least an hour or more. They spent the majority of their time relating to two broad types of "current breaks," eddies and slack water. The eddy and slack water areas used by walleyes are shown in the aerial photo.

The eddies contained current speeds varying from "slow" to "strong." Maximum depth in the eddies was about 21 feet, but six-to-twelve feet was more common. The bottom content in eddy areas was usually sand.

Use of specific areas near Lock and Dam 7 of the Upper Mississippi River by nine different radio-tagged walleyes during spring, 1976.

Areas	Number of Tagged fish using Area	Hours in Area
Eddy Areas		
C	7	12.41
D	2	0.82
F	4	21.96
G	6	34.62
H	4	9.28
J	1	33.95
K	1	3.9
L	4	6.47
N	4	25.7
O	1	3.17
Slack Water Areas		
A	5	111.22
B	1	2.25
E	2	64.75
I	2	5.45
M	2	23.31
Total eddy use	9	38.7
Total Slack Water Use	6	52.7

Eddies occurred at the points marked C, D, F, G, H, J, K, L, N and O. Wing dams or small points jutting into the river caused the eddies at H, N, J and L, while eddies F and G formed at the dam gates as water funneled out. Eddies C and D were backwashes from current as it cut under a bridge. A fallen tree formed eddy K and a submerged sandbar created eddy O. Interestingly, area G was the eddy the walleyes used most frequently.

Slack water areas contained no measurable currents. Maximum depth in the slack water was 22 feet, but depth averaged six feet. Bottom content ranged from muck to rock to sand with mixtures thereof. The smallest slack water area covered less than one-half square mile, and the largest about nine square miles.

Slack water areas are labeled A, B, E, I and M. The walleyes used area A most frequently. On the whole, the walleyes used these areas (A most frequently) more than eddy areas, spending only 39% of their time in eddies versus 53% in slack water. Remember, however, that the walleyes usually used slack water during their resting periods.

SUMMER WALLEYE MOVEMENTS IN A NATURAL LAKE

This study was conducted on West Okoboji, a mesotrophic lake with a maximum depth of 135 feet and large areas of sand, gravel and glacial boulders. The lake's hard-bottom areas often extend to the 50 foot level, at which point soft bottom "ooze" dominates. Moderately sharp drop-offs occur in many areas and the lake stratifies thermally at about 50 feet during the summer. Light penetration is excellent, so weedgrowth often extends to as much as 30 feet. The fish in this study were found mainly in the largest bay, Emerson Bay, and in the northern one-third of the lake. Both areas have large expanses of dense weedgrowth.

Physical Characteristics of Radio-Tracked Okoboji Walleyes— Their Histories of Observation

Fish No.	Lenght	Weight	Sex	Capture date	Release date	Total elapsed days of contact	Total contacts
00a	25.8 in.	7.0 lb.	F	8 June	8 June	203	76
55a,b	23.1 in.	4.9 lb.	M	15 May	15 May	357	81
66b	25.0 in.	5.7 lb.	F	10-16 April	1 May	371	82
77b	23.0 in.	4.3 lb.	M	10-16 April	1 May	379	62
88a,b	24.4 in.	4.2 lb.	F	6 May	6 May	366	73
99c	23.2 in.	4.2 lb.	M	10-16 April	1 May	86	43

a. Fish capture/release site the same: for other fish, capture site is unknown and release was at random locations.
b. Transmitters that were operational as of late July, 1977.
c. Fish captured by angler, 25 July, 1976.

Of the six fish tracked, five spent the great majority of their time in these shallow areas relating to weeds. Only one of the fish took up residence in deeper water not related to weeds.

These walleyes were found in weeds, not because they had made a migration to feed there, but because that's where they lived. This study is significant because it scientifically documents that walleyes in some environments prefer weeds during the Summer Period, even when there were so-called "classic" rock and drop-off areas present.

Another significant observation from this study is that there may very well be two different types of walleye populations in some natural lakes during the Summer Periods. This is important because the two different populations behave differently. Both populations were most active at night, but the shallow, weed-oriented fish were by far the most active in terms of distance moved.

Even during the day the shallow fish moved the most. The single deep fish being tracked stayed in a very small (within one-quarter mile) area all summer long. This fish moved in the predictable pattern usually associated with walleyes—the proverbial deep to shallow water nocturnal movements. When this fish moved it usually traveled from about 30 feet of water up a tapering rock bar into about 18 feet of water. It rarely came into contact with weed edges and never ventured into the weedbeds. The five weed fish, by comparison, made movements that were predictable in the sense that they usually stayed within the weeds and close to their activity center. One common error made by anglers is thinking that walleyes can only find their way around

12

weedbeds by following edges. Scattered, indiscriminate movements seem to best describe the activity of the weed fish.

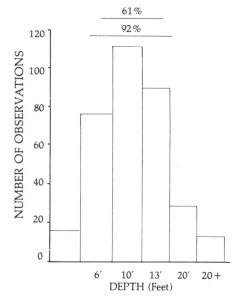

The Most Commonly Used Depths for 5 Weed-Oriented Walleyes in Lake Okoboji.

The accompanying chart shows the depths most commonly used by the 5 shallow water walleyes tracked in Lake Okoboji. The fish were observed in 10 to 16 feet of water approximately 61% of the time. They were foiund in depths between 6 and 20 feet approximately 92% of the time—clearly demonstrating that under the right circumstances walleyes will spend the majority of their time in **the weeds.**

EXPLORATORY EXCURSIONS AND HOME AREAS

After establishing an activity center, each fish stayed within the center except for occasional "exploratory excursions" to other areas. These excursions lasted up to two days and covered distances up to three miles. The fish always returned to their home activity center after these excursions.

Evidence shows that fish really don't need so-called "structure" in order to navigate across flats—or anywhere else! It's becoming more apparent that fish do relate to edges and unusual objects, but they use them as holding areas and not so much for navigational purposes.

One of the fish tracked was captured from its summer activity center, and taken about three miles away and dropped off in the center of the lake. Within two days the fish was back at its home area. We've all heard stories about cats and dogs traveling miles back to their homes after being lost. Apparently, fish have this homing ability, too.

Thus far, research studies have documented that walleyes do set up home areas in lakes and reservoirs during the summer. The fish being tracked in Okoboji were observed to be most active at night, but there were two well-defined activity patterns during the night hours. A major activity period occurred from 8:00 P.M. to 12:00 midnight, and a minor period from 5:00 to 8:00 A.M.

An interesting aspect of aquatic weedgrowth became apparent as the summer progressed. The lower leaves and branches died, presumably as a result of shading by new growth as well as by accumulations of marl deposits. As the dead leaves and branches fell from the main stem, a space of up to two feet was created between the bottom and the lowest living branches of the plant. This

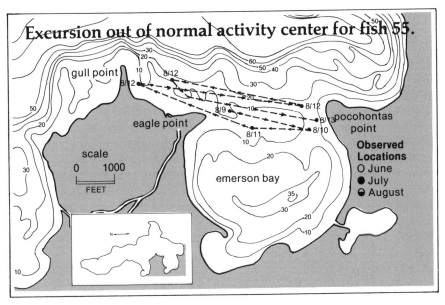

Here's two examples of fish suddenly breaking their established behavioral pattern for no evident reason. Why does a walleye that was functioning very well in a specific location suddenly take off for greener pastures? Who knows? What tracking studies do tell us is that we still have a lot to learn about fish behavior.

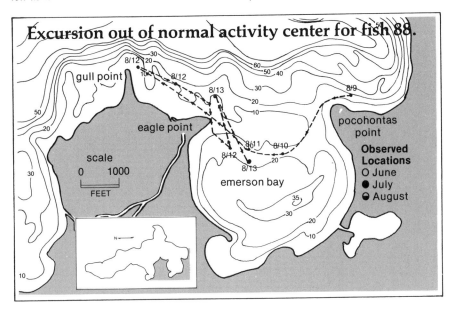

resulted in a habitat comparable to a canopied forest where fish can rest or move about freely in the open spaces and still be protected from the sun.

Another interesting change occurred in the fall when the weedgrowth started to die off. The fish, robbed of the light-screening vegetation, headed for deeper water and moved to the types of areas that the deep water fish in this study inhabited all summer.

The walleyes seemed to be wanderers—except during the summer when they set up home areas (and even then they took exploratory excursions.) Many folks imagine themselves fishing different groups of walleyes when they move two miles or so down a lake to a different bar. However, that may not be the case. Two days—or even two hours later—you might run into the same group of fish that you encountered before.

There are countless other examples of how walleyes adapt to and operate within different environments. Walleyes in the western basin of Lake Erie exhibit a pronounced pattern of suspension most of the summer, due, no doubt, primarily to the fact that their available prey suspends at this time.

On the other hand, in the plateau reservoirs of the Dakotas, walleyes have been caught in 60 to 80 feet of water and have been netted as deep as 125 feet. Elsewhere, walleyes in Lake Superior run the shorelines from the St. Louis River in Duluth eastward in the summer. But since water temperatures on this mammoth, frigid lake can be quite unstable due to shifting currents, the walleyes can be anywhere from 4 to 100 feet deep.

Yes, a walleye is a walleye wherever it swims. But the fish definitely adapts to the environment it lives in. These adaptations determine first, location—where you look for the fish; and second, presentation—how you go about fishing for them! This book covers both of those concerns and relates each to many environments.

Chapter 2
An Introduction
to
CALENDAR PERIODS

W hy classify waters and talk about Calendar Periods? Because the two subjects are vitally important to consistently catching walleyes.
 Throughout this book, the various fishing techniques to use, the different times to fish, and the diverse types of underwater terrain to look for are constantly under discussion. However, in order to put these factors together in a meaningful way, you must realize that there are *certain* times to apply *certain* techniques within *certain* locales on *certain* bodies of waters. A fish catching technique or method may work well on one body of water at a given time of the year, *but not at a different time or on another body of water type.*

Often, fishermen learn of a new method, color or lure that is supposed to work wonders. But, they try to apply it on a different body of water—or at the wrong time of the year—and wonder what happened when it doesn't produce fish.

Viewing angling as an isolated mechanical act is a very common mistake. Folks get so hung up on method, lure color or technique that they fail to realize that this is simply one phase of the angling procedure.

The purpose of WALLEYE WISDOM is to make you aware of the different ways a walleye will respond to different environments and how it will probably react at different times of the year. The key is learning to read body of water types and conditions, plus interpreting the mood and seasonal habits of the walleye. Once you are armed with this knowledge (wisdom), you can then select a method of presentation that is best suited for that specific situation.

Many anglers have difficulty with how walleyes adapt to different kinds of lakes, rivers or reservoirs. Fewer still are aware that walleyes react in different ways and display different moods at certain times of the year.

Recognizing this, we have established guidelines that any angler, anywhere, can learn to recognize. We call them "CALENDAR PERIODS." Since fish do not respond to dates on a calendar, but, rather to impulses brought about by the climate, our "CALENDAR PERIODS" are based on easily identifiable functions of nature. This is independent of our man-made calendar, but fits the mood and activity of the fish.

We add this knowledge to the body of water classification system, which provides the knowledge to identify specific types of lakes, rivers or reservoirs—and how they function. The body of water type has a great affect on fish movement and location throughout the year. These two dimensions enable you to recognize exactly what kind of body of water and what specific time frame is under discussion in order to employ a specific fishing presentation.

Therefore, before we ever get down to the brass tacks of lure types, line diameter, retrieve techniques and the like, it's important to first understand *when* and *where* to employ the technique under discussion. Then and only then can you use this wisdom to enhance your angling success.

Now, let's take a close look at the Calendar Periods and water classification systems.

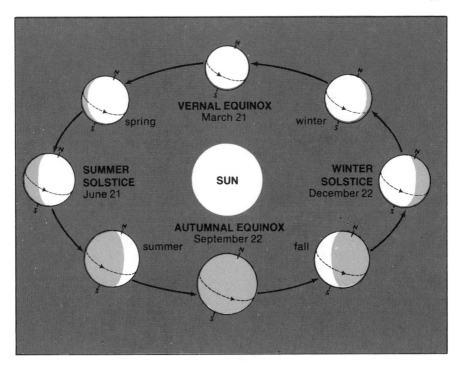

Chapter 3

CALENDAR PERIODS

When does a year begin? Some ancients believed that the pagan god Janus ruled the light and was the protector of all beginnings, and set the beginning of the year at the winter solstice (December 21-22). This was Janus' Day. The solstice marked the time of year when the length of daylight began increasing in northern climates. Later, a medieval Pope set the date of January 1st as a starting point for the western world's year. Our calendar is still based on this decision. However, the natural order (which, of course, includes walleyes) does not recognize this calendar.

Spring, summer, winter and fall are events common only to the temperate world. The tropics, on the other hand, display alternating cycles or rain and wind that signal to the various life forms that the earth's angle to the sun is changing. In the inhospitable polar world, spring, summer and fall are but a brief pause in an otherwise harsh, constant gloom and cold. Only the middle (temperate) zones of the earth experience the four distinct seasons. And it's here the pendulum swings noticeably enough between periods of darkness and brightness that we can easily recognize definable patterns emerging within nature.

We know that light (or length of daylight) plays a major role in the day-to-day feeding, movement and activities of walleyes and other fish. We also know that light seasonally controls or regulates migrations and plays an important part in the spawning process. Walleyes usually spawn at twilight, at night or under very overcast conditions. In fact, there are indications that peak spawning "runs" coincide with the increased light and gravitational effects of the full moon. There are exceptions, of course; walleyes can and do spawn earlier or later than this event. But, by and large, the majority of walleyes attune themselves to the rhythm of a cosmic drummer, and that drummer is light—or more precisely, the degree of it.

The basic nature of some species of fish dictates that they are principally *diurnal* (most of their activity takes place during the daytime). Others are mainly *circadian* (most of their activity takes place at night). Still others are *crepuscular* (major activities occur at or around twilight). However, it is not that cut-and-dried, because many species adapt to local or seasonal circumstances, and sometimes become daytime, nighttime, or twilight activists.

Despite this, there are general tendencies, patterns and trends that concern us. The common yellow perch is usually diurnal, for example. During the daylight hours it lives, loafs and feeds. The bullhead is circadian, and moves and feeds mainly at night. On the other hand, walleyes mainly have a crespuscular rhythm; they are usually most active at twilight.

It's common for anglers to fish a sunken island, a hard-bottom flat or a rocky shoreline during the daylight hours, and catch a walleye every once in a while. But come dusk, all of a sudden the fish start biting like crazy. Yet an hour earlier there was no indication of any concentration of fish. In all probability, the fish were there all the time, but simply dormant and holding tight to the bottom, inside crevices of rocks or under some type cover.

What triggered them? In all likelihood the *degree of light intensity*, or, in the case of the walleye, the waning of it (plus a number of still unknown factors). At any rate, light is the signal; it acts as a synchronizer!

Exactly how fish react to light is not fully understood. We do know that each species has uniquely constructed rods and cones (light receptors) in its eyes that are inherited through its specific genetic code. The degree of light picked up and transferred to the nervous system through a species' eyes largely determines if it is primarily a daytime, twilight or nocturnal feeder.

Light often triggers and regulates feeding and activity times. However, the length of daylight varies with season and region of the hemisphere. It is also affected by daily cloud cover and humidity (haze). More than that, feeding periods obviously change not only with season, latitude and longitude, but also with altitude—so there is a lot we don't understand. Indeed, all of nature, and that includes the aquatic world, is "tuned" to these various signals. The best an angler can do is learn to recognize some of the more obvious clues.

On land the many seasonal changes are quite evident, but underwater it's difficult to see nature's forces at work. Consequently, aquatic seasonal cycles are a mystery and very confusing to some people. But, it is in this mysterious and constantly-changing environment that fish live. So, this is something every angler must be in touch with if he is to catch walleyes with any consistency.

A fish's movements, actions and attitudes *are not* arbitrary. There are valid reasons for each and every activity. The most obvious of the myriad of forces that control the aquatic world is the intensity and duration of light. This is related to the earth's yearly orbit about the sun.

In the northern hemisphere, the sun is most direct and the day longest on June 21-22. The sun is least direct and the day shortest on December 21-22. Water temperatures warm or cool accordingly, and this affects each organism from the lowest form of algae to the highest form of fish. Insect eggs hatch to larvae, and larvae in turn become insects. Snails and aquatic worms move seasonally from zone to zone. Plankton periodically blooms, is consumed, and dissipates in a complicated, interrelated web of life.

Our Calendar Periods divide the year into cycles of fish response. There are no such things as weeks or months—only seasonal periods. Periods (depending on weather) which one year might last nine days, could run sixteen days the next year. Since our Calendar Periods depend upon climate conditions from year-to-year, they are elastic in duration. Calendar Periods do not last a fixed number of days, nor do they occur on given dates each year.

Further, some of our Calendar Periods relate primarily to the walleye's biological demands: Pre-spawn, Spawn and Post-spawn. So, in one region of the continent, a period (for example, the Spawn Period) might arrive months earlier than in another part of North America. The later Periods—Pre-summer, Summer Peak, Summer and Post-summer—are based more on the condition of the total environment and the condition of a body of water. In areas of northern Canada, a Calendar Period like Summer might be a brief five weeks long—while in Texas it might be three or more months in duration. Finally, some periods are determined mainly by levels of water temperature, like the Turnover and the Cold-water Period.

There is another fine point that you must understand to view the Calendar Periods in their proper perspective. You might assume that the best time to fish would be a Calendar Period when the water temperature is at an optimum for the walleye's metabolism, causing it to feed the most. But it doesn't always work that way. When predator fish are usually eating the most, the food is also the most plentiful. So, a species' preferred water temperature level *does not necessarily* indicate a time when the fish is easiest to catch.

On the other hand, an adverse water temperature does not always mean fish are hardest to catch. In fact, this is particularly true with late fall walleye fishing, which is often excellent. The available food supply, the timing of the feeding movements, overall population levels and competition, as well as the seasonal density of cover all play an important role in angling success. These are the kinds of factors we took into account when we developed the Calendar Periods.

The Calendar Periods are *not*, as some think, simply the seasonal condition of a body of water. A lake, river or reservoir may be in a seasonal time frame (spring, summer, fall or winter), but the *fish's response to that environment* determines the Calendar Period. Different species of fish in any given body of water can be in different Calendar Periods *at the same time.*

For example, the majority of largemouth bass are in their Pre-spawn or Spawn Calendar Period in spring. They will usually be shallow and quite easy to catch. But, at the very same time, walleyes, which spawn earlier than bass, would be in their Post-spawn Period, and fishing for them would be slow.

One you learn to "read the signs," you'll have little difficulty identifying one period from another and discerning when different species are in different Calendar Periods. The difference between the unsuccessful angler and the truly successful one often boils down to two things: recognizing the seasonal movements and probable response patterns of the walleye.

MOTHER NATURE'S CLUES

If we lived underwater, the walleye's seasonal movements would become obvious. As the food chain developed and move through its cycles, we would see signs of it everywhere: emerging vegetation, schools of minnows and bait-fish relating to their food sources, and growing numbers of developing insect larvae and crustacea. But since the surface of a body of water is all that most of use ever see, we need to be aware of other clues to these changes.

There are other natural cycles corresponding to the Calendar Periods that are plainly visible. Lilacs in bloom usually mean that walleyes are in their Post-spawn Period and will be tough to catch. When the water is warm enough for comfortable swimming, walleyes will be in their Summer Period. In one kind of lake, the walleyes might be in the weeds. But in another kind of lake they might relate to deep, rock-capped sunken islands. Then, as the first fall colors appear on the trees, you'll know that the Cold-water Period has commenced and you can expect the beginning of a fall river walleye run. The fall arrival of massive flocks of coots (mud hens) on some lakes is a sure sign that the Cold-water Period is here, and on certain waters deep, slow-jigging will be an appropriate presentation.

While these signs may vary from region to region, the perceptive angler learns to recognize nature's clues, and changes his location and presentation accordingly. Here is where a log book proves invaluable. The next time you observe a "peak time" on your lake, river or reservoir, take a look around the surrounding countryside. What is going on that can give you a clue? Is a particular plant just coming into bloom? Have you just seen the first robin of the year? How about an insect hatch or the budding of some kind of aquatic weedgrowth? Since these events occur regionally, the signs are many and varied. However, it is amazing how consistent these patterns will be once you learn to identify and recognize them.

Water temperature, of course, is one major key, since it partially controls weedgrowth and dissipation. Water temperature also triggers insect hatches (or their dissipation), etc. Taking constant temperature readings will keep you in touch with many of the Calendar Periods. The patterns you see developing on land are also a function of the same weather conditions that determine some of the underwater patterns. Astute old-timers are well aware of these cycles, and this is one source of folk wisdom that is usually right on target. Old, experienced hands instinctively are able to see, smell and feel a Calendar Period arriving, leaving or holding.

It's important to be aware of how weather conditions affect a lake, river or reservoir. Flowage (impoundment) lakes connected to a river system can warm up incredibly fast as the result of a heavy, warm rain. Yet a self-contained, big, deep lake a few miles away will remain cooler and take longer to warm up. The fish in both bodies of water could be in vastly different Calendar Periods and react much differently.

There are vast numbers of good technical fishermen who have mastered a variety of presentations, but who still fail to understand how the predator/prey link relates to the Calendar Periods. So they run into recurrent problems at various times of the year. Our experience shows that another key to successful angling is understanding baitfish movements and patterns of other forms of prey.

So, not only do different lake conditions dictate different lure presentations and techniques, but game fish demonstrate marked preferences for certain kinds of lures and baits throughout the various Calendar Periods.

In the final analysis, the only way to understand how the different Calendar Periods function on your particular body of water, or any other for that matter, is to spend enough time there to begin identifying these patterns. Comparing notes with other anglers will help you get a grasp of the Calendar Periods. Keeping a daily log of weather and water conditions, as well as fish feeding patterns, also helps considerably. Often, a review of last year's fishing log, during a cold winter night, provides not only a glimmer of past fishing glories, but also an insight into seasonal fishing patterns you never noticed before. In this way, you can learn the seasonal circumstances that trigger fish to respond, and the locational patterns that result from them.

THE TEN PERIOD CYCLE
THE CALENDAR

1. Pre-spawn
2. Spawn
3. Post-spawn
4. Pre-summer
5. Summer Peak
6. Summer
7. Post-summer
8. Fall Turnover
9. Cold water
10. Frozen water*

*Ice cover is actually a phase of cold water, but is used to differentiate conditions.

Normal Calendar	1	2	3	4	5	6	7	8	9	10
Walleye	9	1	2	3	4	5	6	7	8	9	10

THE PRE-SPAWN PERIOD
A Time of Anticipation

Water Temperature Range: Ice-out to Low 40°F's
General Fish Mood: Neutral

Preparation for spawning is the primary motivating factor for walleyes at this time. The major impetus is getting into position and "staging" in the general vicinity of spawning grounds. Therefore, the Pre-spawn Period begins when the urge moves walleyes to abandon their wintering (Cold Water Period) areas and start migrating toward spawning areas. This journey could be short, as in the case of small lakes, or many miles, as on some large rivers, lakes and reservoirs, or on lakes fed by long rivers.

While the fish are not chiefly interested in food during the staging process, they will feed actively—especially in the earlier phases of the Pre-spawn Period. Even near their spawning grounds, walleyes will relate to some element of the food chain and grab targets of opportunity. Males usually exhibit more aggressive behavior, and more males are caught than females. Nonetheless, both sexes, while *not* snapping at everything in sight, are heavily grouped, so you can expect action once you locate fish.

Various walleye groups will start making a pre-spawn movement in relation to the distance they are from their spawning grounds. So *not all* fish on a lake or reservoir make the move at the same time. Even on smaller bodies of water, all the walleyes do not begin making a pre-spawn movement at the same time.

For example, fish which spawn in an incoming river may stage at the mouth, or actually run the river, when the lake or reservoir is still ice-covered (or at a very low temperature). Yet fish groups which spawn in the cold main lake may remain in their winter haunts for some time after the ice cover melts, or until the body of water warms sufficiently to prompt a staging movement.

However, walleye groups on large bodies of water may stage in proximity to the main lake spawning grounds while the water is still covered by ice. It appears they might winter in various sections of the lake, with each mid-winter movement bringing them closer and closer to the spawning grounds. These are gradual movements, as opposed to a specific spawning migration.

At any rate, as soon as the ice melts (or where ice cover is minimal and the waterway starts to warm), you can expect walleyes to start migrating to and staging near prospective spawning grounds, and to be in a neutral mood. This constitutes the beginning of the Pre-spawn Period. During the early stage of this period, the male fish will not be flowing milt, nor can you force eggs out of a female by pressing her stomach. During the later stage, walleyes move directly onto the spawning sites.

Basically, Pre-spawn is *a time of anticipation*—a period when the walleyes' interests are primarily focused on the coming reproduction ritual.

THE SPAWN PERIOD
A Time of Tension
Water Temperature Range: 43°F - 52°F—Peak 47°F - 49°F
General Fish Mood: Negative

This is a brief, variable period usually lasting from one to three days for individual female walleyes and a little bit longer for individual males. The Spawn Period includes the peak spawning temperature range for walleyes (approximately 47°F - 49°F). However, since walleyes may begin spawning at temperatures as low as 43°F, and have been recorded spawning at temperatures in the high 50°F's, temperature is not the only factor. The key indicator for the arrival of the Spawn Period is when the great majority of male fish are milting and the females' eggs have ripened. While technically a fish that has not spawned is still in the Pre-spawn Period, the reality is that the closer the fish comes to actually spawning, the less likely it is to strike a bait, or exhibit other pre-spawn traits.

Feeding activity during actual spawning is minimal to nonexistent. However, cantankerous milting males, cruising around waiting for a female, will make reflex strikes at baits, lures or other intruders in staging areas—but not during the actual spawn. One possible exception is small rivers, where walleyes can be caught during spawning movements. Yet by and large, it is a very poor time for fishing.

Remember, while actual spawning is taking place in one area, there can be groups of walleyes waiting to spawn in other areas, and groups which have completed the spawning ritual in still others. The Spawn Period must therefore be considered a local activity. Yet within any body of water, the great majority of the walleye population will spawn in a two-week period or less.

Most females will deposit their eggs within 24-48 hours. But females will keep making false runs, usually at night, until their eggs are ripe. So their actual spawning period is very short-lived. Some females may not spawn at all. Males, on the other hand, continue producing milt and can spawn several times. While the spawning process itself takes a short period of time for an individual fish, a group of walleyes in a generally ripe condition may spend a week or more in a spawning area. This is what we term the Spawn Period, even if the fish have not actually spawned yet.

Conversely, after a female drops her eggs or a male milts out, the fish is technically in its Post-spawn Period. However, they may "hang" in a spawning area for a short period of time and exhibit attitudes like spawning fish. Yet if there is a food source in or adjacent to the spawning site, walleyes may even remain there to feed for a few days. However, this only occurs under ideal conditions, and it is far more typical for the fish to begin dispersing out of the area very quickly.

Basically, the Spawn Period is *a time of tension*—a period when the walleye is subjected to great stress, and its reactions correspond with this mood.

THE POST-SPAWN PERIOD
A Time of Recuperation

Water Temperature Range: The Low 50°F's
General Fish Mood: Negative to Neutral

The Post-spawn Period is a complex period and difficult to portray in simple terms. Any characterization of the Post-spawn Period in "definite" terms is misleading. This remains a somewhat mysterious period, largely because of the lack of concentrated walleyes and our limited knowledge of exactly what they are doing.

For example, while we can generalize and suggest that water temperatures will usually be in the low 50°F's, water temperature is not the only factor influencing this period. We are dealing with a "recuperation period," so time is also of the essence. Logically, how long it takes individual walleyes, and thereby the entire walleye population, to recover is going to vary.

So, it is very important to keep both time and temperature in mind when considering Post-spawn. We've found that a week or two is usually long enough for the fish to recuperate and move into their Pre-summer Period (characterized by a more aggressive mood). We've also fished enough water to know that water temperatures of 53°F-56°F often distinguish the resumption of aggressive feeding, and thus the end of Post-spawn.

Post-spawn is usually characterized by inconsistent fishing, but there are exceptions. For example, male walleyes seem to be easier to locate and catch near spawning areas, and they are often active. While females are usually accurately described as having extreme cases of "lockjaw," even they are sometimes caught (admittedly in small numbers) by anglers longline trolling or shore casting at night. However, it would be poor advice to plan your annual fishing vacation to coincide with the Post-spawn Period!

Just as there is a Pre-spawn assembly of walleyes, so too is there a Post-spawn dispersal. How fast this occurs depends on a number of factors. Experience shows that basin characteristics affect walleye dispersal. In waters with sharp, distinct drop-offs, walleyes tend to disperse faster than in waters with gradual, sloping shorelines.

Forage can also influence Post-spawn walleye dispersal. At some point during the recuperation process, a walleye's basic being returns to normal; the fish becomes concerned with food and comfort! If there is forage on or near a spawning area, many walleyes may hold in the area to feed. A prime example is a lake with perch populations. Walleyes will key on perch spawning in sparse weedgrowth adjacent to, or part of, the walleyes' spawning areas. Walleyes that spawn near necked-down lake areas that tend to funnel baitfish from one lake section to another may remain to pick off these tasty morsels. Thus Post-spawn is a recuperation period, but it can also be a positioning phase for the next Calendar Period.

Recognizing a general Post-spawn walleye dispersal pattern is probably most important in reservoirs and lakes where walleyes leave the main body of water to spawn in rivers or large creek arms. It's also very important if you fish for river walleyes. In these situations, walleyes leave the spawning grounds, stopping to rest and even feed a bit along the way. If you can visualize the route back to the main lake or reservoir, or to a summer river holding area, you can usually pick out areas where the fish could hold and catch some. By this time, however, the fish are beginning to cross over that thin line distinguishing the Post-spawn Period from the Pre-summer Period.

Basically, Post-spawn is *a time of recuperation* when the walleyes' hormone levels change. Thus, the walleye's biological emphasis switches from that of a fish primarily involved with reproduction to that of a fish primarily interested in satisfying its needs for food and comfort.

THE PRE-SUMMER PERIOD
A Time of Transition
Water Temperature Range: Mid 50°F's to Low 60°F's
General Fish Mood: Neutral to Positive

While the Post-spawn Period is characterized as a resting stage when fish scatter and feed little, a change is imminent. The walleyes' bodies need nourishment, and the resumption of regular feeding activities indicates the beginning of a new pattern, one we call the Pre-summer Period. This period is the beginning of the fish's prime growth time for the whole year. During this and the Summer Peak Period walleyes grow the most in length, though not necessarily in weight.

During the Post-spawn recuperation period, the walleye changes from a fish primarily preoccupied with the reproduction ritual (and its after-effects) to a fish primarily interested in satisfying its everyday needs of food and comfort. While no set temperature level indicates when walleyes enter their Pre-summer stage, the waters, nonetheless, will have warmed to a point where walleyes become more active and their metabolism demands more food to sustain their energy levels. When water temperatures reach the high 50°F's or low 60°F's, you can usually assume they are "back on the bite"—at least on a fairly regular basis.

Pre-summer is a time of emerging weedgrowth and a developing food chain. Generally, water temperatures vary less from section to section of a lake compared to the earlier spring periods, although certain sections of lakes and reservoirs can be warmer than others. Rivers, however, usually exhibit more constant temperature levels.

Prior to this and depending upon the area of the lake, different groups of walleyes could have been in a Pre-spawn, Spawn or Post-spawn attitude within the same broad time frame. But during the Pre-summer Period, most of the walleye population begins to exhibit much the same mood. Fish are scattered.

In Pre-summer, a body of water itself offers the most pertinent clues to walleye behavior. Pre-summer is a time when fish are hard to pinpoint—often here today and gone tomorrow. Indeed, a prime characteristic of the Pre-summer Period is the variety of definite fishing patterns; you may catch several walleyes rigging live bait in deep water, several more fish crankbaiting mid-depth flats, and even take a few fish in extremely shallow water.

This is one of the most effective periods of the year for night fishing. More walleyes are caught at this time of the year by the average fisherman than at any other time, largely because more patterns are available. Slowly, though, as water temperatures continue climbing upwards, there is a gradual tendency for walleyes to start keying on specific food sources.

Basically, Pre-summer is *a time of transition* when a body of water transforms from the cooler environment of spring to the warmer environment of summer. Fish begin regrouping and patterns begin to emerge.

THE SUMMER PEAK PERIOD
A Time of Fulfillment

Water Temperature Range: Mid 60°F's to Low 70°F's
General Fish Mood: Positive

As the summer progresses, the Pre-summer Period develops into what we term the Summer Peak—a short period of fast-action fishing. It is impossible to walk in the woods, along a beach, or down a country road at this time and not feel nature's increased rhythm. Nature is alive, conscious and moving.

The final trigger that pushes walleyes from the Pre-summer Period into the short-lived period of intense feeding we term the Summer Peak always appears to be the same: Namely, a span of relatively calm, very warm weather. In many cases this is the first really hot, summer-type weather of the season—and more importantly, the first hot nights of early summer.

The Summer Peak is one of the best times of the year for peak walleye fishing. Not only do you encounter schools of fish, but schools of aggressively feeding walleyes, *if* you are tuned in to the walleyes' movements.

Most of a lake's ecosystem reaches its maximum fruition during this cycle. All the cool and warm water species have spawned in most cases. The transformation from a colder to a cooler to a warmer water environment is complete. Insect hatches explode. Most major rooted weedgrowth begins to mature. Most distinct weedlines and edges are perceptible, and plankton are multiplying. Almost everything is reaching its peak of production. Fishing is excellent.

Here are some basic rules of thumb to go by. For example, the summer surface temperature of what we term meso (middle-aged) lakes usually hovers around 72°F - 74°F. It may eventually climb into the upper 70°F's or even low 80°F's, but this typically happens *very slowly*. Thus, the Summer Peak Period —for walleyes—seems to begin with the end of the rapid, early-summer rise in water temperature. In cooler Canadian lakes the water temperature might only reach the mid-60°F's, yet the principle is the same.

A combination of environmental factors stimulates this Summer Peak walleye activity. These three seem the most important: (1) The fish are hungry and, thus, aggressive. This is the period when most of their yearly growth occurs; (2) This is the first time since spawning that *big* females group together. Their competitive group activity helps stimulate even more intense feeding activity; (3) There are plankton of all sorts and hordes of fish fry; the entire lake is blooming and brimming with food. This spurs vigorous food chain activity on all levels. Oblivious to surroundings and with little finesse, there's intense, competitive feeding activity before things settle down to a more normal (Summer Period) pace.

The Summer Peak is basically *a time of fulfillment*—and potentially a "red-hot" period for stringers of large walleyes.

THE SUMMER PERIOD
A Time of Plenty

Water Temperature Range: Maximum Water Temperature
General Fish Mood: Positive to Neutral

The Romans believed the dog star Sirius rose with the sun, giving the days of July and August a double measure of heat. Thus, the term "dog days" was thrust into angling. It's a misnomer that implies lethargy, but this is an illusion. More than at any other time of the year, nature is converting the sun's energy into living matter in full gear. We call this interval the Summer Period.

Abundant prey is available in the form of fry and fingerlings. The lake has blossomed with food, and fish become more selective in their choice of meals. Controlling factors like thermoclines, sunlight, increased metabolism and presence of prey all demand order. Plus, there are a host of other factors. Nature responds by regulating feeding times.

Summer walleye fishing can be perplexing. While the fish feed, the abundance of food and the density of cover can make walleye fishing tougher, especially on some lakes where the fish penetrate weedlines. Feeding activity may be short and fire off at short intervals. Movements may be of short duration, yet very intense.

River walleyes often spread out, and as the groups become less concentrated, the angler must cover more water. Yet in certain reservoir types, summer walleye fishing can be consistent and outstanding. Flatland and plateau reservoirs, for example, provide some of the best and most consistent summer walleye fishing.

Basically, the Summer Period is *a time of plenty*—plenty of food, plenty of cover and plenty of distraction in terms of increased boat traffic, sun penetration, cold fronts and the like. This completes the warming peak for the year.

THE POST-SUMMER PERIOD
A Time of Impending Change

Water Temperature Range: The Water Begins Cooling Quite Rapidly from its Generalized Highest Temperature Range
General Fish Mood: Neutral to Positive

Post-summer, in effect, is the reversal of the Pre-summer process. It is a time when a body of water changes back from a warmer to a cooler water environment. This period takes place during the tail end of summer. Hot days with dead-calm periods, followed by cool nights, are typical. The days grow shorter, and this becomes the cosmic signal to the ecosystem that things are slowing down.

Most of the food in any lake, river or reservoir has already been produced for the year, and the summer (time of plenty) is slowly giving way to reduced food stocks. The density of the weeds, too, begins to noticeably diminish. Insect hatches dwindle, and, in some cases, water levels can be quite low. Last, but not least, baitfish start shifting position as they mature, are lessened in numbers by predators, or as cover diminishes. In fact, during Post-summer everything slowly shifts as the water abruptly cools.

Walleyes respond to these environmental changes in a variety of ways; therefore, a variety of patterns can emerge. Interestingly, marginal anglers manage to catch a few fish—just as they did during the Pre-summer and Summer Peak stages—and for much the same reasons. Just prior to this in the Summer Period, various fish groups were *not* doing a lot of different things. Thus the angler had to be very specific in his presentation, and many times his approach had to be quite refined. But now, in Post-summer, these very defined patterns break down and fish start moving about more. In many cases, fish from one area mingle with other groups, forming concentrations. Walleyes also now tend to linger longer in feeding periods. So when you add up all these factors, fishing is easier, so it can be good—sometimes fantastic.

The internal workings of the environment trigger these changes in a walleye's pattern of operation. Summer fish, depending upon the kind of lake, river or reservoir, might have been restricted from doing a lot of things. But come Post-summer, many of these restrictive factors disappear.

For example, in certain mesotrophic lakes, thermoclines (which often limit oxygen in the depths) might have pushed walleyes out of the deep water during the summer months. Direct sunlight (for long periods of the day) might have further kept these shallow water fish buried in cover like weeds; they might only have fed for brief periods during low-light periods. But come Post-summer, the sunlight is less intense and the fish might wander out of the weeds for longer periods.

With the cooler water temperature, walleyes start mingling with other walleye groups. Since the food supply is less plentiful, it takes longer to fill them to the full. So, in this case, we vividly see how the environment affects fish activity—and, of course, "catchability."

In some rivers, walleyes which spent the summer scattered in shallow stretches might, with the low water levesl so indicative of the Post-summer Period, begin regrouping with other fish and relating to deeper holes—or moving to washout holes under dams. Again, the change in environment makes for a change in fish operation.

Basically, Post-summer is *a time of impending change*, when a body of water (and the aquatic life in it) goes through the transition from a warmer to a cooler environment.

THE TURNOVER PERIOD
A Time of Turmoil

Water Temperature Range: Variable
General Fish Mood: Very Negative

Described as a time of turmoil, the Turnover Period is relative. First, all bodies of water do not stratify during summer, so they do not as such "turn over." Most rivers are a case in point. Lakes and reservoirs, too, may or may not stratify. Usually, shallow bodies of water—which the wind periodically stir up—or ones with a lot of current flowing through them, are immune to the stratifying process. Consequently, the fish in these waters do not experience the amount of stress as fish in waters where the transition from a warm to a cold water environment is an explosive event. Nonetheless, the change from a warmer to a cooler to a colder water environment demands some adjustment.

The most classic (drastic) turnover situation occurs in bodies of water which set up (or stratify) in distinct temperature layers during summer. Since cold water is heavier than warm water, the warmer water stays on top and the colder water sinks and builds up on the bottom; in between lies a narrow band of rapid temperature change from warm to cold called the thermocline.

On these waters a thermocline condition usually remains in effect throughout most of the Summer Peak, Summer and Post-summer Periods. But during the tail end of the Post-summer Period, as the sun grows less direct, seasonal hard, driving, cold winds and rain begin chilling the surface temperature of the water very quickly. As the heavier (colder) water begins sinking, it comes in contact with the warmer water below. This action forces the lighter, yet deeper warmer water back to the surface. Eventually the narrow thermocline layer ruptures and a mixing or "turning over" process takes place. As the wind beats the water, the mixing action continues until it thoroughly homogenizes the water to a point where the whole body of water is the same temperature. This process also *reoxygenates* the water.

Turnover usually occurs after several days to a week of the first late summer cold snap characterized by a succession of dark, cold, wind-driven rainy days. This is a signal that the Cold Water Period is about to arrive.

At times, you can actually smell the stagnant bottom water as it rises to the surface. You might even see dead weeds, decomposed fish and other bottom debris floating on the surface or washed ashore.

The *actual* Turnover process itself takes place once the thermocline layer ruptures. But the turmoil that takes place usually adversely affects the fish for a period of time *before* and *after* this event actually occurs. Fishing doesn't pick up again until conditions stabilize. In general, once water temperatures drop to about 55°F and the water clears perceptibly, cold water fishing patterns emerge.

Fishing during the Turnover Period on bodies of water that actually thermocline is tough, to say the least. However, since all bodies of water do not turn over at the same time, it is usually best to switch to waters which have already turned over—or bodies of water which have not yet begun to—or to waters which actually don't thermocline and turn over so drastically.

Exactly what happens to fish, and walleyes in particular during Turnover, has yet to be documented. In fact, anglers are some of the best sources of information about this turbulent time.

Basically, the Turnover Period is *a time of turmoil* when fish activity grinds to a halt, although action will pick up as conditions gradually stabilize.

THE COLD WATER PERIOD
A Time of Tranquility
Water Temperature Range: 55°F and Down to the Lowest Temperature of the Year
General Fish Mood: Neutral

We term the entire time span from the end of the Turnover to freeze-up as one singular period (Cold Water). Generally, the walleye's metabolism slows a little in response to the changing ecosystem. However, Cold Water Period walleyes can be quite active.

Walleyes will hit a moving crankbait sharply in the early Cold Water Period, yet slow to prefer a jig-and-minnow "teasing" presentation by the end of the period. Thus, as the water cools, you should slow down your approach. The walleye angler must view this entire period within these parameters.

The Cold Water Period is a gradual slowing down of the entire ecosystem. The water regresses to the lowest temperature of the year, and the walleye's metabolism follows. As the days grow steadily shorter, weedgrowth, insect hatches and plankton blooms slow down. The big female walleyes' eggs will already be fairly well developed, and they will occasionally feed quite heavily to sustain themselves.

In lakes where walleyes inhabit weedy flats in summer, the fish may now drop down and concentrate on steep drop-offs or move to deep flats. These areas are usually located near the deepest depths of the lake.

In rivers, walleyes may move from shallow stretches to stage in deep holes.

Migrations start for an early staging towards the spring spawning areas. Current plays an important part in fish location.

In reservoirs, walleyes can move off deep flats and gather around points. Drop-offs with forage hold the key to fish location.

The exodus from the shallows in the early stages of the Cold Water Period often results in tighter concentrations of fish. Feeding intensity, however, can vary, ranging anywhere from intense to lockjaw, depending upon a host of circumstances.

The entire cooling process, from Post-summer through the Turnover and into the Cold Water Period, is one of preparation. The mixing process and reoxygenation of deeper water opens up formerly uninhabitable areas to groups of shallow water fish which otherwise would perish with the coming of ice cover. Understanding this process is important, because the fall cold water season can offer some of the finest walleye fishing of the year *if* you understand fish location.

The Cold Water Period, however, is still *a time of tranquility*; even though the walleyes may bite well, everything seems to move at a slower pace.

THE FROZEN WATER PERIOD
A Time of Rest

Water Temperature: When a Body of Water is at its Coldest
for an Extended Period of Time
General Fish Mood: Neutral

Most bodies of water which contain reproducing populations of walleyes experience ice cover at some time during the year. Yet, because all lakes do not ice over, we define the Frozen Water Period as the longest period of coldest water of the year.

Depending upon latitude, the Frozen Water Period could last six months, a few days—or not at all. Rivers may freeze over completely, but most normally have some ice-free sections. These open sections usually occur under dams or near warm water discharges. On some reservoirs, ice cover may briefly occur in coves and wind-protected bays, while the main lake never ices up. The point is, the Frozen Water Period occurs when a body of water is at its coldest range for an extended period.

By late fall there will be substantial egg development in walleyes. Yet studies indicate that walleyes must spend a protracted period of time in water below 50°F for their eggs to develop properly.

During this time span, the entire ecosystem of a lake, river or reservoir slows. Yet walleye feeding does take place. Indeed, female fish must feed regularly to maintain their eggs and bodies. On some bodies of water, the biggest walleyes of the year are taken ice fishing.

However, the Frozen Water Period is basically *a time of rest*. Not that walleyes sleep—or that activity ceases completely. It's just that the whole ecosystem seems to move at a slower pace than during other Calendar Periods.

Calendar Summary

A VEST POCKET GUIDE TO THE CALENDAR PERIODS

Period	Description	Key Factors
Pre-spawn	Length varies from species to species. Movement from late winter location to the spawning grounds. Some heavy grouping and super fishing at times.	Water temperature. Hormone level. Bottom conditions. Length of daylight
Spawn	Timewise a very short period, but all spawning for a species does not take place at same time. Fishing poor.	Water Temperature. Hormone level. Bottom Conditions.
Post-spawn	Recuperation period for females. Males may be more responsive in feeding than females, but usually slow fishing.	Gradual dispersal from spawning area.
Pre-summer	Movement from spawning area to summer locations. Fish are beginning to regroup. Fishing usually slow and patterns difficult to pinpoint.	Developing food chain.
Summer Peak	Fish are grouped but the lake's food chain is just starting to develop; thus there is an insufficient food supply. This means super fishing. This period could last from 1-3 weeks depending on location.	Developing food chain. Emerging weed beds.
Summer	The bulk of the fishing season for most anglers. Natural food chain is in "high gear" and fish have lots of food to choose from. Patterns are identifiable and presentation becomes the key. Some deoxygenation in certain lakes.	Food chain developed. Weed beds developed. Oxygen becomes a factor.
Post-summer	Prior to actual arrival of first cold fall weather. Lake food chain slows down with less sunlight. Fish activity excellent for a week.	Food chain slows down.

Fall Turnover	First really cold nights cause top layer of water to sink and a general mixing of the water. Fish disoriented, schools break up and fishing is very difficult for 3-10 days.	Water temperature. Oxygen.
Cold Water	Excellent time for walleyes. Good night movements of walleyes.	Location of available food.
Frozen Water	Fishing fair to good.	Location of available food.

When viewing the Calendar Periods it is important to keep in mind that these time frames are elastic. Each year the weather varies and so too will each Calendar Period. Some of these periods may be shorter than a month; others might last two or more months. The timing and length of each period depends on water temperature, light intensity and duration, and other natural influences that affect the various species' hormones and consequently their behavior.

Beyond the differences that can occur in a specific body of water, regions of the country also play a big role. For instance, in northern Canada, the first nine periods of an entire cycle can take place in four months or less. Yet in the deep South, the Pre-summer, Summer-peak, Summer, Post-summer and Turnover Periods might last nine months.

The lake type has a great bearing on when these periods take place. Small dark lakes warm faster than large clear ones, so lakes across the road from each other will not necessarily find the same species of fish in the same moods.

SUMMARY

By now we know that spring may officially arrive on March 21st, but to the walleye, dates on our calendar mean very little. After the Frozen and Cold Water Periods of the winter months, the duration of sunlight, the daytime and nighttime air temperatures, and the amount of rainfall determine the water temperature of a body of water. So, the factors that influence and govern water temperature are decisive and not a nominal date on a calendar.

These conditions may vary greatly even within a limited geographic area. This means that the walleyes in *all bodies of water do not necessarily function in the same way at the same time.* Even in areas where weather conditions are similar, there will be differences from one body of water to another. With this kind of knowledge, a sharp walleye angler moves from lake to lake and hits the peak times on each.

Beyond this, there are vast numbers of good technical fishermen who have mastered a number of forms of presentation and can "read" structure, but who still fail to understand how the predator/prey relationship relates to the Calendar Periods. So these otherwise "good fishermen" consequently run into recurrent problems. Our experience through the years has been that one big key to successful angling is understanding baitfish/prey movements. Strange as it seems, those ferocious predators are actually at the mercy of the prey they feed on. When the prey moves, the predators have to follow!

In reservoirs, or big, shallow flat lakes where walleyes feed on open water prey like shad, shiners, etc., their patterns of movement are quite different from walleyes which principally prey on the burrowing nymph of the mayfly.

Most state fisheries departments do regular test nettings, with accompanying stomach sample analysis, so information on the important baitfish and prey in most lakes, rivers or reservoirs is available. By understanding how prey movements dictate gamefish movements, we can eliminate much of the guesswork and begin understanding the reasons for fish location and attitude in each of the Calendar Periods.

Methods of presentation obviously vary throughout the Calendar Periods. Once you have learned to identify how the walleyes react in a given body of water during the different Calendar Periods, it will become evident that by varying your presentation you can become more and more successful. Sometimes presentation calls for fast movement, while at other times slow is best. Sometimes presentation is more effective on the bottom, while at other times a mid-level approach is best. Sometimes artificial lures are the ticket; other times it's live bait—sometimes nightcrawlers will attract more fish than minnows—or vice versa.

While confidence in a particular lure or bait is a big part of fishing success, too many anglers stick by their favorite lure under totally inappropriate circumstances and end up being "sometimes successful."

During the Summer Period when weedgrowth is at its greatest, and walleyes might be relating to it, some forms of presentation that did well in the early spring might not work that well. This means not only a change in lures, but a change in tackle to cope with the thicker weedgrowth. Water clarity also changes during the Calendar Periods, and this can make a difference in presentation.

So, not only do different lake conditions dictate different presentations, but walleyes in certain lake types actually seem to prefer certain kinds of lures and baits throughout the various Calendar Periods. This can be a trial and error thing, but there are also guidelines to follow.

These varying preferences have to do with both the developing food chain and the metabolic activity of the walleye. It's very probable that the walleyes' normal preference for minnows in the Pre-spawn, Spawn, Post-spawn and Pre-summer Periods has to do with the general lack of baitfish of preferred size during these particular Calendar Periods. Yet as a body of water begins producing numbers of minnows of a size that walleyes can feed on, perhaps a switch in presentation to 'crawlers and leeches will trigger more fish. With all those baitfish around, maybe a leech or 'crawler is a welcome change from the routine!

Finally, water temperature has a predictable effect on fish metabolism. Fishing for walleyes during the Cold Water Period, for example, requires a slow presentation. Walleyes slow down a lot once the water temperature dips below 45°F. A fast-moving crankbait that might be super in Pre-summer might not produce, while a jig and minnow worked slowly might just turn the trick when the Cold Water Period sets in.

The main thing the Calendar Periods teach you is that fish (in this case walleyes) *do not* respond the same way to the same things, day in and day out, month after month. The walleye fisherman who ties on a jig and beats a rocky drop-off from the beginning of the season until the end will obviously have some good days, but he will also experience many, many dry ones. By the same token, a live bait fancier who trolls a deep flat from spring until fall will also have his days, but he will also miss out on a lot of fantastic fishing as well.

In the final analysis, the only way to understand the different Calendar Periods on your particular body of water, or any others for that matter, is to spend enough time there to begin to identify these patterns. A water thermometer will help, but a keen eye on Mother Nature's clues is even better. Comparing notes with other anglers will also help you get a grasp on the Calendar Periods. And, of course, keeping a daily log of weather and water conditions, as well as fish feeding patterns, will help considerably. Often a review of last year's fishing log during a cold winter night provides not only a glimmer of past fishing glories, but also an insight into seasonal fishing patterns you never noticed before.

Remember, fish movement and feeding patterns may not always be predictable. But you can learn the seasonal circumstances that trigger fish to respond and the locational patterns that result from them. Combine this knowledge with the right presentation, and you have reached that fishing plateau that separates the real angler from the "sometimes successful" fisherman.

Chapter 4

An Introduction
to

THE BODY OF WATER CLASSIFICATION SYSTEM

Every time a new lure or system gets popular, people naturally want to get in on the action. But few folks stop to consider the kinds of water these tactics were designed for. And to complicate matters even more, many anglers are in various stages of the learning process, and have difficulty putting the whole picture together.

The scenario repeats itself again and again. For example, an angler buys a new weight-forward spinner and some 'crawlers—a system that is just clobbering walleyes on Lake Erie. On a fine summer's day he motors out to his type of lake, and expects to clean up on ol' marble eyes. But, he strikes out! What happened? Naturally, he figures he either did things completely wrong, or was sold a bill of goods.

Confused, he ponders the problem. He's heard the stories about the magnificent strings of walleyes taken by the countdown system, but is dumbfounded to know why the method doesn't work on his lake. But if he understood the basic differences in the bodies of water, his questions would have been answered.

A horse is a creature of the plains; a mountain goat one of the peaks and ledges. Each functions extremely well within its own niche, but is at a distinct disadvantage out of it. So it is with walleyes. They can make do in small, shallow, warm, silty, weedy lakes, or in timbered impoundments with tremendous water level fluctuations. You may even find them surviving in narrow, rock-strewn, cold, fast-running streams. But in the long run they do much better in large, medium-deep, gravel-based mesotrophic natural lakes, certain highland, hill-land and plateau reservoirs, and middle-aged rivers. These bodies of water are ideal homes for the walleye.

On the other hand, if the total environment is not that suited to the walleye's basic nature, you can find waters which produce numbers of small fish—but few big ones—or waters which produce big walleyes, but few of other size. Therefore, when you fish for walleyes, first think of the body of water type. Then, and only then, can the ramifications of location, feeding times, methods or presentation be viewed in the correct light. In the following sections, we'll examine the various types of lakes, rivers and reservoirs and explain how to identify each of them. Then you'll understand how walleyes will most likely operate under these circumstances.

We will begin with our *Natural Lake Classification System*. Then we will analyze the various river categories, and lastly, investigate the different kinds of reservoirs. Each type of lake, river or reservoir is *more* or *less* conducive to walleyes, and you will learn how to recognize one from the other.

Chapter 5
NATURAL LAKE CLASSIFICATION SYSTEM

A basic understanding of the different types of natural lakes is essential to becoming a consistent walleye angler. Most natural lakes in North America were created by the retreat of glaciers northward during the last ice age. The earth was first subjected to a great variety of natural forces, and when the glaciers receded, the myriad cuts and gouges in the landscape filled with melt water, forming lakes.

All lakes go through a natural aging process called eutrophication. The initial stages can take thousands of years, but the final ones may happen quickly—especially with the addition of man-made causes. Throughout this process, the total environment of a lake—its structural condition, food chains, vegetation levels and dominant fish species—change considerably. Man-caused eutrophication, or aging, is due of course to the expanding human population and disposal of waste products. These have caused changes in lakes so quickly that man has accomplished in a generation what it would have taken nature hundreds or thousands of years to do.

Consequently, WALLEYE WISDOM views and classifies natural lakes according to their condition, and not necessarily their chronological age. A lake is either young, middle-aged or old. Since some lakes lie between types and almost defy classification, our classifications are not to be taken as absolutes. Instead, each category is meant to be a convenient point of reference—a definition we can start to work from.

As lakes "age," their character changes. Generally speaking, geologically "young" lakes are deep and clean; older ones are shallow and murky.

The natural order is such that on one end of the scale we find young lakes with a type of chemistry which can support fish like lake trout and whitefish. At the other end, we find lakes with another kind of chemistry which can only support fish such as carp and bullheads.

Obviously, a lake trout cannot live in a shallow, murky, weedy, low-oxygen lake in the midwestern prairies. And carp have a tough time making it in the rocky, ice-cold, weedless environment of a trout lake. But between these two extremes lie lakes of all sorts—each of which are more or less hospitable to certain species of fish.

Walleyes, for example, have quite a bit of latitude in their genetic make-up and can at least exist in varying degrees in all but the very young or extremely old bodies of water. Sometimes this aging is determined by fertility—the youngest lakes being infertile while the oldest are very fertile.

All classifications of natural walleye lake types lie within three very broad, but basic categories:

1. **Oligotrophic** *(infertile)*—(young) (cold-water environment)
   LATE STAGE ONLY. Low in number, but big fish of 9-14 pounds. Old fish.

2. **Mesotrophic** *(fertile)*—(middle-aged) (cool-water environment)
   BEST! Lots of fish, and big fish. 2-8 pounds is common. Fair amount of fish 8-11 pounds. 12 pound top-outs.

3. **Eutrophic** *(very fertile)*—(warm-warm environment)
   FAIR FISHING ONLY. Good average of 1/2 to 4 pounds. Common big fish is 6 pounds. *Exception:* Some lake's produce lunkers 8-12 pounds. These fish are low in numbers.

When you analyze a particular lake, remember that these categories are simply points of reference to work from and may overlap into other categories. As you become familar with the system, you will be able to recognize a lake as being early stage eutrophic—instead of late stage meso.

The youngest type of lakes—oligotrophic—typically have rock basins and are found almost exclusively in the upper portions of the North American continent. They usually have steep, sharp drop-offs, few weeds, pine-studded shorelines, and a fish population that is composed of cold water fish like lake trout and members of the whitefish family. The nutrient level of the water is usually low. Thus, the lake is termed infertile.

As this type of lake ages, the shorelines become less gorge-like, and the

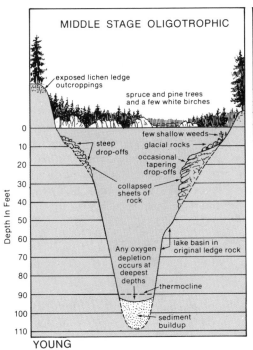

MIDDLE STAGE OLIGOTROPHIC

exposed lichen ledge outcroppings

spruce and pine trees and a few white birches

Depth In Feet

steep drop-offs

few shallow weeds

glacial rocks

occasional tapering drop-offs

collapsed sheets of rock

lake basin in original ledge rock

Any oxygen depletion occurs at deepest depths

thermocline

sediment buildup

YOUNG

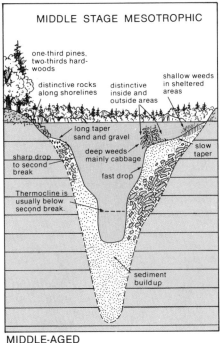

MIDDLE STAGE MESOTROPHIC

one-third pines, two-thirds hardwoods

distinctive rocks along shorelines

distinctive inside and outside areas

shallow weeds in sheltered areas

long taper sand and gravel

deep weeds mainly cabbage

slow taper

sharp drop to second break

fast drop

Thermocline is usually below second break.

sediment buildup

MIDDLE-AGED

LATE STAGE EUTROPHIC

flat terrain, farmlands and sparse hardwoods

Most of lake is shallow and weed choked; one hole exists.

heavy weeds to surface and to shorelines

thin reeds

cattails

sand and muck

sediment buildup

OLD

drop-offs less abrupt and steep. Big boulders turn to smaller rock, and more sand and gravel become apparent. Weedgrowth develops. The trees that bound the lake also tend to change. Since the surrounding terrain changes, the water quality takes on a new character (more nutrients).

These are the first signs of the transitory process between our oligotrophic and mesotrophic categories. Naturally-sustaining populations of walleyes exist in very low numbers in the early stage "oli" lake, but become more numerous as the lake ages to its mid or late oligotrophic stages.

Little by little, the lake changes and eventually develops characteristics typical of a middle-aged, mesotrophic lake. When a lake reaches its mid-mesotrophic stage, much of the exposed rock, except right along the shoreline, is gone. Sand and some gravel now prevail in the lake's basin. The shoreline tapers become more gradual, more weeds appear in the shallows and the trees that surround the lake begin changing from evergreens to hardwoods. A distinct thermocline is usually present. Walleyes and perch are most likely the dominant species. In fact, these waters are the most ideal for walleyes to survive, and indeed, thrive.

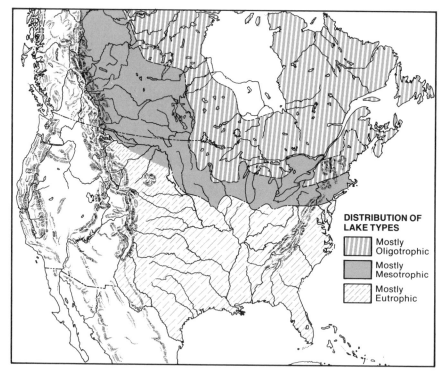

DISTRIBUTION OF LAKE TYPES

- Mostly Oligotrophic
- Mostly Mesotrophic
- Mostly Eutrophic

The advance and retreat of continental glaciers altered the landscape. The massive ice sheets scraped much of Canada down to bedrock, leaving behind shallow areas which are now lakes. They also pushed the north's fertile soil southward. Because of this, lake types follow a pattern. In Canada, for example, if you go east of Lake Winnipeg, you're in "lake trout water." Go west and you're in "walleye water." Generally speaking, most oligotrophic lakes lie in one region; mesotrophic lakes in another, and eutrophic lakes in still another. The rockies and Appalachians formed "barriers" of sorts, yet between these ranges the distribution of lake types—with exceptions—hold fairly true.

FOOD CONSUMED BY WALLEYES ON DIFFERENT LAKE TYPES

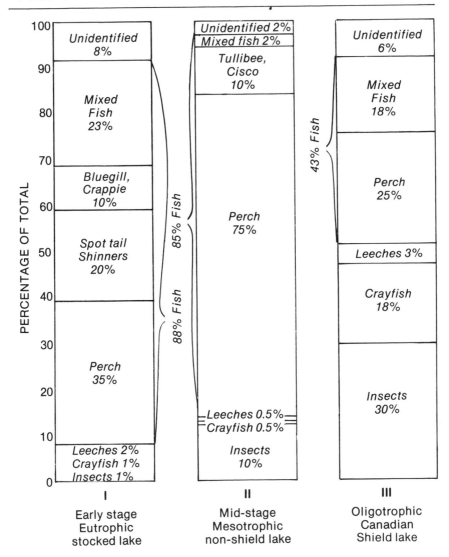

By combining a number of fishery reports on walleye food habits in July and August from various lake types, we were able to compile this chart. It should provide you with clues to walleye movements on various lake types.

By the time the next transition (mesotrophic to eutrophic) stage occurs, a lake, by geological aging standards, is getting old. First off, it is getting shallower. Sand begins turning to muck or clay in certain sections, and the erosion process results in less extensive shoreline tapers than in the mid-meso classification. Secondary drop-offs in the deep water are obliterated or less defined.

Marshy areas usually dot certain adjacent sections. Hardwood trees and flat shorelines rim the lakeshore, rather than steep cliffs or high hills. The lake is changing from a cool to a warm water environment. Self-sustaining walleye populations start becoming marginal.

When a lake moves into its mid-eutrophic stage, it is now a true warm-water environment. In its oligotrophic stage this body of water was a cold-water environment; in its "meso" stage a cool water environment; and now in its eutrophic stage a warm water environment. Largemouth bass and bluegills now predominate and natural walleye populations are negligible to nonexistent, although stocked fish can survive.

By geological standards, this lake is now quite old. It has become very shallow, and the erosion process is near completion. Farmlands usually surround these waters. Thermoclines generally don't develop or last a long time. Weedgrowth is thick and sandy areas become quiet soft. Water color becomes darker, so weeds grow to lesser depths, and the shoreline just sort of blends into the basin of the lake. Walleyes, even stocked ones, start to find life pretty tough in these waters.

In a nutshell, this is the aging process all natural lakes go through. Study the accompanying drawings carefully, so you understand the different types of natural lakes. Most importantly, as you learn to recognize lake types, you'll learn what to expect in terms of walleye size and probable density of their population. In the final analysis, this will help you fish smarter—not harder!

Chapter 6

RIVER CLASSIFICATION SYSTEM

River fishermen face more sudden, dramatic changes in water conditions than a lake fisherman can ever imagine. Most lakes are "a piece of cake" when compared structurally with rivers. Water levels in natural lakes remain relatively stable over long periods of time. It usually takes a long-term drought or heavy rainfall to bring about severe high or low water levels in a lake. Yet river anglers are always fighting rising or falling water levels. More than just contending with water level "flux," they must adjust to bottom structure that is here today and gone tomorrow. Sandbars come and go. Flow patterns can change in a subtle manner with a shift of the stream's course or an increase in current speed.

Changing bottom conditions obviously will also affect fish location. As rapidly as water levels rise or fall, a key fish-attracting current break like an eddy can suddenly appear or completely vanish, and affect fish location accordingly. A pile of submerged rocks that might hold walleyes during the high water of spring might be high and dry a week later. Remember, the ability to read current is the key to successful river fishing. Take the time to learn how it functions with rising or falling water levels, creating or eliminating fish-holding areas in the process.

Fish like walleyes relate to structural elements one way during high water, and another way when the water is low. The water depth and speed around an object produces those all-important "current breaks" that determine sections of slack water where food accumulates and fish gather. Fish will hold and set up feeding stations at these points.

A list of some of the major structural elements found in the various types of streams would surely include most of the following:

(1) MAIN, FEEDER AND SIDE CHANNELS
(2) POINT BARS ON THE INSIDE BENDS OF RIVER CURVES
(3) MAN-MADE STRUCTURAL ELEMENTS
(4) SLOUGHS OF DEAD WATER
(5) NATURAL LEVEES OF HARD MATERIAL LEFT BY FLOODS
(6) BACKWATER AREAS
(7) SANDBARS
(8) POOLS
(9) RIFFLES
(10) EDDIES
(11) CURRENT BREAKS
(12) THE INTERSECTION OF A TRIBUTARY STREAM
(13) AREAS BELOW A DAM

Most streams contain these various components in differing combinations.

Patterns of Current Flow in River Bends

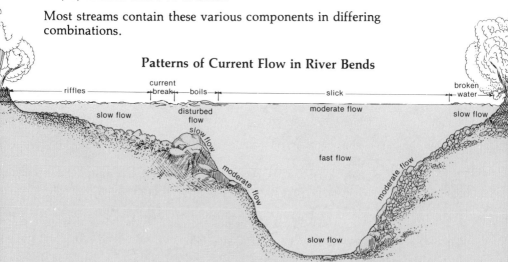

River fishing provides some of the most consistent walleye fishing available. Weather affects rivers the least of all waters. Rivers are the most underfished water in the world.

Wing Dams

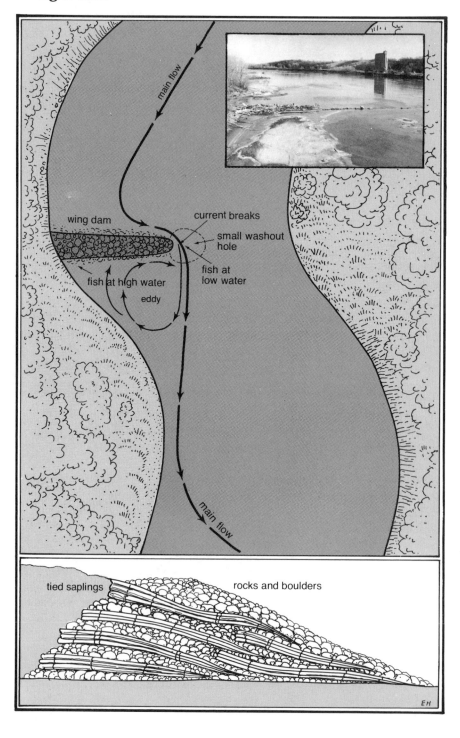

Wing dams are the spot of spots on many river stretches. The preceding sketch shows how they are constructed and how they affect flow. Note that some wing dams are interlaced with alternate rows of saplings and rocks. These provide both a hiding place and a food source for small fish. Insects and other edible organisms lodge in the saplings. Most anglers fish in back (downstream side) of a wing dam; this spot is usually the best fish magnet. There are times, however, when the front face (upstream side) can attract and hold fish, so it should be checked out. Note the location of the fish at high and low water. It is best, when fishing the "low water" spots, to anchor upstream from the hole and cast a jig (tipped with live bait) to the fish. The same goes for the "high water" spot except that you would anchor downstream behind the wing dam in slower current.

Just as lakes are formed through the forces of nature over long periods of time, so are rivers, and therein lies the clue to our categorical approach. Like lakes, rivers follow a natural development pattern from young to old.

Geologists refer to rivers as being "young," "middle-aged," or "old." Since rivers do not thermocline, terms like oligotrophic, mesotrophic and eutrophic (although having some application) do not really describe a stretch of river's condition or nature. Instead, "young," "middle-aged" or "old" better describe the condition of the landscape carved by the river, more so than the actual age of the river itself or its primary environmental condition. On some big rivers like the Mississippi, Missouri, Ohio and Arkansas, there are sections where you can see huge, well-developed plains—evidence of an old river. Here, the original banks are miles away and hundreds of feet higher than today's existing stream bed. That's what we mean when we say the surrounding geography and generalized shape of the riverbed are the main clues to a stream's age.

In its flow, a young river plunges rapidly downhill, cutting through narrow valleys. As a river matures, it moves downhill more slowly and meanders a little more gently through broad valleys bounded by smoothly rounded hills. In "old age," a river curves widely across level flood plains surrounded by worn-down hills.

For a stream, the major catalyst to aging is erosion. In general, the longer a stream extends in length, the more aging occurs in the form of erosion. *The process of erosion actually carries the aging process upstream.* So, as time goes on, older geological conditions which form at a river's delta continue to move further and further back upstream.

Since there are variations in the aging progression in successive sections of a stream, as well as some overlap between the abundance and presence of the cold, cool and warm water fish species, the only way to view a stream is by *stretches.* In this sense, a particular stretch can be young, old, or somewhere in between in terms of geological make-up. For instance, a stream might be quite shallow, have a slow taper for several miles, and possess a number of backwater areas with a soft bottom and aquatic weedgrowth. Here large-mouth bass and/or northern pike might be able to find adequate habitat. But all of a sudden, this same stream might break into a sharp gradient as it shoots through a rocky, cliff-like area, creating a rapids and finally pouring into a boulder-based pool. This younger stretch, although further downstream, could house smallmouth bass and possibly stocked rainbow trout.

Different stretches of the same stream will have different personalities and different fish species. Rarely is a stream the same from beginning to end, because few regions are geographically consistent. Within any lengthy run of walleye river, there are sections which are conducive to supporting walleyes, and sections which are not.

Because of these limitless variations, we devised the following method of classifying streams. With these categories, we can identify and recognize most river stretches found in North America. Of course, there will be exceptions: Usually those parts in transition between types, much like a natural lake that has eutrophic bays, while the main body of the lake is mesotrophic in character.

These classes are best viewed as guidelines that will help you toward a better understanding of the rivers you fish and the quantity and types of fish you could expect to find in them. For our walleye interest, we'll use only the adult, mature and middle-aged rivers. These classifications hold the bulk of the walleye population.

(1) VERY YOUNG — Brook trout and/or grayling
(2) YOUNG — Stocked trout
(3) ADULT — Appearance of cool water fish (walleyes)
(4) MATURE — Good populations of walleyes
(5) MIDDLE-AGED — "Hawg" size walleye
(6) OLD — Disappearance of walleyes
(7) VERY OLD — Mostly rough fish
(8) TIDAL — Backwaters of the ocean

	ADULT	MATURE	MIDDLE-AGED
SHAPE OF CROSS SECTION	Prominent Vegetation. Gravel Deposits Begin to Build. Erosion really flattens out the stream bed.	Flood Plain. Sand and Gravel Deposits	Channel Bottom is Completely Smooth. Broadened Flood Plain. Sand and Mud Deposits
GRADIENT & DEPTH	Gradient: Two to three foot drop per mile. Depth: Six to ten feet average with intermittent deep and shallow stretches based on the amount of sand and gravel present. Most pools following rapids are eight to ten feet with occasional isolated holes of fifteen to twenty feet.	Gradient: 1.5 to two foot drop per mile. Depth: Depth will vary with some stretches four to five feet deep, while deeper holes can be fifteen to twenty feet. There is a lot of eight to ten feet deep water.	Gradient: One to 1.5 foot drop per mile. Depth: Depth will vary from shallow one foot deep weedy backwater pockets to forty foot pools. Runs of twelve feet are common. Under dams, gouges of fifty feet can occur.

	ADULT	MATURE	MIDDLE-AGED
KEY I.D. FEATURE	Trout can no longer reproduce naturally. The appearance of cool water fish. (Walleye, Smallmouth)	The ability to produce quantities of preferred game species such as Walleye, Sauger, and Northern Pike. Deep pools provide refuge, and rock and gravel tributaries provide spawning grounds. A mature stream can produce good populations of several kinds of game fish; sandy, rocky sections with fast water will hold Smallmouth while the deeper, slower sections or pools will contain Walleyes.	The presence of naturally reproducing Walleye and Sauger mixed with fair levels of Largemouth Bass. This is the river of "hawg" walleyes. There is a diversity of habitat for just about any kind of fish. This is the last stage for quantities of naturally reproducing cool water fish. (Walleye and Sauger)
GEOGRAPHICAL MAKE-UP	The stream bed is alternating sections of gravel, sand, fist-sized rocks with sporadic boulders and no silt. There will be shallower sections and some rocks dressed with moss. (Weed growth is scarce). Shoreline banks composed of fist-sized rocks, trees, and brush. Occasional wing dams will be present.	The main channel is composed mostly of sand. Siltation is now a significant factor; wing dams sometimes are constructed to control this. There are some rock outcroppings. Aquatic growth is common along with a higher nutrient level.	Flows mostly through soft sedimentary rock and sandy subsoils. Sand is the dominant riverbed material. Time and erosion have pulverized the various rocks and gravel. There will be a few rock outcrops along the banks of the river. This stage will exhibit well-developed flood plains; flooding is common. Siltation is now a factor. Wing dams to control siltation are common.
PROBABLE SPECIES	Generally cool water fish such as Smallmouth Bass, Northern Pike, some Walleye, and maybe some Carp. Possibly a few Muskies.	Walleye, Sauger, some Smallmouth, Northern, Muskie, Catfish, Silver Bass, Sturgeon, few Largemouth, Perch, Crappie, White Bass, Crap, Sucker, Buffalo, Rock Bass.	Sauger, Walleye, Northern, few Muskie, Silver Bass, good Largemouth, Catfish. Certain sections of a Middle-aged stretch will be more hospitable to one species because of the structural make-up even though they cut through the same terrain.

	ADULT	MATURE	MIDDLE-AGED
SOURCE & ECOLOGICAL DRAINAGE AREA	This stretch can be of highland or farmland origin and will drain a more expansive area: marginal hardwood forests that contain mixed pine, fringe agricultural areas such as truck farms and farm feed lots. At this stage, the river has its maximum number of tributaries that will drain generally infertile, sparse areas. The source is usually a young river or could be a lake or spring in the lower foothills or in a sand or gravel locale. Sometimes adult streams come from "meso" lakes or highland reservoirs. There are almost no intermittent streams acting as feeders.	This stretch may either emerge from or cut through farmland, and is usually composed of sandstone and other subsoil types. The drainage area can include farmland as well as major urban and industrial areas, which can have a major impact on pollution levels. The number of tributaries start to decrease at this stage.	This stage often has a farmland origin. The drainage area is very large with high weed growth adjacent to agricultural areas. Tributaries consist now mainly of adult rivers.
WATER QUALITY	The water is semi-clear but can become very murky during heavy rains, particularly in farm areas or small urban areas. Premature aging may occur in areas of intense agricultural activity when nutrient levels are high or where pollution is substantial.	The water will be semi-clear to semi-murky. During high water periods, it will be very turbid, especially around agricultural areas, usually taking four to five days to clear up. Slower running water will make the temperature higher. Aging will accelerate because of agricultural and industrial pollutants.	The water is murky to quite turbid most of the time because of suspended mineral and soil particles plus increased organic nutrients. Turbidity is a constant factor because of the large size of the watershed, a situation that makes angling difficult. Where this river broadens into a large lake, settling will occur and water quality will temporarily improve.
TYPICAL ILLUSTRATIONS	These stretches are found in western Pennsylvania (Appalachia), Arkansas (Buffalo), the St. Croix in Minnesota, and the upper stages of the Mississippi, the upper Potomac River and stretches of the Shenandoah.	These stretches can be found in major drainage areas in any part of the country. For example, large stretches of the Mississippi and the lower Allegheny River in Pennsylvania.	The St. Lawrence River bordering the U.S. and Canada has middle-aged stretches, as does the Detroit River, and, of course, a good part of the Mississippi and Ohio Rivers.

	ADULT	MATURE	MIDDLE-AGED
R E M A R K S	This stretch contains a higher nutrient level, warmer and slower moving water than the very young or young stretches. Typical of this stretch is alternating "riffle" or "slick" sections. Gone are the roaring, cascading rapids replaced by mini-rapids that are not dangerous. There is increased fertilizer runoff and sewage input. Damming is more frequent, and occasional islands will be found. Sand and gravel bars have become a prominent feature.	Rapids nonexistent; at best a few shallow "riffles" will occur. Mature rivers can and do overflow. They will begin to meander and develop flood plains. Dams, on this river stage, actually create miniature impoundments. Although they are called "pools," they function much like reservoirs. At certain times of the year, usually spring or fall, all the gamefish species could be stacked up against the dam! This stream is an In-Fisherman paradise and is the first stage that produces multiple quantities of preferred game fish.	This stretch usually flows by river towns and metropolitan areas where pollution can be a severe problem. It is at this stage that the river really starts to show the buildup of nutrients, erosion, and pollution. Except for trout and salmon, just about any type of fish can survive. This stream will offer the most pounds of game fish per acre provided it is unpolluted. Flood plains can create backwater sloughs or flat, high, fertile fields. A dredged, mid-ship channel is usually maintained for barges, and dams with locks are common.

Chapter 7

THE RESERVOIR CLASSIFICATION SYSTEM

Just as lakes and rivers fall into distinctive and descriptive categories, reservoirs, too (by way of make-up and function), fall into various classifications. Remember, a reservoir is simply an impounded body of water held back by a dam across some type of river. This artificially impounded water floods natural terrain such as marshes, plains, hills, plateaus or canyons.

Taking a number of cross-sections of North America, you would see that in some areas the terrain might be low, sort of swampy or marshy, or rather flat like the old flood-plain regions of the large river systems. In other places, the terrain is hilly—not high ridges but simply a series of rolling hills.

Still, in other areas, mountains and highland ridges rise up from the earth's surface to form foothill areas. Usually, these are low mountain ranges like the Boston or Ouachita ranges in Arkansas, the Appalachian chain in the east, the Cumberland highlands of Kentucky and Tennessee or the low coastal ranges

Location of U.S. Walleye Reservoirs

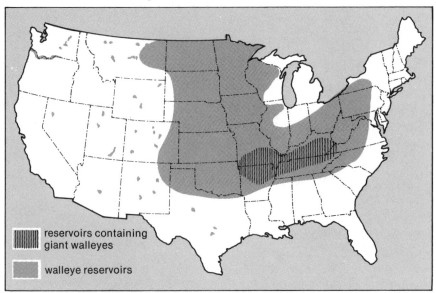

reservoirs containing giant walleyes

walleye reservoirs

As you can see, walleyes are present in many reservoirs east of the Rocky Mountains. But interestingly enough, the lakes producing the real monsters are confined to a relatively small area. Once you get outside of Missouri, Arkansas, Tennessee and Kentucky, your chances for a world record drop abruptly.

Although it generally is thought of as a river, the entire upper section of the Mississippi River is actually a series of reservoirs formed by the many dams placed back-to-back along its path. Even huge Lake Winnibigoshish in Minnesota functions as a reservoir. And the Wisconsin River flowages—Lake Wisconsin, Castle Rock and Petenwell—are actually flatland reservoirs, although locally no one calls them by that name. Both Wisconsin and Minnesota contain numerous small reservoirs that offer excellent walleye fishing.

Up until now, the reservoir walleye fishery of the United States has seen comparatively little attention. Isn't it time that you considered giving reservoirs a try?

on the West Coast.

In the plains west of the Mississippi, you encounter what are termed "high plains." Just west of them is an immense plateau that lifts step-like across the mid-section of the continent. This plateau area is adjacent to the rugged Rocky Mountains.

Reservoirs built in the canyons of the mountains take on long, snake-like shapes, and their cross-sections have towering, sharp, almost vertical walls.

Further investigation shows that fish within similar types of reservoirs repond in much the same manner. In other words, walleyes in various shallow, warm, dark water, lowland (flowage) reservoirs tend to exhibit like patterns of movements and responses, while walleyes in deep, clear, cool, highland reservoirs respond somewhat differently. What becomes obvious is that reservoirs constructed in similar kinds of land forms (even if those land forms are in distant parts of the country), are enough alike that we can fit them into six basic groups.

IMPOUNDMENT CLASSIFICATION

Canyon Impoundment

Most canyon reservoir walleyes live in a vertical habitat near the shoreline, often suspending out from the shore break. These impoundments hold fair populations of walleyes in the 2-4 pound range. A big fish is 10 pounds plus. Canyon reservoirs are the newest walleye fisheries and are still largely unexplored. Lake Powell in Utah is a good example.

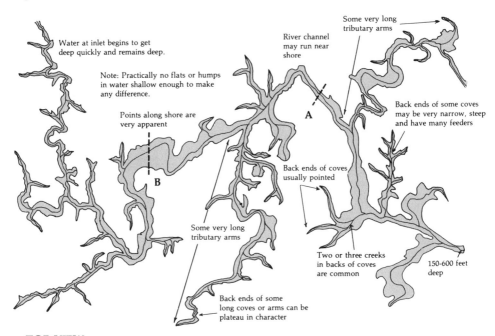

Some very long tributary arms

River channel may run near shore

Water at inlet begins to get deep quickly and remains deep.

Note: Practically no flats or humps in water shallow enough to make any difference.

Back ends of some coves may be very narrow, steep and have many feeders

Points along shore are very apparent

A

Back ends of coves usually pointed

B

Some very long tributary arms

Two or three creeks in backs of coves are common

150-600 feet deep

Back ends of some long coves or arms can be plateau in character

TOP VIEW

CROSS-SECTIONS

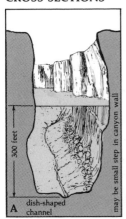

300 feet

may be small step in canyon wall

A dish-shaped channel

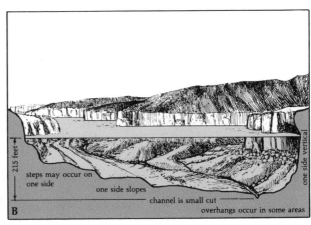

215 feet

steps may occur on one side

one side slopes

channel is small cut

one side vertical

B overhangs occur in some areas

Plateau Impoundment

Plateau reservoirs have very good populations of walleyes in the two to seven pound range. A big fish is nine pounds plus. Like flatland reservoirs, the walleyes are fast growing and short-lived. The Missouri River impoundments fall into this classification.

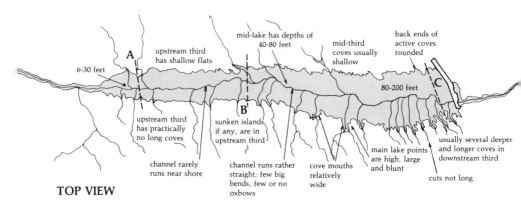

TOP VIEW

CROSS-SECTIONS

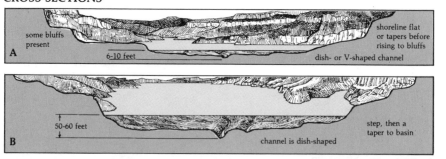

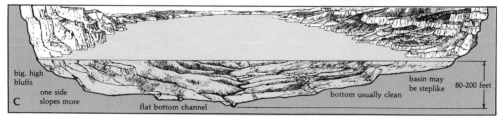

Highland Impoundment

Highland reservoirs usually have good populations of walleyes in the 4-8 pound range. A big walleye is 12 pounds plus—or even larger. Highland reservoirs produce real lunkers. Included in this classification are such waters as Greer's Ferry in Arkansas, Cumberland in Kentucky, Dale Hollow in Tennessee and Bull Shoals and Stockton in Missouri.

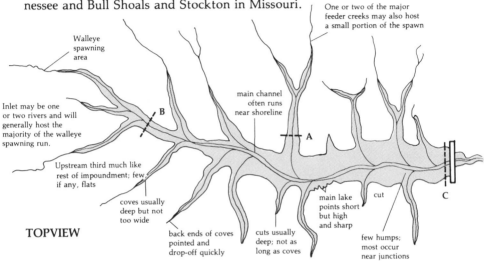

One or two of the major feeder creeks may also host a small portion of the spawn

Walleye spawning area

Inlet may be one or two rivers and will generally host the majority of the walleye spawning run.

main channel often runs near shoreline

Upstream third much like rest of impoundment; few if any, flats

coves usually deep but not too wide

TOPVIEW

back ends of coves pointed and drop-off quickly

cuts usually deep; not as long as coves

main lake points short but high and sharp

few humps; most occur near junctions

CROSS-SECTIONS

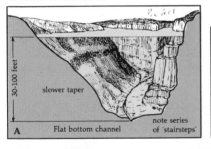

slower taper

30-100 feet

Flat bottom channel

note series of 'stairsteps'

A

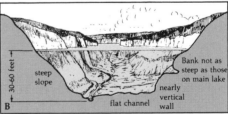

steep slope

30-60 feet

Bank not as steep as those on main lake

nearly vertical wall

flat channel

B

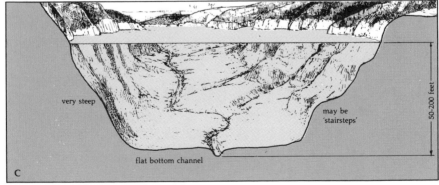

very steep

may be 'stairsteps'

50-200 feet

flat bottom channel

C

Hill-land Impoundment

Hill-land reservoirs generally have low numbers of walleyes. The average good fish runs from 4-8 pounds. A big walleye is 10 pounds plus. Lake Shelbyville in Illinois falls into this classification.

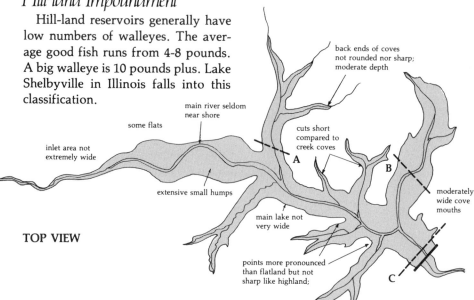

back ends of coves not rounded nor sharp; moderate depth

main river seldom near shore

some flats

inlet area not extremely wide

cuts short compared to creek coves

moderately wide cove mouths

TOP VIEW

extensive small humps

main lake not very wide

points more pronounced than flatland but not sharp like highland;

A

B

C

CROSS-SECTIONS

moderate drop-off

flats

no humps

flat creek bed

slope to basin is moderate

6-12 feet

A

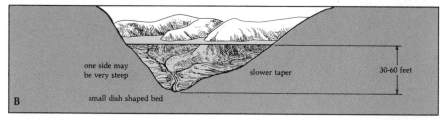

one side may be very steep

small dish shaped bed

slower taper

30-60 feet

B

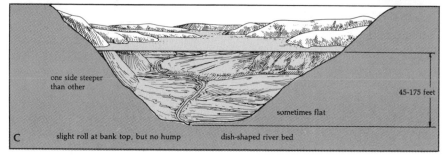

one side steeper than other

sometimes flat

45-175 feet

slight roll at bank top, but no hump

dish-shaped river bed

C

Flatland Impoundment

Flatland reservoirs can have good to excellent populations of walleyes. The fish are very fast growing, but short-lived. Average size runs between 1-3 pounds. Anything 6 pounds or over is considered a big fish. Castle Rock and the other Wisconsin River flowages are good examples.

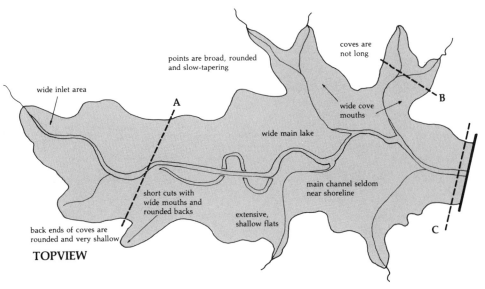

coves are not long

points are broad, rounded and slow-tapering

wide inlet area

A

B

wide cove mouths

wide main lake

main channel seldom near shoreline

short cuts with wide mouths and rounded backs

extensive, shallow flats

C

back ends of coves are rounded and very shallow

TOPVIEW

CROSS-SECTIONS

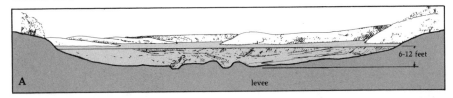

6-12 feet

A

levee

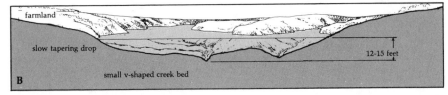

farmland

slow tapering drop

12-15 feet

B

small v-shaped creek bed

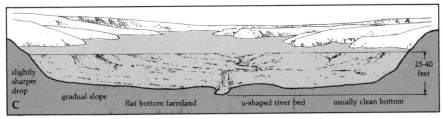

25-40 feet

slightly sharper drop

gradual slope

flat bottom farmland

u-shaped river bed

usually clean bottom

C

Lowland/Wetland Impoundment

Most lowland walleye reservoirs have high numbers of small fish. A large fish here would be around 5 pounds plus. Many section's of the Flambeau and Gile Flowages in Wisconsin are good examples.

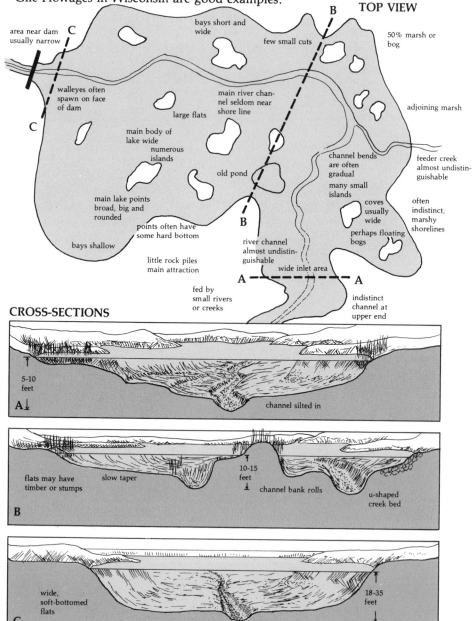

TOP VIEW

area near dam usually narrow

C

bays short and wide

few small cuts

B

50% marsh or bog

walleyes often spawn on face of dam

C

main river channel seldom near shore line

large flats

adjoining marsh

main body of lake wide numerous islands

old pond

channel bends are often gradual

many small islands

feeder creek almost undistinguishable

main lake points broad, big and rounded

coves usually wide

often indistinct, marshy shorelines

points often have some hard bottom

B

perhaps floating bogs

bays shallow

river channel almost undistinguishable

little rock piles main attraction

wide inlet area

A

A

fed by small rivers or creeks

indistinct channel at upper end

CROSS-SECTIONS

5-10 feet

A

channel silted in

flats may have timber or stumps

slow taper

10-15 feet

channel bank rolls

u-shaped creek bed

B

wide, soft-bottomed flats

18-35 feet

C

narrow, u-shaped creek bed

In this unit, we'll only cover the major natural and man-made characteristics that place an impoundment into one class or another. Many, because of limited water, sometimes challenge orderly classification. Remember that some impoundments just plain defy cozy placement. For now, remember that *basic shape*—not content—is what counts within our major reservoir classifications.

SUMMARY

Reservoirs are some of today's walleye fishing hotspots. You'll find consistently big fish in the plateau and canyon reservoir of the Midwest and West. The biggest fish of all, if not in numbers, are available in the highland impoundments of the South where the growing season is longer.

Interestingly enough, most reservoirs are underfished. But the word's getting out, and already the Missouri River system is getting increasing fishing pressure, as is the pre-spawn run at Greer's Ferry in Arkansas.

But there are a whole host of western reservoirs where walleye fishermen are few and far between. For example, the Columbia River basin in the state of Washington is producing terrific walleye fishing for the few taking advantage of it. North Dakota has some remote waters that produce great walleye fishing, such as Bowman-Haley Dam in the southwestern part of the state.

Our bet for the sleepers of the '80's are the reservoirs lying west of the Missouri River, where walleye fishing pressure is comparatively light and there are often plenty of walleyes.

Chapter 8
THE PRE-SPAWN PERIOD

"A Time of Anticipation"

The length of the Pre-spawn Period can vary depending on how you look at it. Theoretically, it begins when walleyes start shifting toward or assembling in their spawning areas. However, this can actually begin to occur while a lake, river or reservoir is still covered with ice—especially where a warmer inflowing stream raises the water temperature in a localized area.

For angling purposes, we consider the walleyes' Pre-spawn Period to begin shortly after ice-out, or as water temperatures reach the upper 30°F's. Fish movements are tied to water temperature, water levels, weather conditions and the angle of the sun's rays. Overall, the rising water temperature and length of day triggers the walleyes' biological clock and starts them moving toward their spawning grounds. The fish will usually begin spawning somewhere between the low 40°F's and 50°F.

Males generally lead the pre-spawn movement to the spawning grounds, and actively cruise these areas at night when the water temperature reaches the mid 40°F's. Females begin joining the males in the shallows at night toward the end of this period.

Egg-laden female walleyes are at their peak trophy potential for the entire year, weighing considerably more than they will during the rest of the growing season. Thus this is one of the top Calendar Periods to go after a trophy. However, many northern states and Canadian provinces have closed walleye seasons at this time, so be sure to check the local fishing regulations.

Now, let's get down to a typical breakdown of location and presentation for lakes, rivers and reservoirs. We've picked a prime example from each of these body of water types to demonstrate how you match your tactics to the conditions.

NATURAL LAKES

Once the ice disappears from a lake, the warming rays of the sun penetrate the upper layer and heat the surface water. The depths remain very cold. Walleyes are powerfully drawn to the shallows and cruise the shoreline in search of baitfish. Since food is seldom plentiful and hungry walleyes often concentrate in the vicinity of their spawning grounds, fishing can be excellent.

Prime locations during this period are the fringes of bulrush points, shallow sand flats (no more than 10 feet deep), flats around the mouths of inlet streams, and shallow, rocky, mid-lake sunken islands. Pre-spawn walleyes typically hold in slightly deeper water just off the edges of these areas during the day, and then move up shallow on them at night.

Since walleyes spook easily in shallow water, try anchoring and casting rather than trolling. Best baits at this time are: (1) small jigs (bright color in murky water, lighter colors in clear water) tipped with a small minnow, (2) a plain minnow (preferably a shiner) fished on a slip-sinker rig or a slip-bobber, or (3) an imitation minnow lure like a Rapala or Rebel.

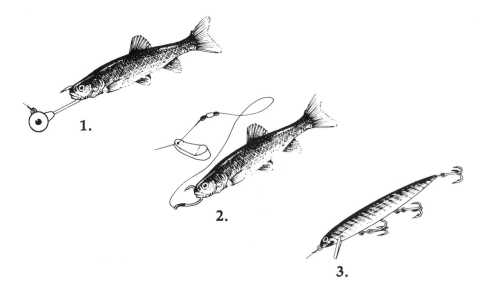

As daylight fades, walleyes are drawn even shallower. If you can find a clean sand/gravel area along shore, try casting with floating Rapalas or other minnow imitators. Don't be afraid to cast within a few feet of shore. Pre-spawn walleyes will edge unbelievably close to shore at night. To locate concentration areas, slowly cruise along shore pointing a Q-Beam spotlight in the water, and look for the reflections from the walleyes' eyes. Once you locate a group of fish, shut off the light and be as quiet as possible. Any noise in the boat will scatter the fish.

A word of caution: Don't expect shallow water walleye fishing to be consistent. Even a slight cold front can drop the temperature of the inshore water a few degrees, causing the walleyes to head for deeper water. So don't stubbornly stick to shallow water just because walleyes were there yesterday. The successful fisherman "reads" the changes and adjusts his techniques accordingly.

The Pre-spawn metabolism of walleyes is still slow. Fish your lures the same way—super slow.

RESERVOIRS

Pre-spawn walleye fishing in highland reservoirs is your best chance at a real trophy during the '80's. After all, when you are talking 20 pound plus walleyes, this has to be the top pick for trophies.

One word of caution, though, the action is not fast for these huge walleyes. But, when you catch one, it'll likely be a giant.

Highland reservoirs generally have one or more major river arms which host a large portion of the spring walleye spawning run. Many fish leave the main reservoir and swim upcurrent to spawn in shallow, rocky rapids in 2-4 feet of water. They hold in slightly deeper pools during the day and then move directly into the rapids to spawn at night.

The exact portion of the river the fish use depends chiefly on the prevailing water level and current, and can change somewhat from year to year. Yet even though the exact stretch may vary, it only takes a bit of experimentation in the general vicinity, or posing a few questions to local anglers, to narrow down the most productive river section.

TYPICAL PRE-SPAWN LOCATIONS

The accompanying map depicts a typical highland river section approximately 2-3 miles above the point where it joins the main body of the reservoir. These narrow rivers generally wind through the mountains and are bordered by towering rock bluffs. The rivers themselves contain numerous areas of broken rock, forming rapids where the water is sufficiently shallow. These are key walleye spawning sites. Pre-spawn walleyes congregate in the deeper pools immediately above and below these rapids during the day, and when conditions are right, spawn in the rapids at night.

Although the bulk of the spawn usually occurs in about one week, walleyes nevertheless inhabit these areas for a good month or so. Once the water temperature rises above 40°F, they begin appearing in the pool/rapids areas

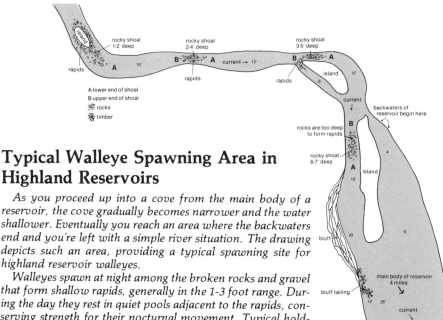

rocky shoal 1-2' deep
rocky shoal 2-4' deep
rocky shoal 3-5' deep
island
rapids
A
B
A
current →
12'
rapids
B
A
rapids
island
12'
6'
A-lower end of shoal
B-upper end of shoal
rocks
timber
current
backwaters of reservoir begin here
rocks are too deep to form rapids
B
rocky shoal 6-7' deep
A
island
12'
bluff
20'
5
main body of reservoir 4 miles
bluff tailing
12'
25'
current

Typical Walleye Spawning Area in Highland Reservoirs

As you proceed up into a cove from the main body of a reservoir, the cove gradually becomes narrower and the water shallower. Eventually you reach an area where the backwaters end and you're left with a simple river situation. The drawing depicts such an area, providing a typical spawning site for highland reservoir walleyes.

Walleyes spawn at night among the broken rocks and gravel that form shallow rapids, generally in the 1-3 foot range. During the day they rest in quiet pools adjacent to the rapids, conserving strength for their nocturnal movement. Typical holding spots are **Areas A,** the lower (downstream) end of the rocky shoals, and **Areas B,** the upper ends of the shoals. In these areas the walleyes are able to drop down out of the current and still remain very near their spawning sites.

The distance that walleyes run up the river depends on water level. In years of low water, walleyes need to move very little since they are able to find areas of shallow rocks quite near to the cove. In years of high water, however, these same spots may be too deep, and it would not be unusual for walleyes to move many miles upstream until they find the proper combination of current, depth and bottom content to enable spawning.

At the water level shown in the accompanying drawing, the shoals (1-3 feet deep) pictured at the upriver end of the drawing would most likely see the spawning activity while those that are downstream would be too deep. These deepr ones, however, will attract and hold walleyes as they migrate on their way up or back downstream. The shoal near the largest island, for example, would be one of your initial contact points at the beginning of the walleye run. Later, as the spawning run progresses, you'll likely encounter the bulk of the walleyes farther upstream.

Heavy spring rains cause the water level to rise, and signal that you should keep moving upriver. Look for areas that have shallow rocks adjacent to quiet pools containing 10 or 12 fet of water. Shallow pools are questionable walleye producers, whereas those having 10-15 feet of depth are often very good.

As a final note, examine the bluff tailing at the downriver end of the drawing. While it is not a pool, it does have a ledge at the 12 foot level before it drops into the river channel. An eddy also forms here since the bluff diverts the main current flow out into the center of the cove. This can be an exceptionally good holding spot, providing that it is out of the main current and lies at the proper depth.

and remain in the general vicinity until spawning peaks in the upper 40°F range. After that, they disperse downriver back into the main lake.

PRESENTATION

Once the walleyes leave the reservoir and enter the river, simply approach the fishing as you would any other shallow river situation. The simplest way to catch walleyes is by fishing the deeper pools with either a jig/minnow combination or weighted crankbait during the day, or trolling crankbaits across the shallow pool sections and edges of the rapids at night. These basic systems all catch fish under these conditions.

During periods of mild current flow, simply drift the pool sections during the day and gently bounce a jig and minnow on and off the bottom. Jigs in the 1/8-1/4 ounce range, tipped with a 2-3 inch fathead or shiner minnow, usually work best under these conditions. When the current is strong, however, you may have to resort to 3/8-1/2 ounce jigs to keep your bait on the bottom. Or,

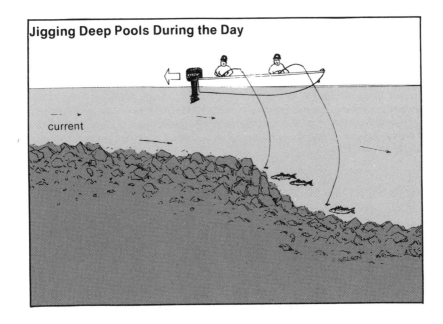

Jigging Deep Pools During the Day

current

if you prefer, troll a 2 ounce Bait Walker-type rig and a 4-5 inch long, thin crankbait on a 3 or 4 foot dropper line. Rapalas, Red Fins, Rebels, Bagleys, etc., work just fine. In fact, you can even anchor at the ends of pools, cast, and slowly retrieve these rigs back to the boat.

Night fishing calls for different tactics. Pre-spawn walleyes are generally far more active at night, roaming the shallower portions of the pools and the edges of the rapids. It's very easy to catch them trolling a large, thin, deep-

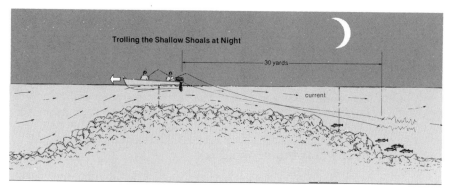

Trolling the Shallow Shoals at Night

Trolling large crankbaits on top of shallow rocky shoals at night produces some of the largest walleyes taken each spring. Adjust the length of your line and the size of the lure to allow the crankbait to occasionally scrape the bottom. By heading upriver into the current, you can move along as slowly as you wish, making the crankbait a perfect target for large walleyes.

diving crankbait like the Rebel Deep Runner. Let out about 40-50 feet of line and slowly troll back and forth across these areas. Most of your strikes occur as you move upriver. A deep diver runs about 7 feet deep on the troll, and you should be able to feel the lure occasionally nick, but not smash and get stuck in, the rocks. This is perhaps your number one big fish pattern. You may catch more small fish on jigs during the day, but night owls trolling crankbaits typically catch the largest pre-spawn highland reservoir walleyes every spring.

Once again, the river fishing usually peaks with water temperatures in the 40°F-50°F range. In addition, the hottest action typically occurs about 1½-2 days after a spring rain. The rain warms the water a bit, and once the muddy river begins to clear, the walleyes usually go nuts.

As far as tackle goes, stick with 6-8 pound test line for daytime jig fishing. Highland rivers are typically very clear except for brief periods of rain-muddied water, so you'll want to stick with spinning gear and light line during the day. Nighttime crankbait trolling, however, is usually a lot more punishing on equipment, so you'll want to beef up your tackle by using casting gear and 10-14 pound test line. Carry both and match your tackle to the conditions.

A RIVER PRE-SPAWN CASE HISTORY

The accompanying schematic map shows a 2-1/2 mile middle-aged river section which, for descriptive purposes, we have divided into three broad areas. They are as follows:

AREA A: Immediate dam area

AREA B: Ship channel and lock area

AREA C: Downstream sections

Each of these areas, because of their structural make-up, produce different patterns of current flow and velocities at high or low water. Of course, the fish adjust to these forces accordingly. Water temperature is approximately 34°F-46°F in each of the following conditions.

AREA A—LOW OR NORMAL WATER LEVEL CONDITIONS

The first thing to check when approaching any dam is where the flow is coming from. On our drawing of *AREA A* (low water condition), note that the gates are open on only one side of the river, so this is where the strongest current flow will occur.

Experience has shown that walleyes tend to stay clear of areas of very strong current when the water is cold. Most of the "catchable" fish tend to be located in the slacker water areas. Even though it looks good, the wing dam nearest the dam has too little slack water to consistently attract walleyes.

The middle wing dam will occasionally hold some walleyes during times of low/normal levels, and should be checked out. Usually the front, shallower face of the wing dam holds the walleyes.

The third wing dam presents a different set of circumstances. At times it will hold walleyes both above and below. This entire section is shallower than the other two wing dams. This wing dam will most often (under these conditions) hold the biggest fish that are holding on the side of the river with the fast current.

The structural differences between each of the three dams are evident. As each gets progressively bigger and has more shallower slack water about it, the more walleyes will be present.

A few walleyes could be found downstream from this point, but the major attraction is obviously the large flat that juts out from the bank. This spot is cleaned by the sweeping motion of the current flow. A clam bed and a scattered rock patch in the 8-15 foot depth level are prime spots. These sites attract small forage fish, and are the major attractions for the walleyes. This flat is the prime walleye water for this section of the river.

What is not apparent on our map are the many small saucer-like depressions and irregular rolling ridges along the bottom. These elements act as flow deflectors and are current breaks just like wing dams. Fish will "hole up" in these critical spots. They can usually be detected by a number of consecutive drifts or trolls, lots of "feel" and an eagle eye on the depth finder.

In summary, during low water conditions at Pre-spawn time, look for

Schematic Map of a River Section

This illustration shows the general make-up of a 2-1/2 mile section of a dam on a middle-aged river stretch. We've divided it into three basic areas because each is affected differently by the rising or lowering water levels.

Our example shows the ship channel and lock as separate from the main dam, but they may be attached on some dams. By the same token, some dams have side stilling basins. Nevertheless, in all cases water level and the resulting velocity plays a major role in fish location. We used the split channel type of dam as an example, because it incorporated more variables.

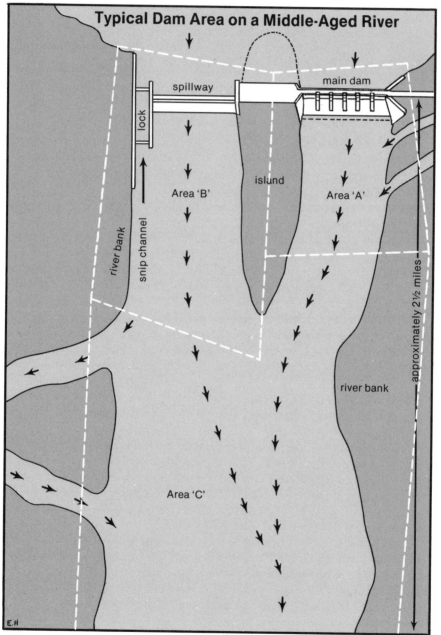

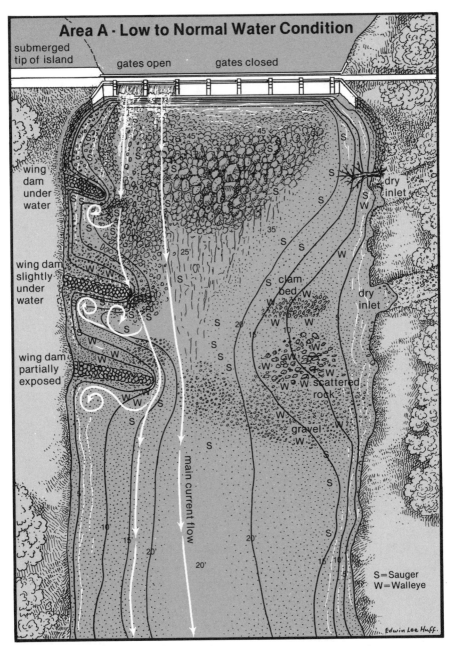

Area A - Low to Normal Water Condition

submerged tip of island

gates open gates closed

wing dam under water

wing dam slightly under water

wing dam partially exposed

dry inlet

clam bed

dry inlet

scattered rock

gravel

main current flow

S=Sauger
W=Walleye

Edwin Lee Huff.

walleyes to congregate in the 6-12 foot deep levels on areas of clean, hard bottom where the current flow is not fast. Usually, the most extensive 8-10 foot flats are best, and the more rocks or some sort of obstructions present, the more they will hold walleyes.

AREA A—HIGH WATER CONDITIONS

As spring rains and run-off accumulate, water levels rise. When they do, more and more dam gates are opened to let the larger volume of water flow through. While it is still important to watch which gates are shut, at high water it makes less of a difference as to which side of the river the majority of the fish will be on.

High water and fast current tend to push the fish to the banks, up to the apron of the dam, or against the bull noses of the columns. They also may just move out of the area entirely.

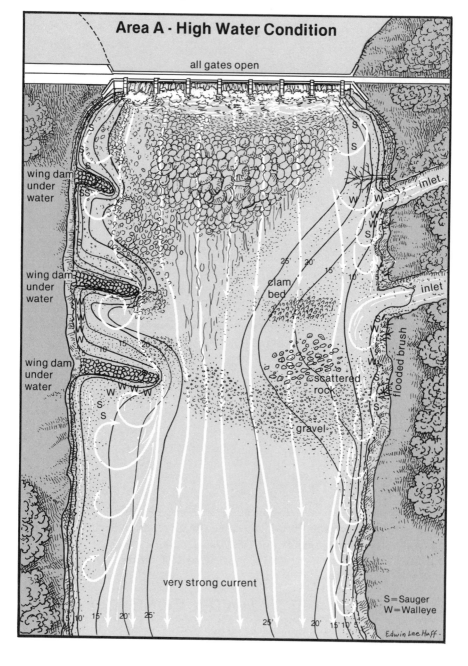

Looking at our map of *AREA A* under high water conditions, we see that with a rise in water level of 5 feet that the rock and clam bed are now evacuated. Even fish that were previously laying along the rim of the drop-off have left. Now the banks and any shore obstructions like felled trees, rip-rap or cut banks all assume a new significance that was absent during low water.

One substantial difference is that while the wing dams were only "so so" walleye spots in low water, they become major locational factors during high water. With the general rise of the water, all previously 8-10 foot deep flats out away from the banks are now 13-15 feet deep—too deep and too washed by strong current to attract and hold fish.

On the other bank where there is an absence of current breaks like wing dams, the fish will now hug tight to the shore. Felled trees, like the one close to the dam, create a large eddy and attract fish.

With the high water, formerly dry inlets now have a flow of water coming out of them. As they merge with the river's waters, they create additional eddies and thus attract fish.

The remainder of the "bank-hugging" fish will relate to whatever land vegetation is flooded over. In fact, many fish will enter the flooded forest of trees and brush.

In summary, the difference between high and low water conditions are obvious. High water reduces the amount of preferred depth levels with proper current flow in the main stream of the river, and the fish move toward whatever structural elements offer the best current breaks along the shore.

AREA B—HIGH WATER CONDITIONS

The side ship channel does not draw any amount of fish in low water. It only becomes important during high water. What happens is that the high water and fast current severely reduces the amount of preferred depth levels immediately under the dam. The areas against the banks and behind the dams cannot accommodate all the fish, so some fish groups must move. In this case, the adjacent ship channel (*AREA B* at high water), with its reduced current and general structural make-up, provides such an area of retreat.

Note that the banks on both sides of this channel are rip-rapped. During low water this rock does not extend too deep into the water, but is now partially covered and draws fish.

The island that separates the dam from the locks is covered with willow trees and brush. During low water it is high and dry, but with a rise of 5 feet or more it becomes inundated with water, and a cross-flow sets up from the waters coming from the dam.

This entire situation provides favorable conditions for walleyes, so they are pulled from *AREA A* to *AREA B*. The entire flat extending from the tip of the island (that was previously too shallow to host a lot of fish) now has a considerable amount of water at the right depth with the right amount of current, due to the breaking action of the trees and brush. As a result, this spot now becomes a prime fish holder.

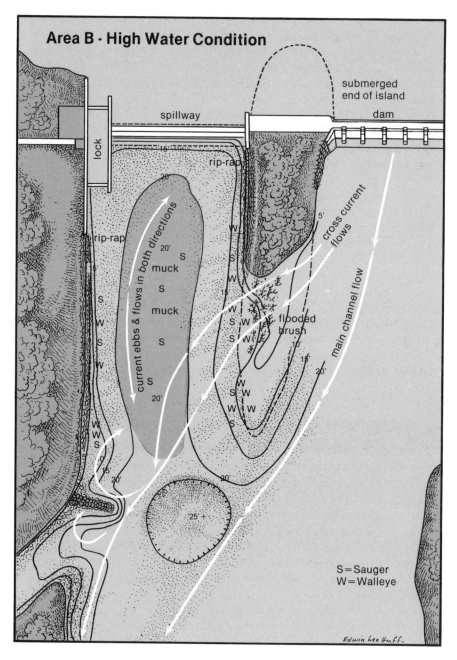

Area B - High Water Condition

spillway

submerged
end of island

dam

lock

rip-rap

rip-rap

15'

20'

cross current
flows

main channel flow

current ebbs & flows in both directions

5'

20'

S

muck

S

muck

S

flooded
brush

15'

10'

15'

20'

S

W

W

S

W

W

S

W

W

S

W

S

S

W

S

W

S

W

S

W

S

W

S

W

i

W

S

20'

W

W

S

5'

15'

20'

20'

20'

25' +

S=Sauger
W=Walleye

Edwin Lee Huff

Old marble eyes will be up on the flat off the tip of the island. In high water, walleyes will also run up and into the flooded timber and brush. If they move in quite a distance, conditions make lure presentation so difficult that it is better to concentrate your efforts on the fish which come out and hold at the edges.

AREA C—HIGH WATER CONDITIONS

While this downstream site can and does hold fish both during high and low water periods, we will only show the high water circumstance. During low water the fish simply move farther out from the banks, much the same as they did in *AREA A*.

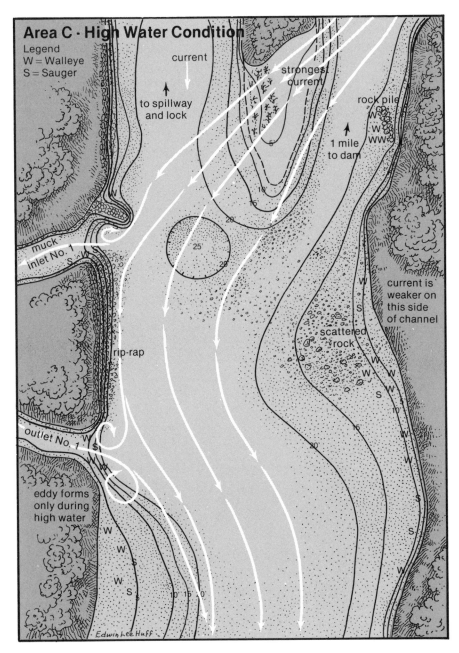

Looking at the map of *AREA C* (high water) we find a classic river bend situation. The wash of the water builds-up a flat with gravel and scattered rock on one side, but cuts the other bank and keeps it deeper.

As stated earlier, some walleyes would normally favor the washed rip-rap bank. In high water, though, the current along there is too swift for walleyes. Thus they have to move.

Since walleyes tend to select areas with mild current and fairly shallow depth, they would be present in the eddy formed below the outlet from the backwaters. Along the opposite bank, the flat jutting out from shore (which would normally hold walleyes in the shallower 8-10 foot depth levels), would now have fish below it, tight to shore. You might even find some fish holding directly behind the small rock pile farther upstream. In short, they'll use most anything that breaks the current at the right depth.

Chapter 9
THE SPAWN PERIOD
"A Time of Tension"

Timewise, the actual spawn in a localized area occurs in a very short period. Yet all spawning does not take place at the same time on a given lake, river or reservoir.

Since spawning is largely controlled by water temperature, lakes, rivers and reservoirs which warm the fastest will see this spawn sequence occur earlier than those waters that warm more slowly.

Trying to get a walleye to bite during spawning could be likened to trying to lure an ardent lover out of the boudoir with a candy bar. It is difficult, if not impossible, to catch an individual walleye while its spawning. But, just as different walleye groups spawn at different times, all members of the same walleye group do not spawn at once. The Spawn Period may extend over a period as long as two weeks. So, in a given spawning concentration, there could be pre-spawn fish, spawning fish, and post-spawn fish. As the Spawn Period winds down, only spawning fish and post-spawn fish remain and fishing success grinds to a halt.

The lesson to be learned is that if you must fish during the Spawn Period, fish as early in the period as you can, since fishing success will invariably get poorer and will stay poor until the early spawning fish recover from the strenuous ordeal and begin to feed again. However, our *IN-FISHERMAN* policy is to avoid fishing for spawning fish whether they be bass, northerns, walleyes or any gamefish. We'll fish pre-spawn or post-spawn fish, but when they're actually spawning, it's best to let nature take its course and fish somewhere else. This helps ensure a successful spawn and good fishing in the future.

To summarize the basics, walleyes spawn in rocky inlet streams, along windswept rocky shorelines, or over gravel/rubble shoals or reefs, usually 1-3 feet deep. Males congregate near the spawning areas first, usually when the water temperature reaches about 34°F. When the water reaches 38°F-42°F, they are joined by the larger females.

River inlet spawning precedes lake spawning, sometimes by as much as two weeks, since rivers warm much faster than lakes. And even within the same lake, spawning time can vary by a few days since mid-lake reefs warm more slowly than shoreline spawning areas. Thus the pre-spawn fishing peak would occur earliest in river inlets and latest on mid-lake spawning reefs.

Let's take a look at the factors that affect the timing of this cycle. This is important, because just as different groups of fish in a lake spawn at different times, different lakes warm faster, so the fish in them begin the spawning cycle earlier. The idea behind this, of course, is to stay on the most active fish. This requires an understanding of when walleyes will begin spawning in a given lake as well as their behavior during the cycle.

WHAT DETERMINES WHEN WALLEYES SPAWN?

It's obvious that there are two major spring periods when walleyes are vulnerable to angling. They bite well up until spawning time, and then begin biting again anywhere from 10-30 days after spawning. In order to take advantage of this information, you must be able to make a fairly accurate estimate of when walleyes will spawn in a given lake.

Obviously, the best way to determine when walleyes spawn is to go out and look. If walleyes are heavily concentrated around inlet streams or over shallow, rocky shoals at night, they're probably spawning. These concentrations will thin out as more and more fish complete the spawning ritual.

The problem is, unless the lake you choose to open the season on is close to your home, this system is impractical. Although direct observation is the only sure-fire way to determine when walleyes spawn, you can make an "educated guess" if you understand what controls the time of spawning.

Most fisheries scientists agree that the time of spawning is determined by two factors: (1) water temperature and (2) day length.

Day length, of course, is determined strictly by latitude, and for a given lake it never changes from one year to the next. Water temperature, on the other hand, is affected by many environmental influences including (1) weather, (2) size, depth and location of lake basin and (3) orientation of the lake to prevailing winds and surrounding shelter. Let's discuss each of these influences separately.

WEATHER

Air temperature, sunlight and wind all have a dramatic effect on the rate a lake warms in the spring. Under conditions of high air temperatures, bright sunlight and heavy winds, ice disappears faster and the water temperature rises rapidly. If the weather is cool, overcast and calm, ice persists longer and delays warming. Walleyes may spawn from 2-3 weeks earlier in the former case than in the latter.

Once the ice disappears from a lake, water temperature can rise very quickly if the conditions are right. It's not uncommon for a small lake to reach a sur-

WALLEYE spawning facts...

Walleyes are spring spawners, beginning as early as mid February in some far southern reservoirs or as late as the end of June in northern Canada. The actual timing depends on water temperature. Walleye spawning activity generally begins at about 42 °F and is largely completed by the time the water reaches 50 °F

Where available, a gravel or rubble bottom is the prime choice. Each female may be accompanied by one or more males as they expel eggs and milt across the bottom. The eggs are widely broadcast and adhere to the irregular bottom surface.

No parental care is exercised by walleyes. Sufficient wave action or current is required to keep the eggs clean and oxygenated until they hatch.

Male and female walleyes look much alike, except that the female is usually much larger. Females are also deeper and much more rounded in shape, due to the bulk of the eggs they carry. The white tail spot that is so characteristic of walleyes is also generally much less distinctive on these larger female fish.

Males are the first fish to approach the spawning areas. Females tend to hang back in deeper water until the water temperature approaches 40 °F.

Walleyes often move many miles upstream to spawn.

The white glow of their eyes will reflect a flashlight beam in shallow water at night.

Summer finds most young walleyes to have grown to the 2-4 inch range (6-8 inches in southern reservoirs) and to be feeding on small fish.

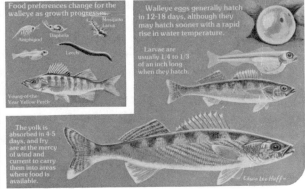

Food preferences change for the walleye as growth progresses.

Mosquito Larva

Amphipod

Daphnia

Leech

Young-of-the-Year Yellow Perch

Walleye eggs generally hatch in 12-18 days, although they may hatch sooner with a rapid rise in water temperature.

Larvae are usually 1/4 to 1/3 of an inch long when they hatch.

The yolk is absorbed in 4-5 days, and fry are at the mercy of wind and current to carry them into areas where food is available.

Edwin Lee Huff

face temperature of 45°F-50°F (normal spawning range) only a few days after ice-out.

If ice cover persists much later than usual, and then a warm front accompanied by high winds causes the lake to open quickly, walleyes may spawn within the first week of open water. Their "biological clock" is controlled by the length of daylight, and even though the lake remains covered with ice, they sense that spawning time is near. Then, when the lake opens, they ripen quickly in an attempt to "catch up."

But the reverse is also true. If the lake opens much earlier than usual and then warms quickly to 45°F or 50°F, walleyes tend to put off spawning even though the water temperature is in the range where they normally would spawn.

Thus, the influence of the biological clock tends to even out the peaks that would occur if spawning time was controlled by water temperature alone.

SIZE, DEPTH AND LOCATION OF LAKE BASIN

You've probably noticed that shallow lakes always open earlier than deep lakes in the same area. The reason for this is simple and can be explained by the surface area to volume relationship. A lake with a large surface area relative to its volume warms faster and opens earlier than a lake with a small surface area relative to its volume. The lake with a large area to volume ratio is obviously influenced more by air temperature, sunlight and wind because a larger percentage of its water is exposed to the elements. Thus a lake with an

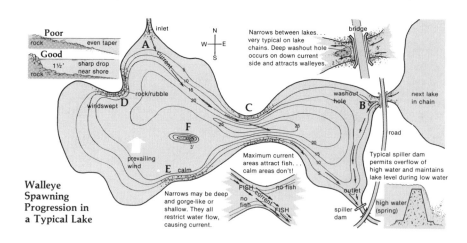

Walleye Spawning Progression in a Typical Lake

FOLLOW THE ACTIVE FISH

Here's a map that Al Lindner uses to explain some of the fine points of spring walleye location. You'll be surprised at how many subtle factors are involved.

The lake pictured here is typical of many natural walleye lakes found across the north country. It's part of a chain of lakes, has a feeder stream for a water source, and a spiller dam to regulate the water level. Let's take a look at what's available to the fish and how they make use of it.

The key attraction for early season walleyes is a rock/rubble bottom in shallow water, swept by either current or wave action. This combination provides an ideal surface for walleye eggs to cling to and develop in an oxygen-rich environment.

This rocky bottom is present in several areas of the lake. Each of these areas thus becomes a potential candidate for spring walleyes, although further examination reveals they're not all equally good. There are numerous factors that combine to make some areas more productive than others, or at least to make them attract walleyes at different times.

The first rocky areas to warm up in spring naturally attract the first pre-spawn walleyes. This typically occurs in areas with current. The inlet (**Area A**) or the narrows between the two lakes (**Area B**) are classic examples of areas with current flow. They are also the first areas to warm, and will attract the first pre-spawn walleye movements.

Less distinctive, but perhaps just as good, is the narrows in the main lake (**Area C**). High spring water levels set up a current through such areas. After all, water must pass through **Area C**, even though its effect may be less obvious than in extremely narrow places like A and B. But if there's current, the walleyes will find it.

Consider how current moves through the lake. The water flows in at **Area A**, and ever-so-slightly brushes the north shore as it passes through **Area C**. Then it crosses the lake and passes along the south shore on its way to the spiller dam. The current not only passes through the narrows—it also brushes certain portions of the shoreline more than others. These current areas attract spring walleyes—the others don't. It's a subtle influence, but can be extremely important to fish location.

As the water continues to warm, and as the fish in **Areas A, B and C** near spawning, other areas also begin attracting fish. A rocky shoreline point like **Area D** is a classic. A similar rocky stretch lies along the shoreline at E. Are D and E equally good?

Probably not. The predominant wind is from the southwest, south or southeast at this time of year. **Area D** is exposed to the wind, and receives much more wave action than E, the protected shoreline. All else being equal, D looks like a better bet than E for early spring walleyes.

Could E be better than D? Perhaps, but only if the bottom composition was more favorable for spawning. Here's a good clue. If the shoreline tapers slowly and continues out into the water at the same slope, chances are it's a poor area. But if the shoreline drops slightly with maybe 1½ feet of water right next to a rocky shoreline, it will attract a lot more fish than a gradual taper. It's a good trick to use for narrowing down your fishing areas.

Let's say a few more days go by and the water continues warming. The fish in the current areas of A, B and C have, for the most part, completed spawning, and the shoreline fish at D and the few at E are starting to spawn. The walleyes in these areas show little tendency to respond to fishing techniques. Is there another alternative?

Yes. Check out the sunken island at F. If it has broken rocks on top, and if it is at least 3 feet or shallower on top, then chances are it will attract some walleyes. If it's deeper than 3 feet on top—forget it. It's too deep to attract spawning fish, but it will most likely be productive later in the year.

The walleyes that spawn at F are the last ones to spawn in our typical lake. It's the last area to warm up, and the fish are perhaps a week or 10 days behind the fish in the current areas in their spawning cycle.

Get the picture? There is a natural spawning progression throughout the lake. Some fish spawn later than others. While some are spawning and not feeding, others may be pre-spawn and still be aggressive. So take advantage of your knowledge and conditions and fish the most aggressive fish.

Get the feel of the lake. Change areas. Try different presentations. Experiment. Don't just automatically anchor at the mouth of the feeder stream. It's a great spot if your timing is right, but if you're a week late you'll probably miss the best fishing.

Successful fishing is more than just presentation. It's being aware of and understanding the environment around you. Some simple locational changes might make all the difference between a wasted effort and a fine catch.

average depth of 100 feet could open 2-3 weeks later than a similar size lake nearby with an average depth of 10 feet. Walleyes would probably spawn from 10 days to 2 weeks later in the deeper lake because of the moderating influence of day length.

Assuming two lakes are identical in all other respects and the influence of weather has been similar, a difference in latitude will result in a different rate of warming and therefore a different time of spawning. Very simply, a lake that lies farther north warms up later than a similar lake to the south.

As a general rule of thumb, the time needed to warm similar lakes to the same temperature increases by one day for every 17 miles north. As an example, a lake at the latitude of Minneapolis, Minnesota will generally warm to 50°F about 20 days later than a similar lake at the latitude of Columbia, Missouri.

ORIENTATION TO PREVAILING WINDS

Again, let's assume that we have two lakes similar in all other ways and exposed to similar weather conditions. The lake with its long axis oriented in the same direction as the prevailing winds will circulate better and therefore warm faster than the lake situated at right angles to the prevailing winds.

SURROUNDING SHELTER

If a lake is protected from the wind by hills, trees or any other type of shelter, the water circulates more slowly and takes longer to warm than a similar exposed, prairie-type lake.

OTHER INFLUENCES

Dozens of other factors can influence the rate lakes warm. Lakes at high elevations warm more slowly than those at low elevations. Clear lakes warm more slowly than dark water lakes. Lakes close to other cold bodies of water, like Lake Superior, warm more slowly than lakes located away from their cooling influence. And lakes with no inlets are apt to warm more slowly than lakes with rivers flowing in.

The accompanying chart will give you a general idea when walleyes spawn in various types of lakes, at various latitudes, under different conditions. Remember that this chart is only a guide—it should not be used as an absolute indicator of walleye spawning time in a certain lake.

By understanding the factors that control spawning time and combining this knowlege with some "local intelligence," you can make a fairly accurate prediction of spawning time in a certain lake. Then you can adjust your lake choice to fish the most active fish—the pre-spawn or pre-summer "biters."

Local contacts such as resorters, bait shop operators, lakeshore residents or fisheries field offices can usually provide the necessary information. If no information is available on the particular lake you're interested in, try to get information on some other lake in the vicinity. Then compare the physical characteristics of the two lakes and decide whether spawning in your lake would be earlier or later.

APPROXIMATE DATE OF WALLEYE SPAWNING PEAK AT VARIOUS LATITUDES IN DIFFERENT LAKE TYPES*

Lakes at Latitude of:	Spawning Peak in Very Early Spring	Spawning Peak in Early Spring	Avg. Date of Spawning Peak	Spawning Peak in Late Spring	Spawning Peak in Very Late Spring
Rainy L., MN - CAN. (49°N.)					
Deep, cold lakes	May 3	May 8	May 13	May 18	May 23
Average lakes	April 26	May 1	May 6	May 11	May 16
Shallow, warm Lakes	April 19	April 24	April 29	May 4	May 9
Winnibigoshish L., MN 47°N.)					
Deep, cold lakes	April 28	May 3	May 8	May 13	May 18
Average lakes	April 21	April 26	May 1	May 6	May 11
Shallow, warm lakes	April 14	April 19	April 24	April 29	May 4
Mille Lacs L., MN (46.5°N.)					
Deep, cold lakes	April 22	April 27	May 2	May 7	May 12
Average lakes	April 15	April 20	April 25	April 30	May 5
Shallow, warm Lakes	April 8	April 13	April 18	April 23	April 28
L. Oahe, SD (45°N.)					
Deep, cold lakes	April 17	April 22	April 27	May 2	May 7
Average lakes	April 10	April 15	April 20	April 25	April 30
Shallow, warm lakes	April 3	April 8	April 13	April 18	April 23
L. Okoboji, IA (44°N.)					
Deep, cold lakes	April 13	April 18	April 23	April 28	May 3
Average lakes	April 6	April 11	April 16	April 21	April 26
Shallow, warm lakes	March 30	April 4	April 9	April 14	April 21
L. McConaughy, NE (42°N.)					
Deep, cold lakes	April 6	April 11	April 16	April 21	April 26
Average lakes	March 30	April 4	April 9	April 14	April 19
Shallow, warm lakes	March 23	March 28	April 2	April 7	April 12
Shelbyville L., IL (41°N.)					
Deep, cold lakes	April 1	April 6	April 11	April 16	April 21
Average lakes	March 25	March 30	April 4	April 9	April 14
Shallow, warm lakes	March 18	March 23	March 28	April 2	April 7
Stockton L., MO (39°N.)					
Deep, cold lakes	March 23	March 28	April 2	April 7	April 12
Average lakes	March 16	March 21	March 26	March 31	April 5
Shallow, warm lakes	March 9	March 14	March 19	March 24	March 29
Greers Ferry L., AR (37°N.)					
Deep, cold lakes	March 18	March 23	March 28	April 2	April 7
Average lakes	March 11	March 16	March 21	March 26	March 31
Shallow, warm lakes	March 4	March 9	March 14	March 19	March 24

*This chart provides approximate walleye spawning dates in lakes at selected latitudes. It is intended to give you a general idea of the spawning peaks in different kinds of lakes within a given latitude. As you can see, latitude and type of lake have a major effect on when walleyes spawn. Also, remember that spawning in tributary rivers or rivers which hold permanent walleye populations usually occurs 1-2 weeks earlier.

Walleye fishing usually peaks 1-2 weeks before spawning and about 10-30 days after the spawning peaks shown in the table. Other influences mentioned in the article can cause spawning dates to vary.

*Credit to Dick Sternberg.

LOCATING RIVER WALLEYES IN THE SPAWNING PERIODS

As the water temperature climbs toward 44°F, the urge to spawn grows stronger and stronger, causing both males and females to move to water only 1-3 feet deep. The sites chosen for spawning vary from shallow sand/gravel bays with very little current off the main stream, to rip-rapped embankments with moderate current, to rocky runs right in the main stream with fairly fast current.

Since river temperature follows air temperature, a few very warm days following a cool spell can shoot water temperatures hovering at 40°F up very quickly to 48°F-50°F. But a fast rise like this does not mean the walleyes' eggs will immediately ripen and spawning will begin.

The eggs of any cold-blooded creature develop faster at a higher temperature, but a certain amount of time is required for development regardless of how high the temperature. So if water temperatures have generally been low, the fish will spawn late even though the water temperature reaches 50°F or more fairly early. By the same token, in years when the water begins to warm early and steadily rises in temperature, the total amount of heat required to develop the eggs is attained early and fish spawn even though the water temperature is in the low 40°F's.

Most big rivers in the northern states usually crest shortly before walleyes spawn and are often still turbid at spawning time. So it would be unusual for the water to be so clear during spawning time to force walleyes into deeper water in daylight hours. Most of the time they stay right in the immediate vicinity—possibly dropping down a foot or two in mid-day.

When the floodwaters climb over the banks and current becomes too strong in the main channel to allow successful spawning, walleyes move into flooded backwater areas. Here they may spawn around flooded trees, along rip-rapped railroad or flood control dikes or over sedge grass meadows or other flooded vegetation. Although the spawning act may last only a few hours for an individual female, she may spend up to ten days in a state of recuperation before moving back to deeper water and starting to feed. Just as males congregate near the spawning grounds long before spawning commences, they remain for several days after the females are gone.

RESERVOIR SPAWNING

Even though the spawn takes place under a rather narrow set of conditions, fish movement, triggered by the spawning urge, begins many months earlier in most reservoirs than in natural lakes. There is a rather dependable pattern of seasonal migration by walleyes in reservoirs, and understanding it will help you locate more fish on a regular basis. Simply realize that *if* suitable spawning conditions are available in the headwaters of the main feeder river or in major creek arms off the main body of water, you can expect the fish to make regular seasonal migrations to those areas.

However, in some reservoirs, suitable spawning conditions do not exist in the creek arms or in the main feeder river. This is a common occurrence in lowland and flatland, as well as some hill-land reservoirs. In lowland and flatland impoundments, the headwaters are often silted in and long creek arms do not exist. As always, the fish will take advantage of the next best thing available, and that might be the face of a rocky rip-rapped dam or gravel on a submerged roadbed. It might even be rip-rap along roadbeds, bridge abutments or railroad tracks.

In Merritt Reservoir in north central Nebraska, however, nothing of the sort existed. So artificial spawning reefs were constructed. Gravel was simply dumped into a small area and some spawning takes place there, though the lake maintains its excellent big walleye population through regular stocking.

Suitable habitat isn't the only thing that attracts pre-spawn fish. Remember that even though the walleyes are now in a reservoir environment, they are the ancestors of *river* fish who historically made long seasonal migrations, *always upstream*. The same thing holds true in natural lakes where there are feeder streams. Walleyes about to spawn are attracted by *moving* water.

There are some conclusions we can draw about the subject of seasonal migrations in reservoirs. In plateau, highland and hill-land impoundments, the spawning run is generally upstream as long as suitable spawning conditions exist in tributaries. If they do not, these lengthy upstream migrations do not occur and the fish tend to use what's available—usually the rip-rapped face of a dam, a submerged gravel roadbed or the next best option. In canyon reservoirs, it appears the fish spend most of the year in the long creek arms and their seasonal migrations are of an upstream nature toward the spawning grounds. In most flatland and lowland reservoirs, the pattern is similar to what we've described except that it is more common for the fish to spawn near the dams on rip-rap because most of the feeder streams and the main river sources do not contain suitable spawning habitat.

Chapter 10
THE POST-SPAWN PERIOD

"A Time of Recuperation"

This is a period of recuperation after the spawn. Some big females which have not completely dropped all their eggs will reabsorb them. Females are in an inactive mood and eat sparingly during the recovery state. The males, although less affected, do not feed heavily either. Fishing is usually slow for females, medium for males.

Why such tough fishing? Well, as with any post-spawn fish, the walleyes have just finished taking a physical beating, particularly the females. Perhaps as much as 20% of their body weight has just been discharged as eggs. Talk about punishment! No wonder they won't respond to your offerings.

The males don't suffer nearly the abuse the females do. They'll remain in or near the spawning grounds for days, usually halfway aggressive and catchable. But the larger females are a different story. All they want right now is a place to rest and recuperate. Post-spawn females typically eat less than 1% of their body weight per day compared to 3-4% during their feeding binges in the fall. They'll eat, but only if it's an easy meal. Anything that requires chasing will be ignored. If you're looking for a big fish, it won't be easy, even if you know where to find them.

THE POST-SPAWN DISPERSAL—GENERAL RULES OF THUMB

A number of questions arise when it comes to locating post-spawn walleyes. How long do they remain in the spawning area? When they leave, how far do they go? Where do they go? All of these questions, and more, are a part of the puzzle.

There are a few general guidelines to get you started on the right track. For one, the males tend to hang around the spawning grounds for awhile. They're the first ones into the spawning area and the last ones to leave. The females, however, usually don't waste any time getting in and out. As soon as they're finished spawning, they start looking for a place to rest.

How fast and how far they move depends on the conditions they encounter. Again, there's a few general guidelines. The flatter and slower the bottom taper, the longer it'll take to leave the general area. So in shallow, flat lakes, dispersal usually takes more time, perhaps a week or more. Conversely, the sharper the bottom taper, the quicker the fish seem to disperse to a recuperation area. So along steep spawning shorelines, a few days might find the fish long gone. It's not a hard and fast rule, but it's a fairly reliable indicator.

Weather, too, has quite an influence. Stable, warm weather warms the water and speeds dispersal. A barrage of cold fronts, however, prolongs both the spawn and the recovery period. Obviously, there's more to it than just a few simple cut-and-dried rules.

Beyond these basic guidelines, the crucial missing link is *where* they go. And that's no easy question, because the kinds of areas that post-spawn walleyes use can be radically different from one lake type or reservoir to another. The only way you'll figure out the answer is by taking a good hard look at what the lake offers and proceed from there.

Once again, we're back to the case of understanding what the environment offers the fish. Where's the food? Where can the fish rest when they're not feeding? In short, where's the most likely place to find the biggest concentration of the most active fish? Well, the most logical answer is, "Look in the closest place adjacent to the spawning grounds where the walleyes can stop to rest, grab an easy meal, and recover from their spawning ordeal."

But first you'll need a good understanding of the walleyes' post-spawn world in order to consistently select the right kind of areas that fit this description.

THE POST-SPAWN ENVIRONMENT

Understanding what the environment offers the walleye during the Post-spawn is the key to making fish contact. There are logical reasons why walleyes are where they are. It's simply a different set of conditions than you encounter during summer, and the walleyes react accordingly. Let's carefully examine this aspect.

First off, lakes generally exhibit a temperature difference from top to bottom during Post-spawn. It's not like a thermocline that develops later in summer. But the principle is basically the same. The sun warms the upper layers of water. This warmth slowly transfers downward, but it takes a long time to do so. At this stage of the season, the lake hasn't had enough sun exposure to warm the lower layer yet. So, in most cases, the fish are faced with two temperature layers—one warm, one cold.

The upper layer is where the bulk of the food is. Most minnow species are spawning around this time, so they'll be shallow. Perch, usually a key walleye forage, are also shallow. Insects are beginning to hatch, some in the shallows and a few varieties in the colder, lower layer. At the same time, in deeper lakes, cold-water species like cisco, tullibee and whitefish, which are fall spawners, suspend and feed on whatever small items they can find.

Nevertheless, the shallow, warm water environment contains the bulk of the food at this time of year. Even though there's a cold water environment beneath it in some lakes, that zone is usually pretty slim pickin's at this time of year. And since walleyes are basically warm water critters, you can expect to

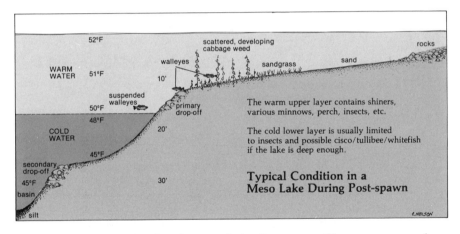

Here are the basics of walleye location during Post-spawn. The upper, warmer layer of a lake contains the bulk of the available food. Most walleyes remain in this zone, either hiding out in shallow weeds, logs, boulders, etc., or else suspending in the shade of a steep drop-off.

Are they all shallow? No. Some fish won't spawn at all, and might never move shallow. They're the few "oddballs." Quite often they're extremely large, old fish, and they'll stay deep and perhaps continue relating to tullibees or cisco for food. Or, perhaps a few post-spawn females will actually drop down into that cold water zone to rest, recuperate, and relate to forage like ciscoes as a food source. But, as for the percentages, the bulk of the walleyes will be found in the warmer, upper zone.

You'll never find all the fish doing the same thing at the same time. There's simply too much variety in behavior. Some fish act as individuals rather than following the crowd. But although you'll never pattern all of them, you can figure out what most will do, most of the time. In this case, most will be shallow, and that's where your percentages for success lie.

Consistent fishing success depends on your ability to put percentages in your favor. In this case, it's concentrating on the bulk of the walleyes, which will generally remain fairly shallow at this time of year.

find the bulk of the walleye population in the upper, warmer zone.

There are a number of ways the walleyes adapt to this condition, depending on what's available to them. This, naturally, varies from area to area. But there's a few simple principles to keep in mind.

By the time they reach their Post-spawn Period, sunlight starts to become an important factor, and the walleyes begin displaying their typical sun-shy behavior. This means that they're going to use whatever means they can to get out of direct exposure to the sun.

There are two ways they accomplish this. One is to hide beneath some form of cover. Logs, stumps, weeds, boulders, etc. in the shallows, if available, provide hiding places to get out of the sun. Such cover allows the walleyes to remain shallow, close to their food supply. Therefore, an area of shallow cover adjoining a spawning area is a prime candidate.

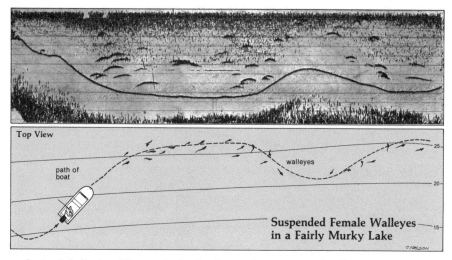

Seeing is believing. The graph clearly shows a loose group of walleyes suspended well above the bottom. In this case, they're just outside a spawning area, suspended in the shade of a sharp drop-off.

The second way for walleyes to get away from the sun is by seeking depth. The sun is still somewhat low in the southern sky this early in the year, so sunlight penetration won't be that deep. Therefore, the walleyes need only drop down a bit to achieve a comfortable light level. However, they'll be reluctant to drop down too deep, because they'll enter the lower, colder layer where food is scarce and the temperature is too low after a spawning cycle spent in the warm shallows.

This option is typical when shallow water cover is poor or absent. Walleyes will drop down to the bottom of the warm water layer, and seek out shaded areas where they can escape from the sun. An example would be the shaded portion of a sharp drop-off. Sharp drop-offs provide better shade than slow, tapering ones, so they're a key feature to look for outside a spawning area.

Now for the complications. For one, fish don't hold particularly tight to the sides of sharp drop-offs. There's nothing for them to lay on top of. They just sort of hang off the side. They'll move around as the sun changes position during the day, hovering in the shade at a comfortable depth level.

Perhaps you can start to see the difficulty. These fish usually won't be right on the bottom. Matter of fact, chances are that they're going to suspend. That's an unwelcome word, because you probably already know how tough catching suspended fish can be.

We have walleyes that are tired out from spawning, sun-shy and inactive, and are usually either buried under whatever shallow cover they can find or else probably suspended. Now you know why we suggest avoiding post-spawn fish if you've got a better option. They're tough!

Our next step is to examine several examples. We'll look at different types of waters, with different kinds of available cover, and see how the walleyes react in each instance. We'll see where they go, what they feed on, and then figure out how to catch them.

RESERVOIRS, SHALLOW FLOWAGES AND TANNIC ACID (STAINED) WATERS WITH POOR WEEDGROWTH

Our first example is common in man-made walleye lakes. Impoundments that contain heavy amounts of stumps and logs normally have a dark water color, stained by the decomposing wood. Weedgrowth is usually at a minimum.

Walleyes spawn in rocky feeder streams or where current sweeps rocky man-made areas like bridge foundations, causeways, dams, etc. Good Post-spawn areas will be somewhere nearby.

Shallow stump flats at the back of the spawning coves are among the first areas to attract post-spawn fish. The walleyes tuck up under the available wood cover at a comfortable depth. The depth depends on the water color—in clearer water it's deeper, in darker water it's shallower.

The walleyes don't necessarily relate to the creek channel, unless, of course, the flats are barren of cover. Then they'll drop down into the channel to get out of the sun.

As the water continues to warm, the walleyes generally move farther out of the coves, into the main lake. Summer can find them a long way from the spawning areas. But in Post-spawn, look for them to be near the spawning site and fairly shallow.

But what about structural elements and their importance to reservoir walleyes? On all reservoirs, shortly after the fish spawn, there is a period of very tough fishing. That's when the fish are recuperating from the rigors of the spawn. On Lake Francis Case, there are some very large mud flats just north of Chamberlain, S.D. You'll find flats like these on nearly every plateau reservoir, especially in the upper sections. However, after the fish recover, they move onto these flats—en masse, especially the smaller males.

It's important to note these large flats are almost featureless. For about a 4-week period, you can drift or troll these big flats with a Lindy Rig/'crawler or a spinner/'crawler combination and catch fish as fast as you can get your bait into the water. It's shallow water, 5-7 feet in depth and the fish don't run large, usually in the 1-2 pound class. But the action is nothing short of fantastic. But what is it that attracts the fish to these seemingly barren flats? There is little change in bottom contour and other than an occasional snag; man, there's just nothing out there. Nothing that is, but walleyes—and in bunches.

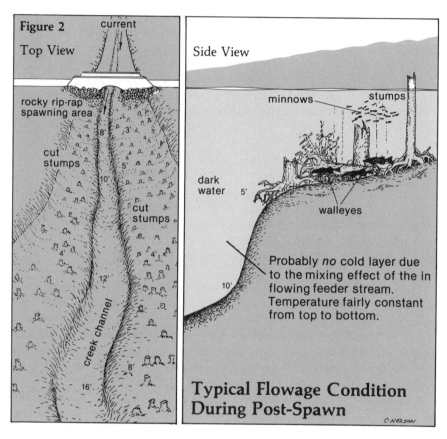

Figure 2
Top View
current
rocky rip-rap spawning area
cut stumps
8' 3'
5'
10'
cut stumps
4' 4'
.12'
creek channel
8'
16'

Side View
minnows
stumps
dark water 5'
walleyes
10'
Probably *no* cold layer due to the mixing effect of the in flowing feeder stream. Temperature fairly constant from top to bottom.

Typical Flowage Condition During Post-Spawn

C. NELSON

Now, if you've been a structure fishing devotee for years, this seems to dispute everything you've learned. You might even lose confidence in your depth finder because it's showing you virtually no structural elements the fish can relate to. Yet, the fish are there. You're catching them, and what better proof can one have?

Finally, in a desperate search for the answers, you examine the stomach contents of some of the fish and find they are gorging themselves on small minnows. You dig into an encyclopedia and quickly discover they are dining on gizzard shad. You read on and find that gizzard shad spawn in early summer, about the same time the walleyes are recuperating from their own spawn. And then you find the clincher! Gizzard shad spawn on large mud flats in relatively shallow water, precisely where they spend most of their Summer Period. On those mud flats, gizzard shad extract organisms from the bottom, all summer long. And the walleyes are right in there feeding on them, despite the lack of so-called structure. In this case, food is more important than any depth changes.

LAKES (USUALLY STOCKED)

Successful walleye spawning may or may not occur in these lakes, depending on whether or not sufficient rock/gravel bottom is present. However, walleyes will make a mock spawning run toward an incoming feeder stream. Good post-spawn areas will be somewhere nearby.

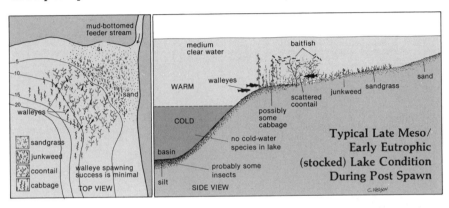

Typical areas are the deeper stands of nearby, available weedgrowth, or perhaps the clean lip area just outside the weeds. Later, in summer, the weeds become choked and thick. The walleyes usually bury in them and are tough customers to catch during the day. But in Post-spawn, the sparse weeds make them fairly catchable.

These lakes generally have no cold water baitfish (like cisco), and lack sufficient oxygen to sustain fish in deep water during the summer. Thus, the walleyes live in the weeds most of the year. Surprisingly, the Post-spawn Period, with its thin weedgrowth and only moderate sunlight penetration, is actually one of the best times of the year to fish these lakes!

DEEP, CLEAR LAKES

These lakes generally contain good amounts of both minnows and perch, often have deep water baitfish like cisco, and produce both numbers and good-sized walleyes. In fact, many trophy walleye lakes fall into this class. Rock for spawning is common in the shallows, along with a lot of clean sand. Weeds are present, but not choked in. They generally grow in a sparse, narrow band, bordering the drop-off.

Once again, the most logical place to look for post-spawn walleyes is near the spawning grounds. But the kinds of areas you'll be seeking are different than those previously mentioned. Unlike the others, these lakes have clear water and relatively little cover on the shallow flats. There's nowhere to hide until the walleyes reach that deep weed zone. So your post-spawn options are generally going to be deeper on these lakes than in the previous examples.

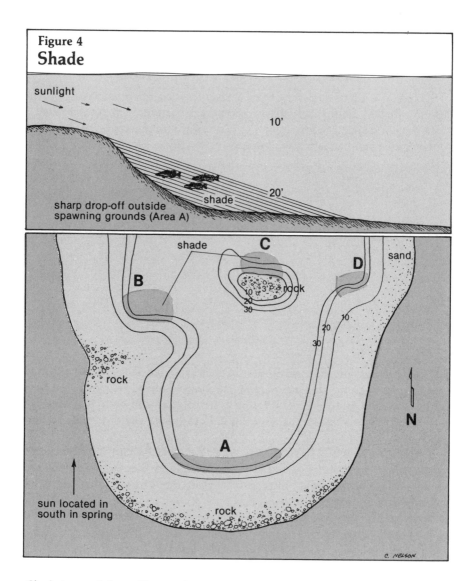

Figure 4
Shade

sunlight

10'

20'

shade

sharp drop-off outside
spawning grounds (Area A)

shade

C

B

D

sand.

10 3' rock
20
30

rock

20 10

30

rock

N

A

sun located in
south in spring

rock

C. NELSON

*Shade is one of the real keys to locating suspended post-spawn walleyes, particularly in clear, deep lakes. As you can see, the south shore of a lake (**Area A**), and the north sides of other structural configurations (**Area B, C and D**) are possible candidates for attracting fish.*

Area A is a sharp drop-off outside a rocky spawning grounds. Area B is the shaded corner of a bar formation, again outside the rocky spawning grounds. Both have excellent potential for post-spawn walleyes.

Area C is the shaded portion of a shallow, rock-covered hump (3' minimum depth) that's shallow enough to draw spawning walleyes. There might be some post-spawn fish lying off the side. Check it out.

Finally, Area D is a shaded corner similar to Area B, except that there's no rock spawning grounds along the shoreline. No rocks—no reason for walleyes to be nearby. Area D would attract few, if any, post-spawn walleyes.

In the event that there's some suitable weedgrowth bordering the drop-off, it'll draw some percentage of the walleyes. They'll lay under the developing weeds to get out of the sun. At night, they'll move around a bit, perhaps munching on spawning perch or shiners. But daytime will see little activity.

If the weeds are poorly developed, though, the walleyes will resort to depth to get out of the sun. That means the fish will drop down the side of the drop-off, or perhaps suspend. You don't know for sure until you check it out. Here's a few clues to narrow down the area you'll have to fish. After all, it pays to save all the time you can.

Keep in mind that the fish will be looking for shade. Therefore, the south shore of a lake, or the north side of a shoreline bar or a shallow sunken island all become potential areas. They're the most consistently shaded areas you'll find.

Now that we've named those areas, don't automatically run to them. Remember, they'll only be productive during Post-spawn if they adjoin a spawning area. That's why the fish are there in the first place. If the walleyes didn't spawn somewhere nearby, you could have acres of shade and still attract few walleyes. It's the combination of the shade and the spawning area that draws fish.

Perhaps the best spawning ground in the lake has very little shaded area adjoining it. Don't despair! That might turn out to be great. It really narrows your search down to that small area. Those big post-spawn sows might be socked into a relatively small shaded area no bigger than your living room.

PREDATORS AND PREY

You're probably all excited by now, but we have to bring one more factor into the picture. Besides having shade adjacent to a spawning area, there must be food present. That can make a big difference, but if you know what to look for, you can use it to your advantage. Let's examine two examples where the food sources becomes the final determining factor.

FIGURE 5 is typical of a good post-spawn area. It's just outside a shallow, rocky spawning ground, and there's some shade present. To keep it simple, let's say there are only two shaded areas. One adjoins a hard-bottomed projection, the other casts its shadow over a deep mud flat. Which is best? The answer? Either, both or neither. It all depends on what the walleyes are eating. Here's why.

Let's say the lake has a good shiner population. They're an important walleye food source. At about the time the walleyes are done spawning, the shiners are getting ready to move in to spawn. So the walleyes and shiners cross paths for a while, making it especially nice for the walleyes since a tasty shiner makes for a good meal.

Until the time the shiners move in to spawn, they'll hang out over the drop-off and suspend. Generally, it'll be over an area of hard bottom, like AREA A in FIGURE 5. Perfect. That's where the walleyes will be.

Think you've got it licked? Well, let's pretend it's the next year, and you go back to AREA A and do poorly. What happened?

Let's say that the strong population of shiners was too strong the year before. There wasn't enough food for all of them to survive the previous year. It was a tough winter, and many of the shiners died off. Now, there are very few shiners compared to last year. Are the walleyes still going to chase the few evasive surviving shiners?

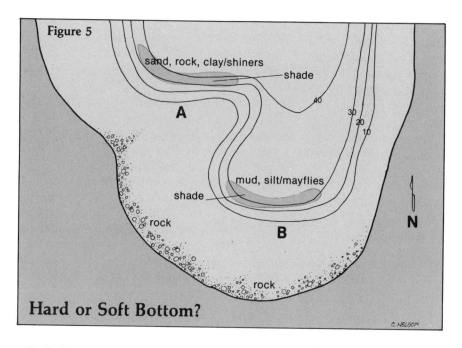

Figure 5

sand, rock, clay/shiners

shade

40

30

20

10

A

mud, silt/mayflies

shade

rock

B

N

rock

Hard or Soft Bottom?

C. NELSON

Probably not. Chances are they'll move down to *AREA B*, over the mud. Ugh! They're not supposed to be near mud, you say? Wrong! Because if there are not enough minnows to eat, they can still pick up a meal from the mud.

How about mayflies? Or more specifically, mayfly nymphs. Throw in some midges and bloodworms too. It may not seem very appetizing to you, but it's right up the walleye's alley. These little critters burrow into the mud, and the walleyes will root around in there to dig 'em out.

At some time in this early season the mayflies begin hatching, leaving the mud and rising to the surface. The walleyes will absolutely gorge themselves on mayflies. Few anglers realize just how important a walleye food source they are, particularly in the spring when the minnow population is usually at its lowest level of the year.

The best mud flats usually top out about 18-20 feet below the surface. The ones shallower than this seem to draw fewer walleyes, probably because of sunlight penetration. But when these flats coincide with a shaded drop-off —it's walleye time.

Here's a clue for locating them. These areas often coincide with the areas that tullibee and whitefish anglers catch their fish in just before the ice leaves the lake. Those fish are there feasting on the insect larvae. Mark their spots, and try them later for post-spawn walleyes.

Adult Mayfly

Walleyes will relate to the most available forage—whether it's shiners in hard bottom areas or mayflies in soft bottom areas. Often they don't have a choice.

For instance, walleye stomach samplings from Lake of the Woods in 1969 showed 60% of the walleye's food intake was tullibees and shiners for the months of April and May. Yet in the following year, mayflies comprised 75% of their diet, and minnows only about 1%—for the same time period! The fish had no choice but to adjust to the changing food supply. When minnows were abundant, they ate minnows. But during a minnow shortage they switched to mayflies.

Drastic population changes are not unusual in nature. When minnows have a good hatch and become too plentiful, they soon run out of food and their survival rate is poor. But when minnows become scarce, insects flourish because there are too few fish to eat them. It's a vicious circle. Populations can swing back and forth, although it's nature's way to eventually bring them back into control again with an inherent system of checks and balances.

Mayfly Larva

It's usually only destruction of spawning grounds or overharvest by man that can push population levels beyond the point of recovery. Nature takes care of itself, providing we don't put too much stress on the environment.

PRESENTATION

Now that we know where they are, let's go get'em. But before we do, let's keep a few basic but very critical points in mind. Walleyes, by their basic nature, are not overly aggressive fish. And post-spawn walleyes are far less aggressive than normal. So you really have your work cut out for you.

In order to tackle this condition, you must work the areas slowly, methodically, over and over again. You'll probably also have to use live bait, which appeals to the walleyes' sense of smell. Nothing is going to happen fast and furious. You'll get 1 or 2 fish at a time. There definitely won't be any feeding explosions. But by the end of the day, a determined effort just might get you an impressive collection of big fish.

WORKING WEEDS AND WOOD

The key to getting walleyes out of this shallow cover is to get some live bait down to the fish, stick it in their face, and let it sit there. Eventually, you'll hit one on the nose and get its attention. It's not very glamorous, but effective.

One of the best ways to work this form of cover is with a tiny jig. Hook a lively shiner or small chub onto the back of an 1/8 ounce jig and pitch it out there. If the cover is real heavy, then hook that minnow up through the skull, solid, so it won't rip off the hook. But if the cover is sparse, try hooking it through the lips only. It'll stay alive, wiggle around, and perhaps attract attention.

Stick with little jigs. That 1/8 ounce jig serves two purposes. One, it sinks very slowly and gives the fish plenty of time to eyeball it. Second, and perhaps most important, it forces you to fish slowly. That's what you need, and a light jig slows you down.

Cast up into the weeds, stumps or log jams. Don't be afraid of the snags. Sure, you'll lose a few jigs, but that's where the fish are. Let the little jig drift down into the cover and sit there. Wait. Wait some more. Then twitch it. Perhaps move it a foot and leave it sit again. You can't fish too slowly for post-spawn walleyes. Eventually, a slight tap on the end of your line will signal the results. Set the hook!

Bill Binkelman's jighead (left) has a light wire Aberdeen hook that's great for fishing in wood. If you get stuck, a steady pull will straighten the hook out and you get your jig back.

Jack Remus' Hawg Jig (right) has a heavy O' Shaughnessy hook that won't bend at all. It's for rearing back and hauling a big fish out of the weeds. The choice is yours. Just be sure to match your tackle to the conditions.

SHINER

CHUB

You can't afford a long duel when you're fishing cover. Try and be a sport and you'll lose your fish. There's too many things to tangle the line on. And with the light 8 pound test line and spinning gear it takes to work these little jigs, you can't let the fish root around in the cover. Otherwise, kiss 'em good-bye.

A light jig can be worked surprisingly well through thick snags. Just keep the line tight so it doesn't wrap around a limb. You can crawl those little devils in and out of the meanest places if you try.

For this kind of "wood fishing," use a light wire Aberdeen jighook, like the kind used in Bill Binkelman's jigs. If you do get stuck, a steady pull on the line will bend the hook open and you'll get the jig back. For weeds, though, you might try one with a heavy hook, one that you can rear back on and force a big walleye up out of the weeds with.

The jig'll do most of your work for you, but you can do a little experimenting. Soaking a shiner on a slip bobber will do the trick, providing you set it deep enough to get down into the weeds or logs. That fat shiner sitting there looks mighty good.

And, if you can manage it, do a little night fishing. Slowly troll a Rapala type lure across the weedy flats or amongst the "wood." Use your electric motor to sneak up on 'em. Go slow. It's probably your all-around best shot, because they're a bit more active at night. At least it's another option when the going is tough.

WORKING DROP-OFF OR SUSPENDED FISH

Once you get off the flats and have an "edge" condition (weedline or drop-off), you can start using a backtrolling approach. Both jigs and live bait rigs will produce. For jigging, use a bit heavier jig than you used up on the flats, perhaps 1/4 ounce. You need the added weight to handle the deeper water. Keep the action to a minimum—no hops or twitches. Just a slow drag, or an occasional slight lift and drop is all you need.

Whether you use the jig or live bait rig, the boat control approach is basically the same. You want to ever-so-slowly creep along, with frequent pauses, placing a tasty piece of live bait in front of the fish. Let's work it through with a live bait rig.

If there are decent weeds for the walleyes to relate to, they usually hug tight to the bottom. Keep your snell length short, like 12 inches. Stick that minnow right in their faces, and go slow.

If the weeds are poor, chances are you're looking at a suspended fish condition. Again, the basic approach is the same, but you will have to modify the length of your snell, and switch over from a plain hook to a floating jighead.

Select a floating cork jig with a #6 or #8 hook—big enough to hold good-sized minnows and handle a big walleye. There are numerous brands on the market. White works very well in clear water, while yellow and orange are quite visible for cloudy water conditions. Pick up a few dozen 2-4 inch shiners to hook on the back.

Here's a super, little-known trick. Pay attention to how your cork jig floats —hook up or hook down. You probably never considered it, but some float with the barb up, others with it down. It all depends on the style of head and hook position. Lower your rig into the water and look at it.

Now that you know which way the jighead rides (hook up or hook down), turn the jig upside down from the normal position, and then hook the minnow through the lips.

The natural buoyancy of the jig wants to make it flip over. The shiner, meanwhile, has to struggle to remain upright. Otherwise he'll turn belly up. So what you have is this minnow down there, struggling like mad, trying to re-

Take a close look at all the floaters pictured here. This is the way they normally float—some hook up, others hook down. It depends on the kind of hook and where it's positioned in the body.

If you want to use the "upside down trick" and make the minnow struggle, turn the jig upside down from normal, and then hook the minnow through the lips.

main level. A lazy walleye will sense the vibrations and pay attention. It might make the difference between enticing a strike or no response at all. You can even fish it in one place—the bait works itself.

If you're fishing over mud bottom with the possible presence of mayfly larvae, try another modification. Take the rubber body off a 1/16 or 1/8 ounce jig like a Fuzz-E-Grub or Ugly Bug, and put the grub body on the cork jig, camouflaging the hook. When a walleye takes it, it'll be less reluctant to spit out the offering. Besides, with the addition of the white or yellow grub body, the offering looks more like an insect and may be enough to turn the tide and get those reluctant fish to strike.

Basically, you'll be backtrolling this floating rig, usually with about a 3/8 ounce walking sinker. Work out from the drop-off, across the adjacent deep water. And watch your depth sounder for suspended fish. This is critical!

Determine how far off the bottom they are, and re-tie your snell to the right length. If you're lazy, you probably won't get anything.

Say the fish are 6 feet off the bottom. Tie about a 9 foot snell. It's enough to get your bait off the bottom and allow for a little bit of angle in your line as you slowly move along (FIGURE 6).

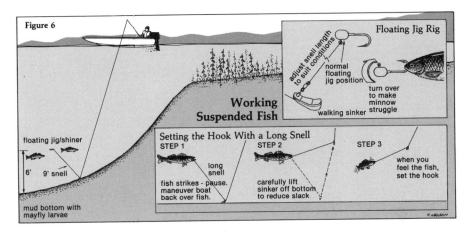

Figure 6

Work, re-work, and keep working the area over and over again once you spot fish. Give them time to respond. It's very common to put in 3 or 4 passes before you entice a strike. Then all of a sudden you'll feel just a touch of weight on your line. Fish on!

Give the fish a little slack and get yourself organized. It only takes a few seconds. Slowly back up over the fish and hover there. That long snell takes a little special effort to set the hook properly.

When you feel the weight of the sinker, slowly lift it up off the bottom maybe 3, 4 or 5 feet. Reel that extra slack line in. Lift a little, reel a little. All of a sudden you'll feel the slight weight of the fish. Set the hook with a quick upward motion. Keep her coming. Get the fish out of the school before they spook and you might be able to get another one.

Remember, these are spooky fish. Be careful. Use a quiet electric motor if available. If the walleyes stop hitting, experiment a little. Try holding a regular 30 inch snell rig 8 feet off the bottom, or even holding a jig and minnow at their level. It might get you an extra fish. Most times, though, they'll spook. Then it's on to the next potential area to try for some more.

Chapter 11

THE PRE-SUMMER PERIOD

"A Time of Transition"

This is a period of regrouping as fish move from the spawning areas to summer locations. Summer patterns take shape as the hormone levels and feeding activities return to normal. Fish activity is rated as active.

The key factor during this Calendar Period is the developing food chain. Our Pre-summer Period begins once the time of recovery from the spawning ritual (Post-spawn) is over. During this time the warming process of the sun, by way of increasingly longer days, is the major influence in transforming a body of water from a cool to a warm water environment. But the longer duration of light has a more profound effect than just warming. All life forms respond to light or the lack of it. Light regulates the growth rates of weeds, insects and, of course, fish.

There is also a corresponding rise in air and water temperatures—and activity. The water in most cases will not have warmed to a point where the various fish species' metabolism will demand a lot of food. And well this is, because food is in limited supply, as all forms have not yet developed to the point where they are of suitable size for the various predators.

Generally, at this time, the water temperature in a lake will vary less from section to section as compared to the earlier spring periods. And from this stage on the weedgrowth in most sections will grow at basically the same rate. In fact, the entire body of water will begin to function more as a unit rather than isolated entities.

In previous Calendar Periods, fish of the same species might exhibit staggered responses. Some could be in a Pre-spawn mood, while others are spawning or have just finished. Now, during Pre-summer, they all tend to exhibit similar responses.

What the fish are doing is readying themselves for the next explosive period—the Summer-Peak, a time when water temperatures, weedgrowth and available food supply mesh in such a way to provide the conditions for a feast. But that time has not yet arrived. Pre-summer is still a period of developing food chains and emerging weedgrowth. Most young vegetation on the flats or the drop-offs lacks substance and definition.

Forage, like small minnows or young-of-the year perch, is not large enough to provide a good one-gulp meal for the larger predators. And these forage species, lacking the concealment of adequate cover, respond to predation by simply roaming around a lot—many times in open water.

It's this kind of unstable environment that's responsible for good catches one day and poor the next. Nothing is consistent. Fish might be quite shallow for a number of days, and then move deeper. Although they feed, the fish aren't aggressive. They tend not to chase food or lures—at least not far. All in all, the Pre-summer Period is a demanding one for the angler. He has to work, but more than that, he must think, for pat formulas don't exist.

One method that starts coming into its own is crankbaiting the reefs in Canadian or U.S. lakes. This is a complex pattern. But, when everything falls together, it is dynamite.

The second is bobber fishing. Both offer special presentations that add to your walleye bag of tricks.

BOBBER FISHING

The resurgence of the popularity of bobber fishing for walleyes has steadily been spreading. Many "smart money" anglers have been using the system on Lake of the Woods. A few "sneaky Petes" have been testing it in the spring on Lake Erie. And when the going is tough with their usual methods, they do quite well with the bobbers. Other knowledgeable folks have been spanking walleyes on Lake Winnipeg in Canada. And a few "in" devotees have been quietly bobber fishing Lake Winnebago in Wisconsin and knocking 'em dead.

If ever there was an oldie but a goodie, this is it. And, as a result of its renewed popularity, new refinements have appeared. Bobber fishing has matured from the realm of amateur night to the level of a proven method. Perhaps its most appealing aspect is that it doesn't take long to learn. Even a green rookie can get the hang of it in a short time. We will cover most of the

Walleye Moods & Positions on a Typical Reef

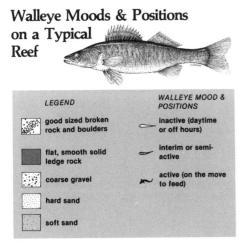

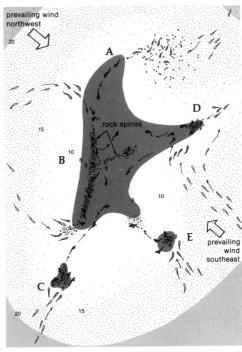

This approach can be used for both patterns (crankbaiting or bobber fishing).

This drawing shows a typical reef and how different fish groups might relate to it during their various activity moods. Basically, there are 3 moods: 1) active (feeding), 2) neutral (fish starting to get ready to feed) and 3) inactive. Keep in mind that from day to day all walleye groups—even the members of the same group—do not necessarily activate at the same time. The percentage of those that are active, neutral and inactive will vary according to local weather conditions and time of day.

Usually, when fish relate to a reef, the deeper fish are inactive and usually won't touch a bait. As they become more active, they tend to move up out of the deeper water to positions just outside the sharper breaks, ledges and boulder piles. These are catchable fish. Then, when they are actively feeding, they move to where most of the food (baitfish) are—in the shallows.

These movements correspond closely with what the baitfish do. In the daytime, young-of-the-year perch, shiners and small ciscoes are usually off the sides of the reef, suspended high up in open water in positions that make it hard for the walleyes to prey on them. Towards evening, however, the baitfish move to the edges and settle at night in the shallows on top of the reef in rock crevices. It's in these positions that the baitfish are most vulnerable. Apparently, the walleyes instinctively know this and react accordingly. Even so, some walleyes may come up and roam the reef during daylight.

This drawing shows fish positions all around the reef. But wait! There are conditions which will activate and draw one group of walleyes quicker than others—especially wind. Experience has shown that those shallow entry areas (sharp breaks in structure) to the reef where the wind pounds in with the most force are usually the spots where the baitfish are most disoriented by motion and reduced light. Thus, these spots receive the most feeding activity—in both intensity and number of predator fish.

While each of the entry Areas A, B, C, D and E show fish present, the direction from which the wind is blowing in the hardest will be the best at that time. In the same sense, those spots on the lee side of the wind will receive less fish use. For instance, if the wind is coming from the northwest, Areas A, B and C will be hot, with Area A probably the *best. In contrast, Areas D and E will be slow. Of course, if the wind reversed itself, the opposite will be true.*

Note also, that when fish are on top of the reef (in this case, shallower than 8 feet), they are very actively feeding. But when they are deeper they may be only semi-active or completely inactive.

It's important to keep in mind that the neutral fish, while not yet feeding heavily, are much more tightly concentrated and in more defined areas than either the inactive or active fish. There are some schools of angling thought that feel these fish, which will strike, are easier to catch than very active fish, because they are concentrated in a given area for a protracted period of time. These fish are quite catchable, and a good catch can be made from these groups if you're right on the money.

In contrast, the active, feeding fish groups atop the reef tend to break into smaller groups and scatter and roam about. If you're in an anchored position, the fish will come in waves. You'll get action for a while and then it will slack off. A lot of times as the fish move about you'll have to reposition yourself. But if you can contact a school just before they move up and scatter, you can really make hay.

basics and acquaint you with what's new. You may even want to add some of your own innovations later.

First off, put away any preconceived notions or ingrained prejudices you have about the system. Realize that this system works like crazy—if applied on the right lake, at the right time, in the right place and in the right way.

Fishing methods, like fish, are the product of their environment. A system is developed to fit a given set of circumstances. This is equally true of bobber fishing.

While the "slip-bobber technique" can be used in a variety of circumstances, its best application is for walleyes on the rocks in certain kinds of lakes during certain seasons. In fact, the revived interest in bobber fishing developed under just these kinds of circumstances.

Why? Well, first of all, walleyes love live bait, almost always to the exclusion of artificial lures. But once walleyes are on the shallow rocks, it's a real problem to present live bait to them. Think about it for a moment. Bottom-walking live bait rigs are nearly impossible to work in these shallow, snag-filled waters. Jigs tipped with live bait, too, are swallowed immediately unless you keep them moving fast—but often a fast-moving offering is not what the walleyes want. Further, free-lining—a plain hook and a split shot with some kind of live bait—sometimes works well on shallow rocks. But there are times walleyes just don't want their food on or near the bottom, so this, too, often rules out this approach. Crankbaits can be very effective in this situation, but they, too, must be used only at certain times.

Long-line trollers with snelled spinners and live bait used to drag their concoctions over the shallow rocks with some success. But there are too many times when the walleyes don't want the bait moving fast. *In fact, there are times they don't want it moving at all.* A bobber set-up is the only method that allows the bait to stand almost still or move very, very slowly without having to fight constant snags and hangups.

There is also another consideration. For any number of reasons, still not fully explained, walleyes and other fish sometimes hover off the bottom when active. And when they do, they seem to be reluctant to pick up a bait on or near the bottom. Apparently, when they are in this mood, an offering must be at eye level or above. There are also times when they won't move any distance to snap at a moving lure or bait or go after one that is passing by quickly. When they are inactive like this, they will grab a bait only after it's been in front of or near them for some time. Taking all this into consideration, bobber fishing is the only method available to us today that solves all these problems.

Now you know why there is renewed interest in bobber fishing and why the system works. The next step is to apply the method in the right place at the right time.

THE RIGHT PLACE

The bobber fishing system works best on the sprawling, windswept classic mid-meso lakes, and to a lesser extent on some reef-studded oligotrophic lakes with extensive meso sections. Typically, these waters have sections of shoreline with fist-sized rock and gravel, bounded by moderately deep sand flats that contain occasional rock rises. In other words, its best application is on those waters that have a certain make-up where the walleye population is high. In different bodies of water, with marginal walleye populations, there may be more efficient methods. So, first off, it's important to use this system on the right kind of lake.

As mentioned, Lake Mille Lacs in Minnesota, Winnebago in Wisconsin and Lake of the Woods in Canada are good examples.

POST-SPAWN AND PRE-SUMMER PERIODS

After spawning the fish do not instantly move out to different locales. On most meso lakes there is more of a slow dispersal that resembles a filtering process.

The fish tend to evacuate the shoreline areas first, and move out to or hang longer on those reefs that lie between the shallow spawning areas and their deeper summertime haunts. As walleyes begin their retreat from the spawning areas, they hold up on these nearby rocky offshore reefs until the water has warmed sufficiently out in the deeper portions of the main lake. When this happens you can expect to have a few weeks of prime fishing on these shoals. It's a classic walleye pattern during the Post-spawn and Pre-summer Periods. The most obvious cases occur on the large, windswept meso lakes, where there are huge schools of walleyes moving from area to area according to the changing seasons.

Lake Mille Lacs in central Minnesota is a perfect example. It's got miles of shallow shorelines for spawning—a clear-cut early spring location. In early summer, the bulk of the walleyes move many miles out into the main-lake, and relate to 20-25 foot deep humps. But where do the walleyes go in the interim? Well, as they begin the retreat out toward the main-lake they hold up for a while on the shallow, nearby offshore reefs until summer arrives. If you think about it, it makes sense.

A similar thing occurs on Lake Winnebago in Wisconsin, Lake Winnipeg and Lake of the Woods in Canada, and on Lake Erie. In fact, it will happen on any lake where there are similar conditions.

Today, Lake Erie is probably the finest walleye lake in the world. Walleyes spawn on the rocky shorelines in spring, and then gradually move out into the main lake as the season progresses. On their way, they'll relate to the closer off-shore reefs first—those nearest the spawning grounds. Then they'll move to ones a little farther out and then later to those still a little farther out. They do this until they establish their normal summertime patterns.

This phenomenon also occurs on some of the oligotrophic lakes of the Canadian Shield, where the deeper water remains cold in the main lake for a long time. Consequently, shallow rocky shoals lying near the warmer mesotrophic arms, bays and sections also become classic Post-spawn/Pre-summer walleye holding areas as the gradual movement out to the main lake takes place.

In summary, in the classic meso waters and some oligotrophic lakes with meso sections, rock reefs and shoals become walleye magnets and holding areas as the fish move from a spring to a summer environment. And it is on these reefs in the Pre-summer Period where bobber-fishing for walleyes has its heyday.

SOME SPECIFICS

Obviously, the bigger the reef the more fish it can accommodate. But there are other factors besides size to consider. The surrounding depth and make-up of the bottom are also important. Fish tend to locate on top of a reef when active and down the sides when inactive. So they spend a lot more time down than up. What this means is that there must be sufficient area to house the fish during the long off hours. Therefore, stairstep reefs with a number of intermittent levels will house more fish than those that just stick straight up, volcano-like, even if they both top-out at the same depth.

The accompanying drawing illustrates a good, better, best principle in regard to reefs. Reefs can be several acres in size—or they may be small enough to cast across. One may rise to a crest and then plunge down again. On another the bottom may roll up and down, forming a series of "mini-humps" on a still larger rocky reef. The kind of reefs you'll find depends simply on the nature of the lake.

Let's say you have a 1 acre rise, 10 feet deep, surrounded by 30 feet of water. On top of the shoal there are various smaller rises scattered here and there that peak out at 3 or 4 feet. It's a large area, with a bunch of irregular features at various levels. Does it sound like a good spot?

You bet it is! A large area like this will definitely attract a lot of walleyes at the right time of the year. The key to fishing it is locating the best fish-attracting areas on that reef.

As we mentioned, inactive fish lay off the sides. When they become active they tend to move shallower. This type of behavior is classic. When they are off the sides it's usually very difficult to get them to strike. When they activate and move on top, they feed like crazy.

Naturally, your first question is, when are they up or down? Walleyes are very sensitive to light levels—more active during low light and less active when there is intense light penetration into the water. As a result, on a nice,

Some Reefs Are Better Than Others

Pictured here are 3 reefs. They all have the same sized top area and all are at the same depth. Nevertheless, if all other things are equal, Reef #3 will hold many times more fish than Reef #1. While Reef #1 will attract fish, its ability to hold them during the off-hours is limited because of its steep drop-off. That's why it can only hold a limited number of fish, even though the top may be quite large.

In contrast, Reef #3 has a series of stair-steps, which provide the fish a more suitable off-hours environment. The walleyes have more room, which translates into more fish.

All reefs are not necessarily equal. Reef #2 is better than Reef #1 because it has a stair-step and more off-hours room. Reef #3 is best because it has more adjacent lateral area and many different levels of stair-steps.

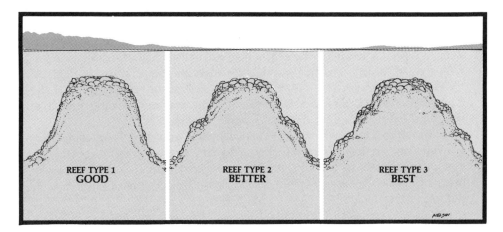

REEF TYPE 1
GOOD

REEF TYPE 2
BETTER

REEF TYPE 3
BEST

calm, sunny day, the fish will be down and inactive. You'd fish the reef much like a sunken island in a smaller lake. You would look for points or projections that extend out toward deeper water. Walleyes tend to congregate down the sides of these ledges or out on the tip of these points. Some may even be out as far as the adjacent deeper flats. By carefully working vertically with live bait rigs or jigs, there would be a good chance you'll pick up some walleyes. But that's the problem...you'd get *some* walleyes. The results, considering the number of fish available, wouldn't be that good. Even bobber-fishing the edges for these inactive fish would be a hit and miss proposition.

Now let's look at a different set of weather conditions—one which can result in some of the finest walleye fishing you've ever experienced. The trees are reeling at the force of a wind that's howling at a good 15, 20 or 25 m.p.h. The lake is churning like a miniature ocean. There are 3, 4 or even 6 foot waves crashing across the tops of the reefs. What do you do now?

Well, if you want to stay on shore and paint the house, no one's going to blame you. That's some pretty mean water. But if you're an experienced walleye hunter on big lakes, it's a good bet you'll be out there. You know that these are perhaps the best conditions to catch a bunch of walleyes from a reef—and not only the eaters, but the lunkers.

When you're reef fishing, realize that local weather conditions have a con-siderable influence on your possible success. Poor conditions are sunny and slick—good are overcast and windy. Wind, even on a sunny day, makes waves and breaks the sun's penetration and helps activate some walleyes. But if you get wind and overcast skies together, you have prime conditions.

On those sunny, slick days the fish usually activate and move up only towards evening or at sundown—and then usually only in limited numbers. Yet, on the overcast windy days you can have hundreds, even thousands, of aggressive walleyes prowling the tops of the reefs scattered in 4 or 5 feet of water all day. Night fishing, too, on some of these reefs can be pure dynamite.

SLIP-BOBBERS

A walleye angler geared for all seasonal conditions must be versatile and possess an arsenal of methods. We want you to understand that this applies to reefs as well. They can be fished, depending on circumstances, in a variety of different ways. You can free-line them (live bait and split-shot), crank them (as we discussed earlier), vertical rig and jig the edges and deeper adjacent flats, or troll the tops with live bait or spinner set-ups. But, as we've mentioned, there is another alternative—slip-bobber fishing—one that has recently been the rage on the reefs of the big, sprawling walleye lakes.

Let's look at a typical situation. The walleyes in your lake have completed spawning and are leaving the shoreline areas. You've located fish on one of the best offshore reefs in the lake. Its top is covered with rock and scattered boulders. The waves are rolling in, making boat control extremely difficult, if not impossible.

Fishing this reef with the standard live bait rigs and any number of other methods would be very difficult. To avoid being hung up constantly; you'd have to fish directly beneath the boat. And in 5 feet of water you know you're spooking the majority of the fish before you get to them. Presentation has always been a problem in this kind of situation. Most other fishermen on your lake, rather than cope with all the snags and lost tackle, have avoided fishing these areas under these conditions. But you stay out and work.

By dark you are back to the dock with a beautiful stringer of walleyes. You only fished a couple hours on the reef, and didn't get snagged even once. And your 6 year old son caught more of the fish than you did. Folks on shore are ecstatic...they ask for your secret method. Coyly, you answer, "...a bobber and leech!" Many of the experienced fishermen might snicker and think, "fluke," or stand by unconvinced. The rookies at the dock, however, would be intrigued.

First off, you would explain you didn't just go "cork fishing." More precisely, you used a slip-bobber that slides freely on your line. It was used in conjunction with a bobber-stop to position your bait at a predetermined depth. The tiny bobber-stop will flow easily through your line guides and onto your reel while the bobber slides down to your weight. Likewise, when you cast, it creates no problems and allows you to fish in any depth of water. The slip-bobber rig is really one of the most simple ways you can catch fish. And that is what probably turns off the veterans, but interests the novice fisherman. All you have to do is cast out and watch your bobber. Your 6 year old son loved it.

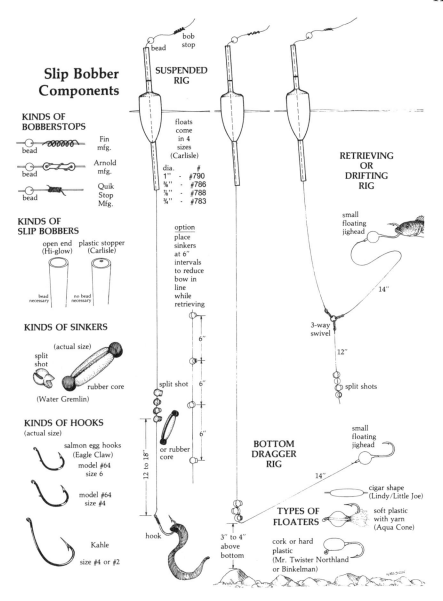

Slip Bobber Components

KINDS OF BOBBERSTOPS
- bead — Fin mfg.
- bead — Arnold mfg.
- bead — Quik Stop Mfg.

KINDS OF SLIP BOBBERS
- open end (Hi-glow) — bead necessary
- plastic stopper (Carlisle) — no bead necessary

KINDS OF SINKERS
- (actual size)
- split shot
- rubber core
- (Water Gremlin)

KINDS OF HOOKS
(actual size)
- salmon egg hooks (Eagle Claw) model #64 size 6
- model #64 size #4
- Kahle size #4 or #2

SUSPENDED RIG
- bob stop
- bead
- floats come in 4 sizes (Carlisle)

dia.	#
1"	#790
⅝"	#786
⅞"	#788
¾"	#783

option place sinkers at 6" intervals to reduce bow in line while retrieving

- 6"
- split shot — 6"
- or rubber core — 6"
- 12 to 18"
- hook
- 3" to 4" above bottom

RETRIEVING OR DRIFTING RIG
- small floating jighead
- 14"
- 3-way swivel
- 12"
- split shots

BOTTOM DRAGGER RIG
- small floating jighead
- 14"

TYPES OF FLOATERS
- cigar shape (Lindy/Little Joe)
- soft plastic with yarn (Aqua Cone)
- cork or hard plastic (Mr. Twister Northland or Binkelman)

COMPONENTS

First, you must be rigged (set-up) right. Depth is the most important consideration. With the aid of a slip-bobber set-up you can successfully bobber-fish at any depth from deep to shallow. Let's take a closer look at the bobber rig itself.

The first and most important part of the rig is the bobber itself. The bobber should be small in size. It only needs to hold your bait off the bottom. The pencil-type bobber seems to work best, because it stands up higher in the water, giving you good visibility, but offers little resistance when a fish takes your bait. This is very important on the days when walleyes are in one of their finicky moods.

The genius of slip-bobber fishing is that it allows you to fish effectively in deep water. And it's easy to adjust the depth of your bait. That's where the bob-stop comes in. This device stops your bobber from sliding up the line, but allows a weighted leech to sink to the adjusted depth.

The stops you can use are numerous. A piece of a rubber band or one of the manufactured stops will do fine. A bead is built into some slip-bobbers, but you may have to slide one on your line between the stop and bobber, if it isn't included.

The sinker can be either a split-shot or a Rubbercor type. The Rubbercor is best because there's no line pinch or slippage.

The amount of weight you use is important! You should have enough for the bait to sink quickly but still allow your bobber to float high enough to detect a strike.

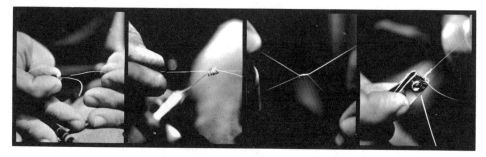

The Bobber Fisherman's Best Friend

The innovation of the bobber-stop was one of the elements that revitalized the cork fishing system. Most of the time you'll be fishing with 5, 6 and sometimes as much as 15 or more feet of line beyond the tip of your rod. With a traditional fixed bobber it would be impossible to cast out, or reel up a fish, with that much line beneath the bobber. This simple little item solves all these problems.

Pictured here is a movable line tie. It's fast and easy to assemble because of its threader sleeve and it reels in like a dream. It also removes all line twist.

Leeches should be hooked through the suction cup when bobber fishing. This allows them to swim (their head is opposite the suction cup) naturally. Minnows should be hooked lightly under the dorsal fin and 'crawlers through the collar.

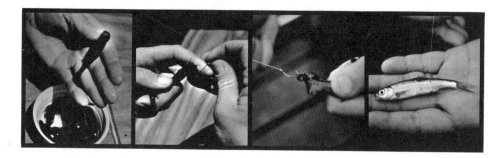

BAIT VS. HOOK SIZE

Proper hook size will depend on the bait you are using. In Minnesota, leeches have become very popular and account for most of the walleyes taken on bobbers. They are probably the best bet for cork fishing.

When a walleye grabs a leech it will roll it up in a ball, frequently around your hook. This is why a bigger hook is required with a larger leech. This also leads us back to the importance of setting the hook hard. At times with a large leech, you may have to drive the point of your hook first through the leech and then into the fish.

Hook your leech through the sucker end of the leech for bobber-fishing. This is actually the leech's tail, contrary to what many people believe, and it will swim away from your hook in an enticing manner.

Nightcrawlers and minnows are also used successfully at times. It's a good policy to hook the nightcrawlers through the collar for bobber-fishing, rather than through the nose as when backtrolling. The resistance of the bobber can pop off a lightly-hooked 'crawler.

Minnows should be hooked through the back, just behind the dorsal fin. Again, hook size should be selected in accordance with the size of your minnow. The smaller the bait, the smaller the hook and vice versa. As a general rule, use larger hooks when bobber fishing than you would on live bait or split-shot rigs.

TACKLE

One of the neat things about bobber-fishing is that it requires only the simplest tackle. An open spinning reel with 6 or 8 lb. mono, a slip-bobber and bobber-stop, sinker and hook is all that is necessary. Heavier mono line, like 12 lb. test, creates a lot of drag. Make sure you use premium lighter weight lines.

When it comes to rods, use a fairly stiff one—a 6½ footer or one of the 6 foot models. Because of the angle of your line, which runs first to the bobber and then down to the fish, it's important to have a rod with enough backbone to set the hook. In fact, this is when most fish will be lost. Also, when you cast out the float, you do it with an upward "stiff arm" sweep so you don't cast the bait off. A stiff-action rod allows you to do this better.

When you first get a bite and your bobber goes under, you should *slowly* pick up the slack in your line until you actually feel the fish. Do this carefully so as to not put any undo pressure on the fish. Remember, it could be swimming in any direction, even towards you, so it is extremely important to get the bow of the line out before setting the hook.

Timing is the key to successful bobber fishing. Each day is different. The fish could be more or less active than they were yesterday or even a few hours ago. You'll constantly have to play it by ear and experiment.

Generally, you can judge the amount of time to let the fish take the bait by the intensity that they strike. Usually, when they hit hard, hit 'em back quick. When they mess with the bait and you see your bobber dancing on the surface or going under very slowly, let 'em run. A good rule is when the bobber finally goes down, wait a second or two, tighten up whatever slack is left, and then crack 'em hard. You must set the hook with authority and keep a tight line or you'll miss a lot of strikes. Trial and error on the amount of time you give a fish to chew on the bait is still your best yardstick.

WORKING AN AREA

Since bobber fishing is best in heavy waves, you can forget about any attempt at trying to troll or drift. Your best success will come from an anchored position. But you obviously don't just anchor anywhere. First, scout the area to find a rock spine or rise that you feel will attract or hold fish. A lot of times you can spot suspended fish near these areas on your depth finder. Flashes high off the bottom indicate active fish in the area. Or lots of high-riding baitfish may also indicate that the fish might be up.

The best way to pin down a probable spot is to crisscross the area you intend to fish and get to know it first. Then visualize how you can best fish it from a stationary position. Once you know how your bobbers will drift, you can choose the best place (or places) to anchor. Then move directly upwind from that spot and drop your anchor. Be sure you have plenty of anchor rope to allow the anchor to hold in the heavy waves. You may need a full 100 feet!

Remember, the bigger the waves the better. On a reef pounded by waves the disoriented schools of minnows are very vulnerable. The minnows try to use the big rocks to hide from the searching walleye schools by sliding into the crevices when attacked. So, both predators and prey tend to congregate in the broken rock areas, and this is where the bobber really comes in handy!

Once your boat is in position, let the bobber do the work for you. When you begin fishing an area, it's best to cast out at a 90° angle to the boat and let the wind and waves sweep the bait around the boat. By working both sides of the boat you can cover quite a large area. It's much like fan-casting. But once you pin-point the location of the fish, it pays to be on the money. Start placing your bait directly into that spot. You may have to cast your cork upwind from the spot and feed line out and steer the cork into position.

Often one person in a boat will catch all the fish using the same bait, even the same set-up his partner is using. Obviously, he is doing some *little thing* that makes a difference. Maybe he is laying his casts so they come right along the edge of a boulder pile instead of skirting too far out. Or he may be sweeping his bait through the crevices by letting it bounce on the bottom and then lift off with the roll of the waves. There can be many little reasons why one person takes fish and the other doesn't—but it sure happens. So it pays to watch for the little things.

Under light wind conditions you can actually position the boat right on top of the reef. It's usually best to do this toward evening or at night when the maximum amount of fish filter up. Then you can work a full 360° around the boat. But this approach is difficult to do if there is a stiff wind, because a light bobber and split shot just do not cast well into the wind.

Finding the right depth to set the bobber at can take some time, but looking closely at the prevailing conditions will usually give you a starting depth. As we mentioned earlier, walleyes are very sensitive to bright light, so they will usually adjust to it by staying in a depth of water that is most comfortable for them. Let's review a few general guidelines.

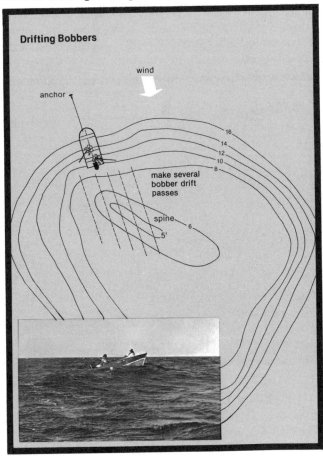

Never Fight the Wind

If you are going to struggle against the wind, you'll probably lose the battle. Instead, use it to your advantage. By aiming your casts and feeding or taking in line you can actually steer a bobber into position.

You can also make it sit in one place, pause in spots or move on. This is the secret that takes cork fishing out of the novice class and places it into the category of a true fishing system.

On a bright day with light or moderate winds the walleyes tend to stay in the deeper adjacent water and will hug the bottom. Some fish will move onto the reef, however, toward evening. These, too, tend to hug bottom even when moving up.

If the winds are blowing—even if it's bright out—the light penetration will be reduced and a few fish will filter up during the day. But the major activity atop the reef itself will still occur again toward evening. During these times (both during the day and evening), whether deep or shallow, the walleyes tend to rise up a bit (about a foot or so) off the bottom.

If it's overcast and windy, light will be reduced considerably, and more fish will filter up during the daylight. But the major, most intense, movements will still occur toward evening. Significantly, when these conditions prevail, the majority of fish, both shallow and deep, will be higher off the bottom—maybe hovering 2 to 3 feet off.

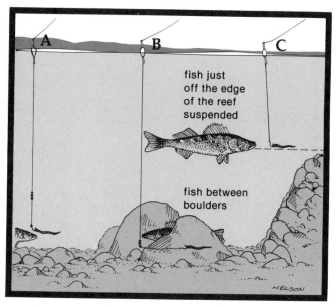

Set Your Depth to Make a Difference

Many folks think of a bobber as only a device to signal a strike. Well, there's a lot more to it than that. A bobber is also a vehicle to set depth, provide action, determine speed and steer a course. Pictured here are 3 different depth sets.

Position A is a rigging set 12 to 18 inches off the bottom. This is the one used most often, since walleyes sitting on or just off the bottom can usually see it well.

Position B is a bottom dragging method. It can be used with a plain hook or a small floating cork. The sinkers are set 3 or 4 inches from the bottom to avoid hang-ups and a foot or so of line is left to trail out along the bottom. Walleyes occasionally sit in the crevices between big rocks or boulders, and won't move out or up much to take a bait. This set-up allows you to send your offering right into their lairs.

Position C is used when the walleyes suspend off the sides of the reef. Usually, this occurs in late morning when the walleyes, along with the baitfish, have evacuated the top of the reef. Sometimes the baitfish will swim directly off the top of the reef and continue at the same level. So you can find walleyes in a similar position in 5 to 6 feet of water. The walleyes are semi-active, and they won't move up or down too much to grab a bait. You can sometimes spot them on a flasher or graph.

In summer, in almost all cases, the majority of movements occur toward evening. When bright and calm, fish tend to hug bottom. When bright and windy, they will lift up a bit. And when overcast and cloudy they will hover up as high as 3 feet or more. So, obviously, predominant light can tell you a great deal about where to properly set your bobber.

Again, when it is bright and calm, during the late morning, noon and early afternoon hours, the majority of walleyes tend to drop off the reefs and lay in the nearby deeper water. But if it should suddenly become cloudy and windy, and light penetration is reduced for a protracted period of time, some fish will start moving up shallower and become more active, even if this happens around midday. The top of the reef would then probably offer some action.

When it is calm, you may have to cast more often. Some days, retrieving your bait slowly along the edges of a reef is the way to go, rather than letting it sit sedentary. On other days, just moving your bait slightly for a foot or two and then allowing it to rest there a few minutes will bring a strike that otherwise would not come. So it just depends.

It's these little considerations that make bobber fishing an intricate fishing method and not just plain old cork-plunking. Awareness of what is happening around you, and making things happen by slight adjustments in position or presentation, is what makes the system interesting—and so much fun.

Since fish move up during low-light times, night fishing can also be very productive with the slip-bobber technique. Usually, if there is a fish movement around dusk and the weather remains stable, there is another sporadic blast around 1 or 2 AM, and another at dawn. For some reason, if there's a half-hearted dusk movement, the entire night is usually a flop.

Night fishermen rig their boats with either electric or gas lights to watch their bobbers, and they bring in some fantastic catches. Recently, lighted bobbers are even being used. One has shown up on the market that operates from a hearing aid battery and buzzes with a strike!

TIPS FOR REEF FISHING

In lakes like Winnibigoshish and Mille Lacs in Minnesota, and some big Canadian Shield lakes, the walleye schools can be quite huge, some ranging from 100 to 200 fish. These groups are usually broken up by year class. Each lake, of course, exhibits different predominant year classes of fish.

The 4-8 pound fish will usually be separate from the 1-3-pounders. The really big lunkers (8-10 pound walleyes), however, are always the exception to the rule. When lots and lots of fish are up, the big ones will be there among them, but when things are slow they are usually absent. The biggies group more loosely than the younger fish, since they eat so much more ravenously. Don't be surprised if one shows up right after you catch 6 little bananas in a row. You never know.

Also, certain bars have a history of producing the very big fish. Others just don't, even though they may house a lot of 4 to 6 pounders. You have to learn the lake to get this kind of information.

The huge walleye schools generally move and meander along the reefs as they feed. Keep an eye out for activity. If lots of boats are present and only one's catching fish of any size, spend only 15 or 20 minutes there and start moving off to the sides and changing your tactics. A half an hour or so is all the time it takes to tell if the fish are active on top of the reef or not.

Bobber fishing may not be the most glamorous way to catch walleyes, but it certainly ranks among the most effective. There are times when the most tried-and-true walleye methods just don't produce.

Chapter 12

THE SUMMER-PEAK PERIOD

"A Time of Fulfillment"

During this cycle the lake's entire ecosystem reaches its fullest bloom. Walleyes are regrouped and feed actively on the developing food chain. This is one of the best times of the year for fast-action fishing. Fish activity is rated as very active.

Key factors include water temperature and the growing food chain. The Summer Peak occurs on reservoirs, lakes and rivers. But, this is a very short, hard-to-observe period.

AN EARLY SUMMER PATTERN FOR MESO LAKES

It's been alluded to; it's been whispered about; but only a handful of anglers are onto it. In lakes where walleyes forage on ciscoes, a feeding binge occurs just before the walleyes establish their summer patterns. Those who recognize and fish this "Summer Peak" consistently corral monstrous walleyes topping 10 pounds.

Although this period is, perhaps, the toughest of all to pinpoint, the fish are so aggressive that it may pay off with the biggest rewards. Over the past 10 years we've taken many 8-12 pound fish during the short time this period lasts. In one case, a small group actually took 14 fish averaging 9 pounds in three days!

On more southern lakes, where perch are a key food source, Summer Peak walleye activity usually keys along weedlines. But in lakes containing both perch and ciscoes, the *big* walleyes apparently prefer ciscoes at this time of year; thus the key activity centers around steep-breaking, main lake areas where ciscoes are found, as opposed to weedlines!

THE SUMMER PEAK PERIOD

In order to best explain when and how the Summer Peak occurs, let's trace walleye behavior from just after ice-out until the beginning of the Summer Peak. Walleyes typically spawn when spring water temperatures rise to the mid-40°F's. The Spawn Period is followed by what we term the Post-spawn Period. We usually characterize Post-spawn as a resting stage when fish scatter and feed very little. Shortly, however, their tired bodies need nourishment, and the resumption of aggressive feeding indicates the beginning of the Pre-summer Period. While no set temperature indicates when walleyes enter their Pre-summer stage, once water temperatures reach the low 60°F's, you can usually assume they have.

Even though the fish feed aggressively (this is the time of year when fish establish most of their growth gains), they are usually still scattered at this time. Indeed, a prime characteristic of the Pre-summer Period is the absence of definite fishing patterns; you may catch several walleyes rigging deep water, several more crankbaiting mid-depth flats, and even a few fishing extremely shallow water for largemouths.

Slowly, though, as water temperatures climb upwards, the fish begin regrouping. There is also a gradual tendency for them to start keying on specific food sources. Yes, patterns start to emerge.

The final item pushing walleyes from the Pre-summer Period into the short-lived, yet intense, period of feeding we term the Summer Peak, always seems to be the same: a period of relatively calm, very warm weather. In many cases this is the first really hot, summer-type weather of the season. This weather often pushes surface temperatures near their summer high. For instance, the summer surface temperature of many meso lakes hovers around 72°F-74°F. It may eventually climb into the upper 70°F's or even low 80°F's, but this typically happens very slowly. Thus, the Summer Peak Period—for walleyes—seems to begin with the end of the rapid, early-summer rise in water temperature.

A combination of environmental factors stimulates this Summer Peak walleye activity. These three seem the most important: 1) The fish are hungry and, thus, aggressive. This is the period when most of their yearly growth occurs. They really have no choice in the matter; they must eat, or they won't grow! 2) This is the first time since spawning that *big* females group together.

Their competitive group activity helps stimulate even more intense feeding activity. 3) There are plankton of all sorts and hordes of fish fry; the entire lake is blooming and brimming with food. This spurs vigorous food chain activity on all levels. Summer Peak walleyes are akin to a group of starving men at a smorgasbord. Oblivious to surroundings and with little finesse, there's intense, competitive feeding activity before things settle down to a more normal (the Summer Period) pace.

LOCATION

As we said before, the location of peak activity seems to depend on the available forage. In lakes where bullheads or perch are the key prey, the most intense activity centers around weedbeds. In reservoirs where walleyes favor smelt or spottail shiners, the activity centers around shallow gravel flats or points. However, in lakes where ciscoes are the principal forage, the activity keys around quick-breaking, hard-bottomed drop-offs in the main lake; that's where the ciscoes are!

Usually, summer fish relate to *gradual* breaks. Once the intense Summer Peak activity is over, our experience shows that even the *big* fish relate to such gradual areas. But for the moment, the key areas are firm-bottomed (rock, gravel, sand, or clay) breaks that drop quickly into deep water. The best areas are typically part of large, relatively flat-topped, shallow shoreline bars or sunken islands. Large sunken islands (small islands seldom produce as well) seem to be especially productive, apparently because they draw roving ciscoes from many directions, as opposed to shoreline bars which might only draw them from one. You see, the ciscoes move through open water and appear to contact walleyes predominantly when they also contact the bar. Some walleyes also run the ciscoes in open water.

That brings up another point: How deep will ciscoes contact the bar, and thus, how deep will the walleyes be? If you think back for a moment, we said that this period usually follows a relatively calm and very hot period of weather. While a thermocline probably forms long before this time, the period of very warm weather generally intensifies the thermocline into a temperature barrier, although not likely an oxygen barrier. It's not that the walleyes won't go through the thermocline; they will. It's just that they apparently prefer not to do so if possible.

Even though surface temperatures may hover around 72°F at this time, 64°F-66°F temperatures probably exist just above the thermocline (temperatures fall precipitously within the thermocline itself). These temperatures are near the walleyes' preferred level. Ciscoes, on the other hand, prefer lower temperatures, but will stay in the upper water levels for a short time. The stable, hot and calm weather that's so important in bringing this period also encourages plankton growth. The ciscoes stay in the upper strata for a short time to feed on plankton. Indeed, you often see schooling ciscoes breaking the surface during early morning.

Now back to our original question: How deep will ciscoes contact the bar, and thus, how deep will the walleyes be? It's not quite that simple, because ciscoes can contact the outside of a bar at all depths in the upper water levels.

124

The Pre-Summer Big Walleye/Cisco Pattern

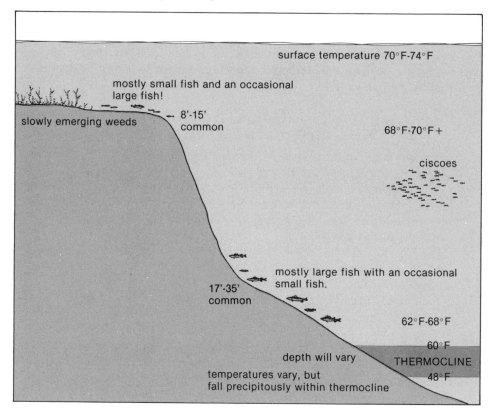

During the Summer Peak Period in lakes where walleyes key on ciscoes, a distinct pecking order sets up with relation to breaks or a breakline. Almost without exception, the small fish relate to the shallow lips on a bar, while the big fish rule the deeper water. While these depths vary depending on the lake, we've found so many big fish in 22-28 feet of water, on so many different lakes, that it definitely bears mentioning here.

Expect some of the projected temperatures to vary. Also remember that large walleyes are usually somewhere above the thermocline (but usually relatively close to it). They do not, however, generally stack up immediately above it as if they were using it as a breakline.

We don't know why, but the walleyes usually establish themselves in a sort of "pecking order," with the largest fish usually being the deepest! Thus, if the top of the thermocline sets up at about 35 feet, and the major lip on the bar breaks from 12-15 feet of water down into the 30-50 foot range, you can expect the smaller (and more numerous) fish to key around the 15 foot lip area—perhaps even moving up to use the edges of slowly emerging weeds. The big fish, however, are nearly always deeper; in this instance, probably down in 20-30 feet of water.

We're not saying that the *big* fish always lay just above the thermocline, although they're usually close. The comparative depths we're talking about are also relative. Typical mesotrophic Canadian lakes (or mesotrophic sections of oligotrophic lakes) are usually shallower than their counterparts scattered across the U.S. The key "big fish" level varies depending on the conditions in each particular body of water. We will say, though, that the 22-28 foot range has produced many fish for us. However, be willing to experiment!

SPECIFIC LOCATION

The reason we've spent so much time on location is because it's half the ballgame in this instance. Presentation is a real "piece of cake" once you understand fish location. We've already stated that the outside edges of large, flat-topped shoreline bars or sunken islands attract most of the roving ciscoes, and thus the walleyes. Now it's time to get more specific, because huge walleyes definitely use certain areas of these large bars or islands as "cisco ambush points."

Picture yourself, for a moment, among a school of ciscoes swimming in open water. Suddenly you come into contact with the deep-breaking edge of a huge bar. Wanting to continue swimming in the direction you were going, but being unable to do so because of the bar, you do the next best thing: continue on following the edge of the bar. Of course, being by nature an open water fish, you stay a short distance away from the bar. You're really building up speed and cruising now. Suddenly there's a distinct inside turn caused by a point in the bar. Ciscoes carom off ciscoes as the entire school attempts to turn and maintain its open water status. In the confusion, a few of the ciscoes, perhaps even the majority of the school, overrun the mark and end up inside the corner. Like savvy warriors who attack only when the opposing army is confused, disoriented, and within range, huge walleyes—which have been waiting in the corner to take advantage of just such a mistake—slash into the school! Flashes of titanic, bronze-sided walleyes intermingle with the silver, streaking ciscoes, and for a moment panic reigns! Like small scouting parties, some huge walleyes follow small groups of confused ciscoes up the break, while others do the opposite. And then it's over! The walleyes slowly regroup in the corner, while the ciscoes—their basic existence ever protected in such skirmishes by sheer numbers—school again and continue on their way.

Although the inside corners formed by projections on a bar are the key cisco ambush spots, walleyes use the tips of points, too. Here the walleyes are also able to surprise roving ciscoes without expending large amounts of unwarranted energy. However, if we had to pick one over the other, the inside corners are usually the best. It also seems that the more distinct a turn or point is, the more productive it is.

But hold on a moment; these areas must be located in the main lake where ciscoes roam! It actually seems very important that these areas be out away from shore. Inside turns on a shoreline point are seldom as productive as inside turns or points way out in the main lake. That's probably why large sunken islands in the main lake basin are so highly productive.

Typical Cisco-Based Meso Lake

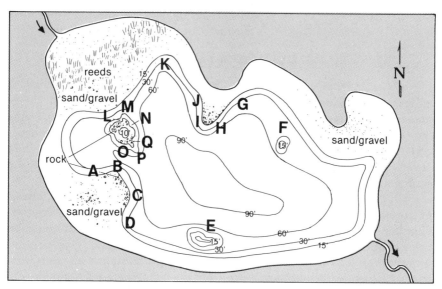

Remember that the walleyes' key forage—ciscoes—roam open water in the main part of the lake. While they may be at any depth—including near the surface—they do not use shallow water over shallow bars during Pre-summer. The prime ambush points, in order of importance are: 1) Inside turns as far out as possible into the main lake area; 2) points as far out as possible into the main lake area; and 3) inside turns near shore on shoreline bars. Also remember that the distinctness of these areas plays a part in how potent an ambush point they are.

Keeping these things in mind, we would evaluate the areas on this lake as follows:

A—An indistinct, shoreline-related, inside turn. Not a key area!

B and C—Although not particularly distinct-looking points according to the map, they are main lake points, and as such, should be checked.

D—A slightly more distinct, shoreline-related inside turn. Still not a key area.

E—The 15-30 foot depths on the main lake (north) side of the island should be checked for distinct ambush points. Forget the back side (south). Possibly a very good spot!

F—Should be checked keeping in mind that small sunken islands usually aren't as productive as larger islands.

G—Same as A.

H and I—Same as B and C.

J—A distinct, inside, shoreline-related turn. Not a great spot, but might be checked.

K—No! Too close to shore.

L—The sunken island spots—L thru Q—are probably the best areas on the map. L is a distinct, inside turn that should be checked. It would be better if it weren't on the back side of the island shielded from the main lake area, however.

M—A distinct point which could very well attract fish!

N—A main lake, inside turn that is definitely worth checking!

O—A distinct, main lake, inside turn. A great looking area!

P—The best main lake point on the map!

Q—The most distinct, inside turn on the main lake and, thus, probably the best "on paper" spot available!

In a nutshell, L thru Q are your best bets. Areas B, C, E, F and I also have possibilities.

If you have time, check them all. Otherwise, concentrate on the distinct turns (L thru Q) on the offshore sunken island.

TIMING'S THE KEY

So there you have it. It's really not so hard to understand where the fish are and how they react. Presentation is, as we've said before, rather easy. The real problem, and thus the reason why so few people key on this pattern, is because Summer Peak walleye activity lasts such a short time. Timing is critical, yet difficult. Many anglers stumble onto this pattern *once,* but are unable to duplicate the catch again. Yet sharp anglers can key on the pattern year after year.

In order to identify this Summer Peak period, you should be fairly familiar with a body of water. This is no time to be hunting for new spots. Alas, sometimes this must be done. Even so, the factors we've discussed eliminate much of the unproductive water in a lake and will help you key on likely areas.

Once the walleyes finish spawning, it is best that you fish the lake often to have an idea how the lake is progressing. Bring on the hot, calm weather! Unfortunately, the weather doesn't cooperate every year. Sometimes Summer Peak activity is far less intense! And don't think that lakes always turn on in a south-to-north progression. The timing is as much a result of depth and other factors as it is latitude. Many large, deep (60-90 feet maximum) central Minnesota lakes experience a typical Summer Peak during mid-June; yet many shallower (40-60 feet maximum) Canadian lakes peak about the same time! On the other hand, Wisconsin's 134 foot deep Lake Geneva, which is much farther south, might not experience this peak until late June.

For such reasons we suggest you stay in touch with what's happening on a few particular lakes if you expect to take advantage of this peak. Unfortunately, it's pretty tough to calculate this "long distance" if you're planning a Canadian trip. Take a guess—then go! You'll probably catch nice fish and have a great trip whether you hit the peak or not. As we said, most of the mesotrophic Canadian lakes that we're familiar with peak during June and then settle into stable summer patterns until late August. Fish a lake once and you'll have a much better idea when to go back next year.

PRESENTATION

Remember backtrolling with a slip sinker rig? Yes, you know—backtrolling with a leech or nightcrawler! Great, because it's just the technique you need to catch fish in this situation.

Backtrolling is, basically, a method of boat control using the motor to pull the boat in reverse. The objective, of course, is to keep one eye on the depth finder and follow a path you think will catch fish. Running the boat in reverse allows you to slow the boat down (splashguards are a necessity during windy, wavy weather). By directing the boat into the wind and periodically shifting the motor in and out of gear, you can hover in place, turn, or move slowly

Up and At 'em

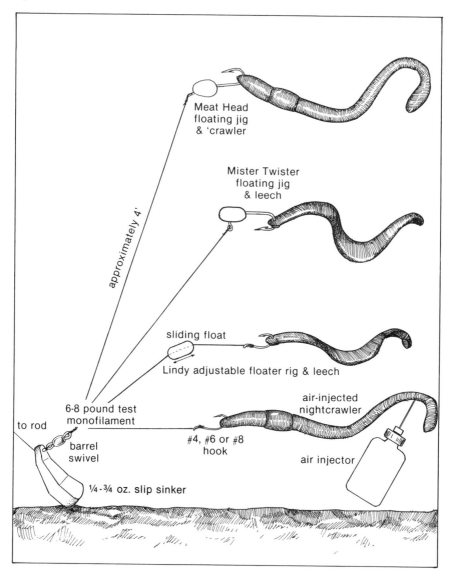

Meat Head
floating jig
& 'crawler

Mister Twister
floating jig
& leech

approximately 4'

sliding float

Lindy adjustable floater rig & leech

air-injected
nightcrawler

6-8 pound test
monofilament

to rod

#4, #6 or #8
hook

air injector

barrel
swivel

¼ - ¾ oz. slip sinker

An experienced walleye hand knows that walleyes can be anywhere from "glued-to-the-bottom" to suspended "way high." That's why you carry an assortment of goodies to cover a variety of depths.

Active Summer Peak fish, as a whole, tend not to be smack on the bottom or way, way off it; they're usually somewhere in between. If you gear your approach to fish about 2-6 feet off the bottom, you're in the ball park. Remember, if you pay attention, you often see the fish on your depth finder. That means they're up off the bottom a bit. Put your bait there, too.

There are a variety of cork or styrofoam floating jigheads on the market. They raise your bait the highest of all the various rigs. However, for a moderate "lift," Lindy's floater snell is quite an innovation. A tiny float slides up and down the snell, enabling *you to adjust both the bait's distance off the bottom and how near the bait you want the tiny float (it serves as an "attractor"). Finally, there's the old standby air injector for inserting a tiny bubble of air into a 'crawler's tail. Don't be afraid to experiment with them all.*

Once you zero in on fish location, it's usually a case of "best presentation = best results." Don't be sloppy. Fish the prime areas very slowly and take the time to adjust your rigs to keep your bait at the proper level above the bottom. Lazy = no fish. It's that simple. But when you have your act together and put your time in, you're locked into one of the best big walleye patterns of the year. Patience = results.

along at a steady pace.

Backtrolling isn't the only method of boat control for this occasion, however. At times it is possible to use a controlled drift, too. Providing the wind direction is correct, it's sometimes possible to drift precisely along a breakline. Use your gas or electric motor to correct your drift slightly should you stray from your intended path.

Obviously, you want to concentrate on the inside turns created by projections in bars, and on the points themselves. Large, obvious projections usually appear on a good hydrographic map. However, many similar smaller areas that aren't on a map can also hold fish at times.

Match your sinker size to the depth of water you're probing and the speed you're moving. If you're searching along a new bar looking for projections and inside turns, you may want to move along quickly until you identify these areas. Such probing (usually in 17-30 feet of water) calls for a 1/2 ounce, or even a 3/4 ounce, slip sinker. We usually prefer to slow down and fish familiar areas with 3/8 or 1/2 ounce weights, however. If, as is often true on Canadian lakes, you find the fish in the 12-17 foot range, consider going to a lighter 1/4 ounce sinker.

If we had to pick one snell length for our live bait rigs, it would be about 4 feet long. That's the length we've taken most of our fish with. But if you consult your graph or depth finder and find the fish are hovering higher or lower off the bottom, you might consider going with a longer or shorter snell. It pays to experiment.

You have two basic choices of terminal hook rigs and baits. First, of course, use 6 or 8 pound test line. Then go with either: 1) a plain #4, #6 or #8 hook, or 2) a similar floating head or floater rig set-up. Couple the plain hooks with a fat'n sassy, juicy crawler. Use a worm blower to add just enough air to the 'crawler's tail to get it floating. Do not—we repeat, do not!— blow the 'crawler up so that it resembles the Goodyear Blimp. It's important that the 'crawler float up off the bottom, but just as important is the 'crawler being able to squirm and shimmy enticingly in front of the fish. Remember, the 'crawler receives stiff competition from the walleyes' preferred forage—ciscoes —so it has to look tempting.

Because it's also important that leeches (make them big, fat, juicy, squirmin', jumbo leeches!) be fished off the bottom, and because they can't be air-injected very effectively, fish them on a floating jighead or a floater rig. Both the Mister Twister Floating Jig Head and the American Luresmith Meat Head Jig have their strong points. The Mister Twister Floating Head imparts an enticing wobble to a bait. The Meat Head's hook, meanwhile, rides point up, instead of down, and increases the bait's hooking potential. There are plenty of other good floating jigheads on the market. What color? Fire orange or red.

Pay particular attention to your depth finder or graph unit. Look for the presence of fish, and how far off the bottom they are. Once you spot what appears to be big walleyes, very carefully work and rework the area. *Slowly* backtroll upwind through the fish, and then *slowly* drift back through them again. Vary the length of your snell and switch jigheads if necessary; try to place your bait at the *exact* level the fish appear to be up off the bottom. This is no time for sloppy presentation. A slow, meticulous, "in-your-face" approach may trigger even inactive fish. If they won't hit, come back and try again later. Patience is the key. Early morning is usually the best time of day to hit 'em, but don't be afraid to try a good spot every couple of hours. You never know when they'll hit. Remember, you're dealing with the largest walleyes in the lake, and they didn't get that big by being reckless. Stay with it, and you'll catch them.

If you're probing new areas, it's certainly A-OK to use your outboard. However, if you spot fish on the depth finder, and it's calm enough to go with your electric motor, by all means do so. Trolling over fish too many times with the big motor will spook them. We even turn our graphs off (but not depth finders) once we contact a group of fish. Sometimes the steady thumping of a graph will eventually turn fish off. Don't take chances.

Can you take a nine, ten, eleven—even a twelve pound plus walleye—early this coming season? You'd better believe it! The Summer Peak, walleye/cisco pattern that we've fished for years can just as easily become a part of your game plan!

RIVER LOCATION AND PRESENTATION

Fishing rivers for walleyes is unique because it is so visual. As you look for spots you can actually imagine the bottom by reading the telltale clues on the water's surface. Once you understand how the current reacts to bottom contours and creates visual signs, you will be able to spot the areas that hold fish well before you come into casting range. Remember, river fish tend to shelter themselves from current whenever possible. They don't want to fight the current anymore than we would like to walk uphill into a 40 m.p.h. wind. Most rivers are strewn with objects such as rocks, logs, boulders, gravel and sandbars which retard the current flow. When these objects occur in shallow water, the river will react by forming eddies, riffles or boils. Walleyes will gather at these current breaks during the summer months.

To get a better understanding of some of the types of areas which will hold fish in an adult river stretch, we've prepared a map to help you visualize the river bottom. Let's take a trip down the river and point out some of the more important areas to look for and the ways to fish them. This pattern will hold all summer long.

AREA A

As we head downriver, the first area that attracts fish is a wing dam. A wing dam is a man-made structure made of alternating piles of submerged rock and brush. They are normally found within the first half mile below a dam. These shore-connected structures are designed to direct the current flow away from the shoreline and into the main channel. Because they break or disrupt the current, they form ideal fish-holding areas. In most cases, a small hole will form at the tip of a wing dam. The wing dam will also create an eddy downstream behind the dam. Along with the eddy a current break (indicated by the lines) will form. Above the lines, in calmer water, is the eddy. Below the lines is the faster water of the main river channel.

This current break is an excellent spot for both walleyes and smallmouth. The smallmouth tend to hold shallower and closer to the wing dam (see *Area A 1*).

Walleyes will usually hold slightly downstream from the wing dam during the summer (see *Area A2*), along the edge where the faster water of the channel and the slower water behind the wind dam meet. Walleyes seem to prefer a current edge where they can dart out into the faster water to prey on forage and then move back into the calmer water to rest. *Area A* is usually a choice spot and should be worked very thoroughly, preferably from an anchoring position.

Area A 2 is the current break that forms below a wing dam. It is usually a little deeper here, and there will most likely be a visible boil or stream of boiled water running in the area of the lines. Walleyes will lie along the current break or edge where the fast and slow water meet. This area can also be reached by casting downstream from our anchoring position. To do this easily, simply let out about 20 additional feet of rope and tie up. (This is where a 100 foot rope comes in handy.) The boat may swing a little more with the current, but it will be in a good stationary position to thoroughly cover the downstream portion of the wing dam. This technique eliminates the need to pull up the anchor for short moves.

AREA B

In *Area B*, there is a shallow, gravel tongue with larger rocks on the inside bend of the river—a very common fish magnet in rivers of this type. In *Area B 1*, a riffle will form where the current flows over the shallow rocks. The lines again indicate the current break which forms as a result of this shoal. Depths may range from 2-4 feet on top of the tongue, usually dropping quite abruptly to 6 feet or more in the channel. In this area, larger submerged rocks will hold smallmouth, both on top and down the drop-off. The eddy, in *Area B 2*, will generally be a bit deeper than the shoal, so it will attract walleyes rather than smallmouth.

Walleyes will lie at the edge of the eddy or on the rim of the small depression created by the eddy. Begin working this spot with the bow facing upstream and the motor in forward, adjusted so that the boat slowly slips downstream with the current. Using the slipping technique, you can cover this larger struc-

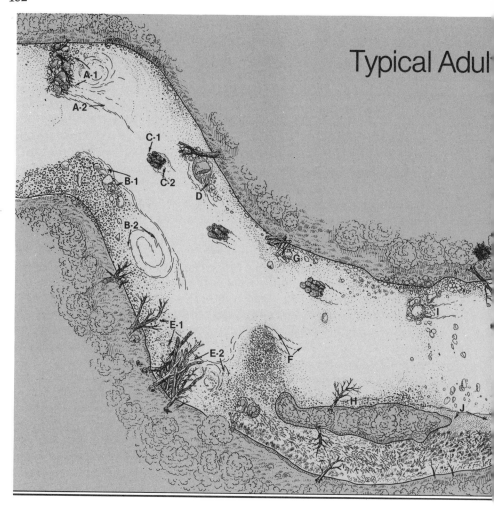

Typical Adul

ture. Anchor only if you find a large concentration of fish.

Almost any casting direction—upstream, downstream or quarter-casting—is fine, as long as the lure is kept vibrating. However, it is difficult to work plugs cast upstream and retrieved with the current. Since you'll lose some degree of control and feel, there is a tendency to miss strikes.

AREA C

Area C includes several log pilings in the center of the river. These man-made structures were created many years ago to aid lumberjacks in floating logs downstream. Groups of these logs are commonly found in a row along one side of the main river channel and are usually spaced anywhere from 30 to 50 yards apart.

Area C 1. It is best to cover this smaller spot quickly from a mobile position, casting as close to the pilings as possible, as smallmouth will hug right next to and in between the individual logs. It is even a good idea to bump the logs as

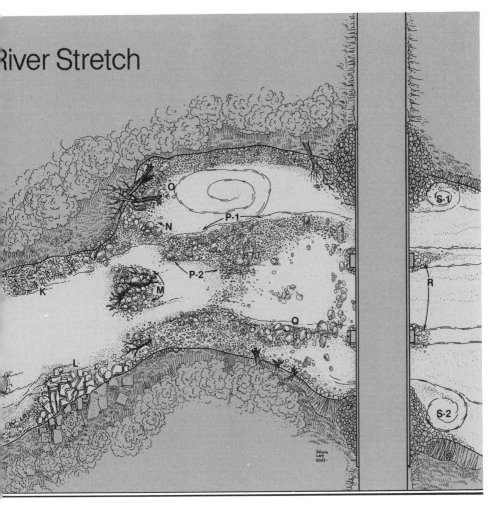

River Stretch

you retrieve your crankbait.

Area C 2 includes the slack water directly below the pilings and the current breaks on both sides. There are usually more fish behind the pilings than in front, both in the slack water and strung out along the two current breaks.

Maneuver your boat so that you adequately cover both sides of the pilings, using the slipping procedure. Accurate casting is the key in this situation. You should be able to tell if there are any catchable fish behind the pilings with 5 or 6 good casts. If you catch a fish or two, take the time to work the area thoroughly.

AREA D

In *Area D*, a submerged log has jammed against a large boulder. Large boulders (both above and below the water) like this are very common in these kinds of rivers. Depending on current and depth, there would be small riffles (shown by the lines) running downstream below this obstruction. This would be a good spot for a few smallmouth bass and possibly some walleyes. It would not hold a lot of fish, but such spots often have big fish.

It's best to work smaller objects like this from a mobile position. Place your casts ahead of the rock, at the tip of the sunken tree. Don't hesitate to cast near or on top of obstructions like this. Follow them with consecutive casts downstream below the boulder. Make your casts across and beyond the rock, retrieving the lure so that it hits the rock. You'll be surprised at how often this will trigger fish. Remember, the current break downstream from the rocks will usually hold fish so don't forget to fire a few casts in this area.

AREA E

Area E combines dead trees that have fallen into the river with an abandoned beaver lodge. Wherever you find this situation you'll find fish, because walleyes are attracted to large amounts of submerged timber.

The top arrow in *Area E 1* points to the fallen trees. Begin here and cast well up into the timber, making your casts as close as possible to the base of the tree and working the plug all the way out to the tip. Cover both sides of the tree, as each could hold fish.

The entire stretch between the fallen trees and the beaver lodge should be fished as you work your way down. The beaver lodge could have fish on all sides, so work it thoroughly. You may even want to anchor when you reach the lodge, especially if you picked up a fish or two while you were moving.

Area E 2 features a current break that runs downstream from the beaver lodge. This area will hold walleyes and is one of the better spots on the map. Why? Because it is found in combination with a number of desirable conditions in a relatively small area.

AREA F

Area F, like *Area B*, is a shallow, gravel bar that could be anywhere from 2 to 4 feet deep on top and drop down to 6 or 8 feet in the channel. Providing it's shallow enough and there's enough current, riffles would form on top of the bar and a current break would trail behind the shoal (again, indicated by the lines). This current break would correspond with the edge of the drop-off. The base of the drop-off along the current break is ideal walleye habitat.

It's best to work a spot such as this slowly, using the slipping procedure to gradually work down the bar. Pay close attention to the current break trailing downstream. The plugs can be cast and retrieved from all angles as long as the current doesn't stop their vibration. If contact is made with any number of fish, anchor and fish the area thoroughly.

AREA G

Area G is an unusual situation that you'll find on some rivers—logs from the logging era that have been driven into the riverbank by the current. There's no need to anchor here, as it will take only a few casts to check for fish.

AREA H

In *Area H,* a large tree has fallen into the water alongside an island, forming a small current break behind the deadfall. Most of the time this area will hold more smallmouth than walleyes. Spots like this will rarely hold large numbers of fish and should be treated much like *Area E 1.*

AREA I

Area I is a giant boulder—above or below the water depending on the level— on top of a stretch of gravel. A few walleyes could be found in a spot like this. Cast beyond the boulder, hitting the rock as you retrieve your lure. For some reason, this technique seems to trigger reluctant fish. Remember to fish the trailing current break downstream.

AREA J

Above *Area J* is an island that is common on a river of this type. These islands generally have a lot of bushes and trees on them which become partially submerged during periods of high water. Behind the island is a shallow side-channel. These side-channels usually are only 2-4 feet deep, and have a very soft silt and sand bottom with little current. Stringy river weeds will often bloom heavily in spots like this, making presentation next to impossible.

Area J is a long sandbar extending from the downstream tip of the island that will hold walleyes. This is very common on an adult river and will almost always draw fish. The sandbar will most likely only be about 1 to 3 feet deep, but will quickly drop off into the channel, and will have a harder bottom than the side channel because of the flushing action of the current. A noticeable current break will form alongside of and downstream from the bar. Work the entire edge by casting on top and parallel to the sandbar.

You might also try front-trolling upstream parallel to the bar. Let out about 30-40 yards of line and troll slowly, occasionally pumping your plugs up and down. You can't troll into the current very fast or you'll have problems controlling your lures. Vary your trolling speed until you find a successful pattern. Watch carefully for any little dip or irregularity in these kinds of sandbars as they can be important fish-holding spots. You should anchor, of course, if any contact is made with substantial numbers of fish.

AREA K

Area K is another small gravel shoal adjacent to a group of weeds growing in sand near shore. These weeds can be long, thin grass, or a miniature version of cabbage. If adjacent to the main channel, these weeds will often hold walleyes, especially if gravel is present. You could pick up a few fish by quickly casting this area.

AREA L

Area L is a makeshift landing with a pile of broken cement slabs (these often appear below dams and bridge pilings as well) which have fallen into the river from one bank. Areas of fractured concrete or transplanted rock (rip-rap) along river banks are very common, since many of these rivers were the transportation routes of yesteryear. These broken slabs can act much the same as boulders and create a current break. Fish will lie along the current break which forms downstream, reacting in the same manner as in areas with large boulders.

AREA M

A pile of rocks and sticks lies in the middle of the main channel in *Area M*. This large structure drops into 6 to 8 feet of water rather quickly on all sides, and is one of the better spots for big schools of walleyes. Since it should be covered thoroughly, it would be best to anchor twice and fish each side, casting as close to the pile as possible. The upstream edge, which will often hold an aggressive smallmouth, should be worked carefully. Distinct current breaks will form downstream on either side of this structure. Make sure to cast these edges for some distance downstream from the pile, as this is where the bigger walleyes will be.

AREA N

Area N is simply a series of three medium-sized boulders near the river bank. Only a sharp eye on the water's surface would spot these if they were a couple of feet under the water. The only clue would be a few boils 20 feet downstream with a trail of foam leading back. These hidden spots are deceiving and will often harbor a real trophy.

AREA O AND AREA P

Area O is a small, sheltered slackwater area with rocks, boulders and fallen logs. Your best bet here is to cast the plug into the shallow-water obstructions and carefully work it back. You may get a few more snags, but you'll also catch more fish. Be sure to work the entire inside edge along the rim of the hole formed by the eddy.

The combination of *Area O, Area P* and the large eddy formed by the outcrop of land at this point in the river combine to make this one of the best spots on the map. In *Area P*, a shallow gravel bar expands in width and is surrounded by the channel on both sides. Alongside *Area P 1*, just below *Area O*, is a large eddy that has molded a small depression in the bottom. The depth on top of the gravel bar would likely be 3 or 4 feet, dropping to 8 to 10 feet in the middle of the eddy. These larger eddies are usually not as visible as the smaller ones. It is the larger areas like these that combine several desirable conditions that contain large schools of walleyes.

Area P 1 is the current break formed along the edge of the gravel bar where it drops off. Walleyes will also tend to concentrate in the deeper portions of the eddy. During periods of low water, walleyes will concentrate in the deeper part of the eddy.

Begin by trolling, as described in *Area J*, along the current break and through the heart of the eddy. This spot should be big enough for several troll-

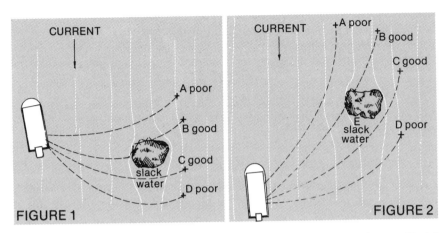

FIGURE 1

FIGURE 2

Figures 1 and 2 show the difference between a good and poor cast with a crankbait in current. Figure 1 shows how your approach should be from the upstream side of an object; Figure 2 from the downstream side.

Figure 1: Casts A and D are poor casts, because the lure is too far from the stump. Remember, a fish won't move very far into the current to strike. The correct way, shown by B, is to cast past the stump and hit the upstream side on the retrieve. This is exactly where an active, feeding smallmouth would be.

Below the stump, D represents the wrong way to cast. Cast C is a better choice, since it covers the slack water directly behind the stump. A resting fish would be here. The lure should be cast past the slack water and pulled directly into it as close to the stump as possible. Be sure to engage your reel immediately—any delay will allow the current to push your crankbait downstream.

Once the lure is in the slack water, you can slow your retrieve a bit. The crankbait is now in that narrow band of productive water behind the stump. Unless speed seems to be necessary to make the fish strike, it's a good idea to slow down your retrieve to keep the bait in the fish zone as long as possible.

Figure 2 shows the right casting position once you've drifted past the stump. Again, A and D demonstrate poor casts—too far from the fish zone. Cast B strikes the upstream side of the stump, which is perfect. Cast C is fine, since the lure passes through the slack water.

Take a look at point E. This would be an excellent spot to place a jig. But with a crankbait, it would be best to cast beyond point E. Then, once the plug reaches E, it will have achieved the proper action. It is always to your advantage when fishing a crankbait to cast past your target. This way by the time your retrieve brings the lure alongside the target, it will be running at the right depth and be vibrating properly.

When drifting past a stump like this, you and your partner will only be able to get about three casts apiece before the river carries you out of range. That's why it's so important to make sure your casts are covering productive water.

ing runs, beginning at the bridge and extending upstream through *Area P.* When you contact fish, note the exact spot. Then, slip downstream and cast toward that spot. If you catch another fish immediately from the same area, you're probably into a good school. In this case, drop the anchor and work the spot thoroughly.

Area P 2 is the other side of this small gravel ridge where a current break has also formed. While this spot would probably not have as many fish as the eddy side, it would be well worth a few casts.

At the base of *Area P 2* (where the right arrow is pointing) the entire midstream area turns into a shallow gravel flat with intermittent rocks. The shallower portions would most likely hold smallmouth. Take the time to cover this spot, both by trolling and casting.

AREA Q

Area Q features a gravel bank that drops off into deeper water. Again, a current edge is created that will draw fish. Both trolling and casting will work here.

AREA R

Area R, a very important part of the river, contains pilings supporting a highway or railroad bridge. The type of pilings depend largely on the age of the bridge or where it is located. Some have a very gradual drop-off into deeper water, while others are sharper. Most pilings have an underwater pile or rip-rap at their base. These pilings are excellent current breaks and will hold walleyes. Both the front and back of the pilings will hold fish, but the downstream side will be better—especially the current break trailing downstream. Again, quickly cast this area, and if you run into a concentration of fish, drop the anchor.

Here is a lineup of lures for cranking rivers. Pictured, at left from top to bottom are Smithwick's Watergator, Rebel's Racketshad, a 1/3 oz. Cordell Spot, and a 1/4 oz. Cordell Spot. At right from top to bottom is a 1/3 oz. Cordell Big "O", a 1/4 oz. Gay Blade, and a 1/8 oz. Gay Blade.

AREA S

Area S 1 and *S 2* are eddies created by the rip-rap from the bridge foundation. Always be alert for eddies in these locations. Place your casts along the rip-rap bank (as parallel as possible) and gradually work deeper. The larger the eddy and the more extensive the rip-rap, the better chances there will be for a big school of fish.

SUMMARY

This map contains representative samples of the better spots on a river that is best classified as adult. And many of these conditions can be found on a mature river as well. Though they are grouped closely together for the sake of convenience, they probably would not occur quite so close together on actual river. Furthermore, since rivers differ and have their own unique characteristics, each time out you'll find new types of spots that produce fish. The ability to learn to spot these areas will take a sharp eye, patience and some experience.

Chapter 13
THE SUMMER PERIOD

"A Time of Plenty"

This is the bulk of the fishing season for most anglers who take summer vacations. Natural food chains are in high gear and walleyes have lots of food to choose from. Patterns are identifiable and presentation becomes a key. Restrictive factors include some thermoclining, the sun's radiation and an over abundance of natural food. Fish activity is generally rated as medium, but this is when most people take their vacations and fish.

Let's take a closer look at our favorite patterns.

BUT THEY'RE NOT SUPPOSED TO BE THERE.... WALLEYES IN THE WEEDS

If you've read any number of fishing articles over the years, you know that most authors perpetuate the notion that all walleyes live in deep water on the rocks. Truth is, that's not the case. Yes, some walleye groups make *seasonal* use of deep water. But weeds play a far more important part in the walleye's lifestyle in natural lakes than most anglers believe.

There's bound to be controversy when the topic of weed walleyes comes up. Some died-in-the-wool "structure" fishermen don't believe they exist, saying that any walleyes caught in the shallows are either accidental stragglers or part of a shallow feeding movement made by a deep water school. Yet, many lakes have a very viable walleye population that lives in the weeds all summer long. The key is determining when and where this situation occurs. Then you can go ahead and catch the fish.

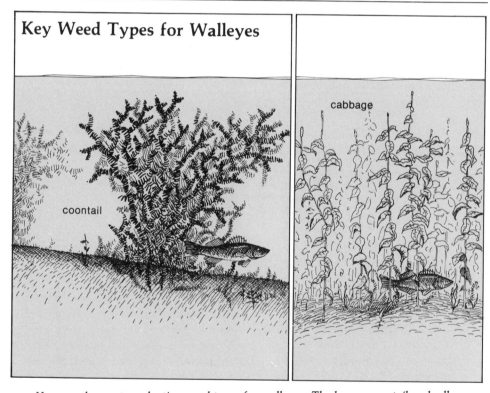

Key Weed Types for Walleyes

coontail

cabbage

Here are the most productive weed types for walleyes. The heavy coontail umbrella (left) is perhaps the toughest to fish because the fish can get back under it and are difficult to reach. Less taxing on the angler are cabbage weeds (center) which are often sparse enough so you can fish down into them. Usually, they also can be easily fished along the edges.

CONDITIONS TO LOOK FOR

Although you'll find walleyes in the weeds in a number of instances, there are a couple of conditions that stand out. In these cases the walleyes are so weed-oriented that fishing elsewhere is usually a waste of time! Let's look at each of them.

In lakes where they are stocked, the majority of the walleyes often live in the weeds. Most of these lakes weren't good walleye lakes to begin with and have a shortage of classic walleye habitat. Many were originally bass/northern pike /panfish lakes with an abundance of shallow weeds, poor oxygen content in deep water and an overall shallow water fish habitat. Walleyes stocked in this kind of lake have no choice but to live in the weeds.

Some heavily fished classic walleye lakes also host sizeable weed walleye populations (especially some heavily pressured metropolitan lakes). If the lake is heavily fished by smart anglers, those beautiful deep water rocky points and sunken islands won't hold the numbers of walleyes you think they do. Those walleye schools have been fished down to a low level. In fact, the strongest, most untapped segment of the walleye population in these lakes often lives full-time *in the weeds.*

Why not? Weeds provide plenty of food, oxygen and cover. And most folks don't fish weeds for walleyes because they're unaware of what's available. They've been brainwashed into always looking for rocks. And chances are they're missing out on most of the fish.

Over the years we've seen the walleye population undergo drastic changes in many lakes, all as a result of man's influence. Some lakes that originally had approximately a 60% deep water/40% weed walleye population now have perhaps a 75% weed-oriented/25% deep water mix. There are two basic reasons for this.

For the first time, these deep water areas were being fished intelligently. Heavy fishing pressure on the vulnerable walleyes occupying deep water points and sunken islands extracted the "biters" like a fine-toothed comb. In the past 12 years there has been a great deal of emphasis on deep water structure fishing techniques for walleyes. The Lindy Rig, live bait/slip sinker system and nightcrawler, leech or minnow combination caught on fast, and anglers began catching and keeping walleyes all summer long. After years of this harvesting, the deep water strain of fish was fished to a low level.

Couple this decline of the deep water walleye with the fertility from leaky septic tanks and fertilizer run-off, which causes the weedgrowth to explode, and you've got a different environment—one where the walleyes use the weeds. It's the same lake, but conditions have changed.

We can think of many such lakes that are supposedly fished out, but the truth is that they're chuck-full of weed walleyes. Either the locals don't realize the fish are there, or they don't know how to fish for them, or both. These "sleeper" lakes are prime candidates for big walleyes in the weeds.

In summary, then, look for a potential weed walleye fishery under two main conditions: (1) shallow weedy lakes that are heavily stocked; (2) heavily fished natural walleye lakes. These are your prime candidates for the tactics discussed here.

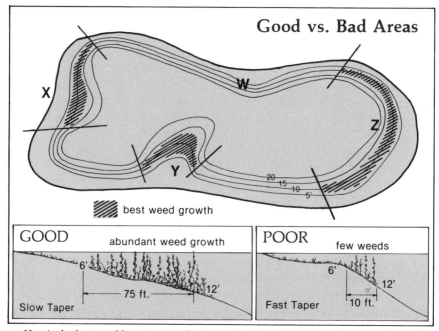

Good vs. Bad Areas

best weed growth

GOOD — abundant weed growth

Slow Taper — 6' — 75 ft. — 12'

POOR — few weeds

Fast Taper — 6' — 10 ft. — 12'

Here's the basics of locating weed-oriented walleyes. In lakes where weeds are the key attractor, look for the wide, sloping areas to grow the most weed growth. A slow, tapering area simply has more space for weeds to grow than a fast, narrow drop-off, and thereby attracts more fish. The slow tapers have more available living space, so they attract more weed walleyes.

Areas X and Y are points with gradual slopes in the 6-12 foot range. They'd grow plenty of weeds and are obvious candidates to host weed walleyes. Less obvious is Area Z which is simply a slow-tapering corner of the lake with no obvious concentration points. Yet, with its slow taper you can bet it'll grow weeds and attract walleyes. True, it'll take some work to find the small turns in the deep weedline or the areas of thickest weed growth that attract the most fish. But such spots do exist. In fact, on some lakes these corners grow more weeds than the obvious points and may be the best summer walleye attractors, even though they may look like real "duds" on a contour map. Each lake has its own characteristics, and you've got to get out there and explore the possibilities.

Finally, look at the point at W. Notice that its sharp taper drops off quickly to deep water and provides little of that 6-12 foot area for the weeds to grow. It's probably a very poor weed walleye spot, even though at first glance it looks promising.

WEED WALLEYE BEHAVIOR BY WATER CLARITY

Walleyes that live in the weeds can show a wide range of behavior. Sometimes they're totally inactive, lying deep under the vegetation and moving little, if at all. At other times they're tigers, and when you drop a lure in front of them their competitive urge makes them fight over it, particularly in lakes with low levels of available food. However, their average daytime mood is semi-active, generally meaning that they can be caught.

As you might expect, during the low light periods of dusk, dawn and throughout the night, it's a different story. Walleyes become more active in the weeds, cruising the tops, up into the shallows or out to the edge of weedlines in search of food. That's when they're most accessible.

TIME OF YEAR

Any time you find an abundance of healthy green vegetation, you've got some walleyes in the weeds. Normally, that's late spring, summer and early fall. Post-spawn walleyes will simply drop just below the first main drop-off to get out of the sun. Then, as the weed beds finally begin to grow and develop, lots of walleyes begin moving in under this canopy-like protection. In dark water lakes where the oxygen content is absent in deep water during the summer, nearly the entire population of walleyes moves into the weeds.

Summer, then, is the prime time for weed walleyes. Particularly in the examples mentioned, walleyes will remain in the weeds throughout the summer. It's not until after the fall Turnover, when oxygen returns to the deep water and the weeds begin to die off, that the walleyes in many stocked lakes begin shifting location and some begin using the deeper structural elements.

A walleye tracking study conducted on Lake Okoboji, Iowa, dramatically proves the existence of the weed walleye. Of six walleyes implanted with electronic tracking devices, five lived nearly full-time in the weeds throughout the summer. The sixth fish remained in the weeds for some time after tagging before dropping down to deep water, and was almost immediately caught by an angler! How's that for ironic? As soon as the walleye left the weeds and went where it was *supposed* to be, somebody nailed it. Yet the others spent a cozy summer in the relative protection of the weeds, undisturbed by deep water walleye anglers. It's a good lesson that shows the vulnerability of deep water walleyes and confirms the existence of walleyes in the weeds.

So, the term "dog days of August," supposedly a time when walleyes aren't supposed to bite, is used by anglers who don't know the facts. The reason walleyes "don't bite" is because most people are fishing where the walleyes are not—in deep water. Yet in many cases the few folks who are fishing in or next to the weeds are catching fish.

What can you do to consistently take summer walleyes? Plenty. Don't give up on old marble eyes until fall. There are a number of methods you can use to make outstanding catches, both day and night. Here are a few tricks to put the odds in your favor all summer long. First, let's examine some typical summer spots.

KEY LOCATIONS

If you had to pick an average depth where summer weed walleyes would be found in *most* lakes, it'd be 6-12 feet. In fact, 7-10 feet might be even closer. It's not an automatic guarantee, but it will be remarkably consistent in most lakes you'll fish.

The reason that 6-12 feet is a key depth range is that, in most lakes, it's the depth where the deepest weedgrowth lies. Large expanses of coontail and cabbage weeds in the 6-12 foot range form a miniature forest where walleyes thrive under the overhead cover.

The chief characteristic of a good weed walleye area is a *slow tapering*, 6-12 foot weedy flat. This kind of area offers the walleyes the most *living space*. The gradual depth change allows a wide band of weedgrowth to develop, as opposed to a sharp taper where the weedgrowth is restricted to a narrow area. Thus the general rule of thumb—fish slow tapers in summer.

The walleyes are randomly spread throughout the entire weedy area—one here, two there. Yet you can still get into a group of fish by locating a key feature that will concentrate a number of them in a limited area.

Cruise up on top of the flat and look for *open* or *thinner* spots in the weeds. And watch your depth finder. These spots are usually associated with a slight dip in the bottom. Or perhaps the bottom composition changes and becomes too hard to support a lot of weeds. Whatever the case, the weeds thin out. Scuba divers repeatedly find large numbers of big walleyes lying in such areas, right up in 7-10 feet of water during the day. Hard to believe—but true!

All these areas have one thing in common. They concentrate *active* or at least *neutral attitude* fish. The ones that are really turned off are way back under the weeds and very difficult to catch. But when you find an *edge* fish, it's preparing to feed, has just fed or is at least half-way susceptible to being triggered by your approach. Those are the fish you want to concentrate on.

AS THE SUN GOES DOWN

It's the classic early morning/late evening walleye feeding time; that's when you want to be out there fishing. As the sun dips to the horizon, the walleyes begin getting restless, moving out to the edges of the weeds, preparing to feed.

Once it gets dark, look for the walleyes to move very shallow. Right up to the shore, in 2-3 feet of water. Gravel points, fallen trees, docks, river inlets—they're all key shallow water cover areas that attract nighttime walleyes. You might even catch more fish by fishing from shore than you could in a boat!

Always look for the proper *combination* of elements when you're fishing this pattern. A shallow gravel point might look good, but could also be a poor producer unless it is adjacent to a weedbed where the walleyes can hide out during the day. Separately they might be mediocre, but lying close together they're the best spot in the lake.

After a number of "night stalking" trips, where we explored the shallows with spotlights at night, it was very evident that the inside edge of a good weedbed where it met a rocky shoreline was a dynamite night fishing spot. We spotted more walleyes in these areas than we did where the inside edge bordered sandgrass or plain sand. There's something about those shallow rocks that really pulls walleyes out of the adjacent weeds after sunset.

PRESENTATION

Daytime weed walleyes can be notoriously lazy, so you've usually got your work cut out for you. The condition often calls for live bait, yet it's tough to fish live bait in heavy weeds. Still, there are a few tricks you can use.

If some fish are along the deep weedline, they're fairly easy to get at with a backtrolling approach. We recommend using an electric motor rather than an outboard due to the overall shallow depth and spooky fish. The outboard may scare them, but the electric will usually do the trick.

Begin by slowly backtrolling the weed edge with a long line and light sinker, say 1/8 ounce. The light weight forces you to run a much longer line than you'd usually use. You'll lose some bottom feel, but with the bait way out behind the boat you'll minimize the spooking factor. A live bait rig, tipped with a leech, nightcrawler or chub and long-lined along the weed edge, is a very effective weapon. Keep that bait right at or slightly up into the weeds if they're sparse enough to work through. This is where the fish are holding.

Experience shows that switching to a bullet sinker is superior to a regular walking sinker for this approach. It's far more weedless than the walking sinker, which is designed to crawl over rocks, not through weeds. It's a little trick that saves a lot of aggravation.

Experiment with your snell type. The plain hook is usually best, but sometimes the attraction of a small spinner may turn a few extra fish. Or, if you find a low carpet of sandgrass or moss outside the weed edge, try using a floating jighead. It'll get the bait above the moss where the fish can see it.

Don't let the fish run once they've hit the bait. Grudgingly feed them a little slack by lowering your rod tip, and then slam the hook home. If you let them run, they'll bury themselves and you'll have a tough time getting them landed. A good stout spinning rod and 8 or 10 pound test line gives you plenty of muscle for hauling them out in a hurry.

CLUMPS

If the weeds or weed clumps are sparse enough, you can use the same slow trolling approach and go right through them. Usually, though, it'll be tough to do, so you'll be forced into a casting approach to work them effectively.

Clamp a split shot 8-10 inches ahead of a #6 hook and pitch a leech, small chub or water dog into the weeds. Nightcrawlers seem to lose much of their effectiveness in the weeds. They tear off too easily or fall victim to panfish. Yet leeches, chubs or water dogs are tough enough to take the punishment.

Lay your casts right next to the edges of the weed clumps. In fact, swing your rod tip to the side and physically pull your line as far under the edge of the clumps as possible. Then retrieve the bait right under the weed clump and let it sit there.

PLASTICS

Sometimes the weeds are just too darn tough to work live bait through. In that case, switch over to a tiny jighead and a plastic tail, like an 1/8 or 1/4 ounce Pow-rr head dressed with a plastic grub or various plastic creatures. Cast that jig right into the weeds and do some rippin'. A good stout graphite or boron rod lets you snap your wrist and tear through the weeds. Then let the jig fall down and just lay there motionless. It may be enough to interest a walleye

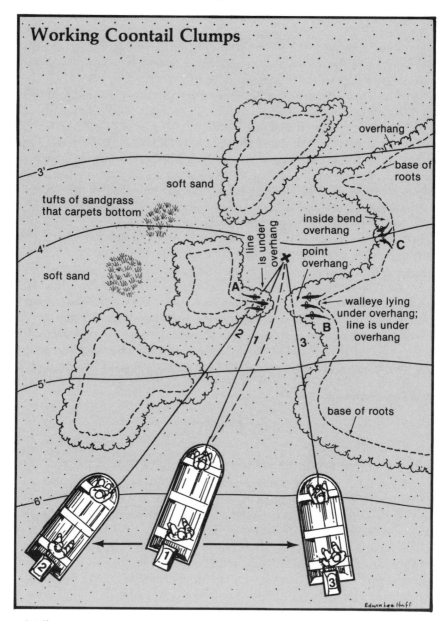

Working Coontail Clumps

overhang

base of roots

3'

soft sand

tufts of sandgrass that carpets bottom

inside bend overhang

C

4'

line is under overhang

point overhang

X

soft sand

A

walleye lying under overhang; line is under overhang

2 1

B

3

5'

base of roots

6'

2 1 3

Edwin Lee Huff

Walleyes are a bit tough to catch in coontail because of the way the weeds grow to the surface and then lay over, forming a roof. You have to get your line under the coontail overhang. That's where the fish are.

Cast past a clump and then either swing your rod tip to the side or physically move the boat to one side. For example, cast from boat position #1 as shown, and then move the boat to position #2 to reach the fish at A. Similarly, moving the boat to position #3 reaches the fish at B. Your retrieve will come back under·the coontail overhang where the fish are, rather than out in the open.

The fish on the inside bend at C are tougher to get at. You'll have to reposition yourself for a good cast. Don't expect the fish to come to you—you have to bring the bait to them. Weed walleyes aren't easy, but they can be had!

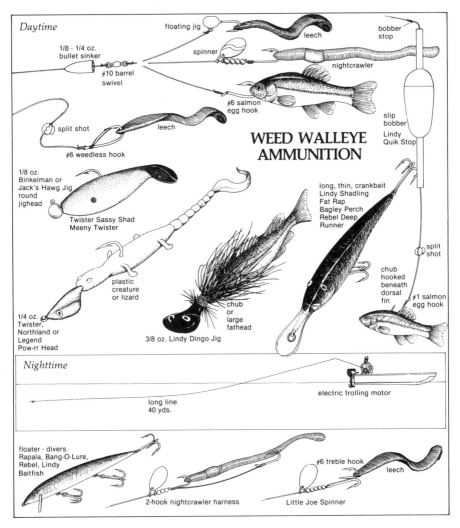

Daytime

floating jig

leech

bobber stop

1/8 - 1/4 oz. bullet sinker

spinner

nightcrawler

#10 barrel swivel

#6 salmon egg hook

slip bobber

split shot

leech

Lindy Quik Stop

#6 weedless hook

WEED WALLEYE AMMUNITION

1/8 oz. Binkelman or Jack's Hawg Jig round jighead

Twister Sassy Shad Meeny Twister

long, thin, crankbait Lindy Shadling Fat Rap Bagley Perch Rebel Deep Runner

split shot

plastic creature or lizard

chub hooked beneath dorsal fin

#1 salmon egg hook

1/4 oz. Twister, Northland or Legend Pow-rr Head

chub or large fathead

3/8 oz. Lindy Dingo Jig

Nighttime

electric trolling motor

long line 40 yds.

floater - divers Rapala, Bang-O-Lure, Rebel, Lindy Baitfish

#6 treble hook

leech

2-hook nightcrawler harness

Little Joe Spinner

to come and take a look. Hits are tough to detect—just a twitch in the line. Slam the hook home and get the fish up and out of the weeds *right now.*

Plastic-bodied jigs may not have live bait appeal, but they do take the abuse heavy weeds dish out. Surprised bass fishermen catch a lot of walleyes fishing plastic worms through the weeds. In fact, if the fish are fairly active, you'll catch more walleyes with a plastic tail because it'll stay on the jig while live bait will rip off the hook.

BOBBERS REDISCOVERED

In addition to being a deadly new approach for both fishing shallow rocks and suspended fish, slip bobbers have turned out to be dynamite for weed walleyes too. The attraction is obvious. Dangle live bait in front of a walleye's nose long enough and chances are you'll trigger a response.

Slip bobbers work best in sparse or clumpy weeds, where the bait can get down through the vegetation or right up against the weedline. A leech or minnow hanging there struggling is bound to attract some interest. And the lack of speed is right up their alley. In fact, after you've jigged a few fish from an area and they seem to quit biting, pitch a slip bobber in there and you'll entice a few more.

CRANKING

Crankbaits also catch a lot more walleyes than you'd expect, providing you use 'em under the right conditions. They really shine in shallow, dark water walleye lakes where the walleyes are up in four or five feet of water relating to the weeds. We've been in on a couple of early spring crankbait catches that were fantastic. No messin' with live bait! It's slam, bang, and toe-to-toe with the feisty walleyes. The method is particularly effective at night, cranking those baits right over the tops of the weeds. And under the right conditions it produces during the day too.

During the day, cast your crankbait parallel to the weed edge and retrieve it right along the weedline, occasionally ripping a weed or two. Or if they're sparse enough, pitch it right up on top and crawl it over the tops of the weedgrowth. Both methods are very effective.

Stick to long, thin crankbaits when it comes to walleyes. They seem to prefer this shape over the short, fat alphabet plugs associated with bass fishing. The wide, lazy wobble of the thin plugs is more attractive to walleyes than the tight-wobbling action that turns bass on. It's a little tip that will pay big dividends.

NIGHT STALKING

Night can be the best time for weed walleyes. As the sun goes down they start becoming active and begin cruising in search of food. You need to work something up above the tops of the weeds where they can spot it.

Casting crankbaits at night is great for small, well-defined spots like an obvious point or shallow rock pile. Yet when you're faced with a large weed flat, you're usually better off trolling. It allows you to cover more water quicker, and with less effort.

Once again, use a long line, electric motor approach. Pick out a shallow running bait, like a Rapala, Rebel or Lindy Baitfish—one that'll run just deep enough to occasionally touch the tops of the weeds. Then cruise back and forth, systematically covering the weed tops. If you catch several fish in an area, stop and cast. It's that simple.

The same approach works with a spinner type lure. Get a big-bladed spinner like a Little Joe or Maynard's nightcrawler harness, hang a nightcrawler on the back, and start trolling. Looks awful—but it works wonders! Sometimes it'll take fish when the plain artificials won't.

Whether you prefer spinners or some form of crankbait, the system works. Nightfishing with Rapala-type lures and nightcrawler harnesses repeatedly takes big walleyes from hard-fished waters. The hardest thing is to get you out there the first time to try it! After that, you'll be convinced!

PLATEAU AND HILL-LAND RESERVOIRS

We'd like to dwell on the Missouri River reservoirs in order to bring across some important points that apply to walleye fishing in plateau and hill-land reservoirs no matter where they are located.

These reservoirs give up walleyes to anglers fishing a variety of methods. But the most productive methods are also the most unusual—at least by natural lake fishing standards! Yet it is our experience that the techniques covered here are the *norm* for fishing plateau and hill-land reservoir walleyes during the summer, and will work wherever they are used.

We don't pretend to know exactly why reservoir walleyes react a bit differently from their natural lake cousins. We think it probably has to do with the size of the impoundments, the forage base and the exceptional walleye populations often existing in these systems. Here are a few other things to consider, too.

Because of the large size of many reservoirs, they are often slow to accept seasonal change. Summer walleye fishing can be uncharacteristically consistent. While the fishing doesn't get "good" until late May or early June on Lakes Oahe and Sakakawea in the Dakotas, once the water warms up, the fishing stays good right into the fall. Peak fishing on the main lakes usually lasts from June to the middle of September. On reservoirs located much farther south, in Kansas and Kentucky for example, this summer period may actually extend from late April into early October.

Forage always has a bearing on fish size and location. Rainbow smelt and spottail shiners constitute the primary food sources available to Missouri River walleyes. These excellent baitfish have turned these fish into some of the thickest-bodied, scrappiest fish you will ever encounter. On the other hand, reservoir walleyes in many other areas of the United States have abundant shad populations to feed on. Down South, walleyes also have the benefit of extended growing seasons and can grow to substantial size.

Hill-Land and Plateau Walleye Reservoirs

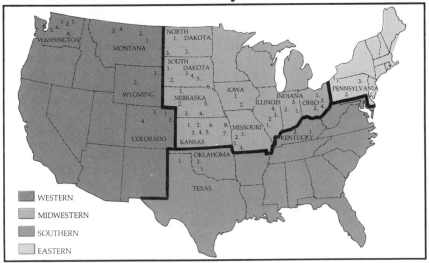

Hill-land and plateau reservoirs, and reservoirs with sections falling into these categories, are found all across the United States. Of course, they don't all hold walleyes, so we've taken the time to pinpoint a few waters for you. Obviously, we can't guarantee that each of these waters will produce walleyes with the consistency of the Missouri River Reservoirs in the Dakotas. Yet the walleye fishing in Washington state appears to

be fantastic, and Kansas reservoirs (some may verge on the IN-FISHERMAN *flatland reservoir category) are relatively untouched. Cumberland in Kentucky is also a good bet, and the Allegheny Reservoir is also hot. Some of the deep eastern reservoirs listed here fall more into the highland variety, but the fishing patterns still apply. For information on the states we haven't listed, contact their fisheries department for more information.*

SOUTH DAKOTA
1. Belle Fourche Reservoir
2. Angostura Reservoir
3. Lake Oahe
4. Lake Sharpe
5. Lake Francis Case
6. Lake Lewis and Clark

WASHINGTON
1. Franklin D. Roosevelt Lake
2. Banks Lake
3. Rufus Woods Lake
4. Lake Pateros
5. Chelan Lake
6. Potholes Reservoir
   and points downriver

NEBRASKA
1. Merritt Reservoir
2. Lake McConaughy
3. Swanson Lake
4. Harlan County Lake
5. Sherman Reservoir
6. Lake Lewis and Clark

WYOMING
1. Keyhole Reservoir
2. Boysen Reservoir

MISSOURI
1. Stockton Reservoir
2. Truman Reservoir
3. Lake of the Ozarks
4. James River Arm
   of Table Rock Lake

ILLINOIS
1. Cedar Lake
2. Carlyle Lake
3. Lake Shelbyville
4. Clinton Lake

OHIO
1. Pleasant Hill
2. Dillon
3. Salt Fork
4. Seneca Lake

COLORADO
1. Sterling Reservoir
2. Bonny Reservoir
3. Horsetooth Reservoir
4. Rifle Gap Reservoir

NORTH DAKOTA
1. Lake Sakakawea
2. Lake Oahe
3. Bowman-Haley Reservoir

MONTANA
1. Fort Peck Lake
2. Nelson Reservoir
3. Lake Elwell
4. Fresno Reservoir

KANSAS
1. Webster Reservoir
2. Glen Elder Reservoir
3. Wilson Lake
4. Kanopolis Reservoir
5. Marion Lake
6. Milford Lake
7. Melvern Lake
8. Clinton Lake

IOWA
1. Big Creek
2. Rathbun Lake

OKLAHOMA
1. Altus Reservoir
2. Foss Reservoir

INDIANA
1. Brookville Lake
   (below Truman Dam)
2. Harden Reservoir
3. Salamonie

TEXAS
1. Lake Meredith

PENNSYLVANIA
1. Allegheny Reservoir
2. Lake Raystown
3. Wallenpaupack

KENTUCKY
1. Big South Fork and
   Cumberland River areas of
   Lake Cumberland
2. Nolin River Lake

Numbers also make a difference. As any fisherman can tell you, presenting a bait to a large school of fish can be a lot more productive than working a small group. Schooled walleyes are often competitive, and they'll smash a fast-moving bait with all the voracity of a largemouth bass.

Because there are often great numbers of fish, location is the key ingredient. The key to location rests with your being able to find and fish areas that attract the largest concentrations of fish. In just a moment, you'll learn how.

In simplest terms, Summer Period plateau and hill-land reservoir walleyes use "classic" structural elements such as points, humps and sunken islands. But there are points—and there are points! And there are islands—and there are islands!

Let's get back to Lakes Sakakawea and Oahe for a moment to illustrate why you must learn how to identify high percentage spots in order to enjoy consistent success. Sakakawea and Oahe are multi-structured bodies of water. Generally, rock/shale points are the key to fishing Oahe, while these same types of areas, as well as sunken islands, are the places to look for old marble eyes on Sakakawea. Yet combined, these lakes cover nearly 3/4 million acres of water! Their contour maps resemble a plate of spaghetti; a one-mile stretch of lower Oahe may contain as many as 20 or 30 likely looking points! If you started at the Oahe Dam at dawn and spent 15 minutes working every point on the west side of the reservoir, by evening you'd still be within sight of the power plant! You'd probably find fish before then, but you'd also be wasting a lot of time fishing unproductive water. Obviously, fishing here can be a locational nightmare for the uninitiated. This is where we begin our all-important discussion of key areas.

HIGH PERCENTAGE SPOTS— CONSISTENT WALLEYES

While we don't claim to have the complete answer to finding summer walleyes on plateau and hill-land reservoirs, there is a system that helps eliminate unproductive water—fast! The thing to do is concentrate on areas that consistently attract fish. Herein lies the key for plateau and hill-land reservoir walleye anglers, whether from Kentucky, Kansas or Washington. Admittedly, the specific conditions facing Kentucky anglers on a hill-land impoundment will differ somewhat from those facing a Kansas or North Dakota plateau reservoir angler. But, the fish-finding principles are the same!

High percentage spots are simply areas that have a variety of features likely to attract and hold walleyes. We're looking for areas with the most variety. Such areas are usually two or three different spots rolled into one, giving the walleyes (and forage) several options under different weather conditions.

POINTS

When the wind blows on Oahe and Sakakawea, the waves pounding ashore loosen the soil and form a mud line. Walleyes like to use this mud line as an "umbrella," allowing them to feed in water as shallow as two or three feet deep. On calm days, however, they prefer rock or shale on a sharp-breaking,

Multi-Featured Sunken Island

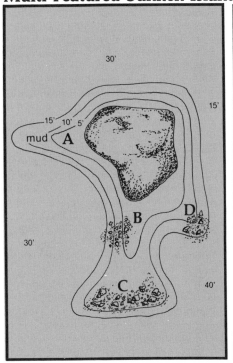

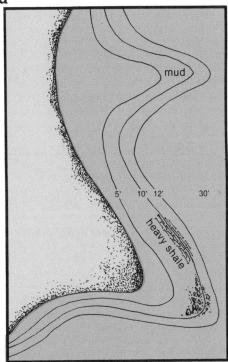

Multi-Featured Point

Dan Nelson:
This island produced an incredible number of big fish for us the past couple years. And it's easy to see why. The mud point (A) offers the fish one option. The small point (B) gives them another, the big hammerhead point (C) still another and the smaller point (D) yet another. Regardless of conditions, the walleyes can find something they like here.

The multi-featured point has a combination of elements forming a super spot. The fish have three options in this small area: the rock point, the soft-bottomed point and the shale bed in between. It takes careful examination to find all these features.

extended point. On some days you may find the fish laying just below the first lip of a drop-off. Some days they're deeper. Thus, stair-step drop-offs add to the attractiveness of a point, and on different days you may find fish on any ledge down into 50 or more feet of water. The point is, walleyes often prefer structural items that allow them the *most possible options* regardless of the weather—high percentage spots.

Any short, hard-bottom point may hold walleyes on a given day. But reservoirs like Oahe and Sakakawea have hundreds of short, hard-bottom points. You're better off passing up the short points and stopping when you find a long point with several kinds of fish-attracting features. A good point might have a stair-step ledge on one side, scattered rock on top and a shale bed lining the other side. The point's shallow inside turn may be soft-bottomed, while the deeper outside turn might break off into another, smaller, hard-bottom point. Such an area is almost certain to hold walleyes, whether it's in Kansas, Kentucky or Cucamunga!

HUMPS

The same principle applies to sunken islands or humps. An island with many points, stair-step ledges, and a variety of bottom conditions is generally better than a smooth, gradual-breaking sand hump. We might also mention that an already good island is made all the better by the presence of a saddle—

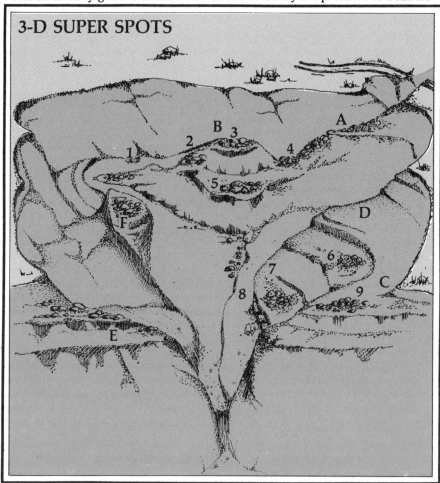

3-D SUPER SPOTS

This three-dimensional picture of a large bay further serves to illustrate the "super spot" phenomenon. Point A is but an average fish attractor standing by itself. But when it's coupled to Island B by a saddle, it becomes part of a "super spot"—a high percentage fish attractor.

Even standing along, Island B constitutes a "super spot" because it offers a variety of bottom conditions and depth options for walleyes to use during different weather conditions. The extended point area 1 serves the needs of deep fish and also attracts roaming fish to the island area. Rock slide 2 and the rock-capped island top 3 are also attractive to fish at different times, as is the deep, hard-bottom lip 5. Saddle area 4 will be fre-

quented by fish moving from Island B to point A or vice versa.

Points C and D and their adjacent features also constitute high percentage areas due to their variety of bottom conditions and stairstep drop-offs. Rock lips 6, 7 and 8 on the inside turn between points C and D should always be checked. Shallow flats like 9 will hold fish under optimum conditions. There are many other areas which deserve to be checked.

In comparison to the "super area" formed by points C and D, point E does not offer many options and will, thus, not attract many fish. The same would probably apply for sunken island F.

a "dip" between two higher spots. One of the best possible conditions exists when a saddle area connects an island with a point of land! Again, the variety of features increases the possibility of mega fish!

We like to apply the "Good, Better, Best Principle." Generally, an extensive, hard-bottom point is good; an extensive, hard-bottom point with several different hard-bottom conditions is better; and an extensive, hard-bottom point with different bottom conditions, stair-step ledges, and perhaps a saddle area connected to a sunken hump, is best. Remember that everything is relative, however. If the best available reservoir area is a moderately long, hard-bottom point, that's a terrific spot on this reservoir!

Without getting too complex, generally look for high percentage structural elements in the middle and lower sections of reservoirs—the true main lake sections. Also remember fluctuating water levels can make last year's unproductive spot pure dynamite this year. As always, you're on a search and seizure mission, with the emphasis being on "the search."

We are giving you only the one most consistent pattern for fishing these waters. There are others! You can explore road beds, rip-rap, creek channels, stump fields, or isolated rock piles, bars and rock slides.

Suspended fish are also common, and there are ways to take them. When you're running across the lake, it's a good idea to watch your depth flasher for schools of baitfish. Vertically schooled (as opposed to horizontally schooled) bait is usually being chased by gamefish, and vertical jigging can work wonders. Generally, though, we suggest checking out the nearest adjacent structural element; there are probably active fish on it, too.

PRESENTATION

There are several important elements making up the art of presentation. Let's look at speed, depth, color and size for a moment.

For reasons we can't explain, a spinner (single-hook or two-hook harness) dressed with live bait seems by far the most productive bait you can offer these summer reservoir fish. Remember now, when you're talking reservoirs from one end of the country to the other, there will be exceptions. And even on reservoirs where spinners are decidedly preferred, yes, crankbaits will work; and yes, slip sinker rigs will work; and yes, a host of other baits. But day-in and day-out, you can't beat a spinner.

For any of you who refute the one-lure theory, remember that suspended Lake Erie walleyes also definitely favor one summer bait, the weight-forward spinner. Spend time on reservoirs like Oahe and Sakakawea and you'll come to the same conclusion. The only reason the spinner isn't the norm on other reservoirs across the United States is that it *simply hasn't been fished.*

After finding a potentially super spot, your first consideration, no matter what bait you're fishing, is depth and speed. It's impossible to rank one over the other in order of importance. One without the other will cut your success considerably.

When you're talking about two entirely different categories of reservoirs, as well as reservoirs spread out across the U.S., it's impossible to talk about definite depths. We can say this, however. Once you've found a depth pattern you can usually depend on it, for at least a day, and perhaps even the entire summer. We're not talking one single depth, mind you, but a variety of depths coinciding with certain weather conditions.

On Lakes Sakakawea and Oahe, it's very common to find the fish loyal to a depth pattern. If you locate a school of fish in 11 feet of water, chances are most of the walleyes you'll take that day will come from this depth. If the wind kicks up, or in other words *if the conditions change,* the walleyes may move into very shallow water along the mud line. The fish might do lots of other things, too, but the point is: As long as weather conditions are stable, the fish will usually hold at a fairly constant depth.

Establishing a depth pattern is relatively easy. Start along the first lip created by the drop-off (15-17 feet in Oahe and Sakakawea) on a point or hump and systematically work shallower with each successive trolling pass until you find fish. Start deeper to avoid spooking any shallower fish. We would suggest fishing several other potential areas before probing much deeper water.

As we've mentioned previously, local conditions can affect fish depth. In 1980 and 1981, Lake Oahe received very little flow from the Garrison Dam. As a result, water levels dropped and the water clarity improved, pushing walleyes down to 40 and 60 feet during late July and August. At the same time, most of Sakakawea's walleyes were coming from 15 feet or less. Obviously, no matter where you fish, you need to take local conditions into account.

SPEED CONTROL

Speed is equally important. You may hit the right speed on one pass and bang several nice fish. Of course, even with a tachometer, staying with a particular speed can be very difficult. A trolling speed device can be very helpful.

Short of a trolling speed device, you need to depend on feel. Start by trolling just fast enough to lift the spinning blade off the bottom. From there, gradually increase the speed until the fish tell you you're moving fast enough. With a sensitive graphite or boron rod, the drag on the line and the pulsation of the blade will tell you approximately how fast you're going. Don't be afraid to move too fast; those walleyes are often super aggressive, and you're usually better off going too fast than too slow.

Incidentally, in order to vary your speed, you may have to start off slowly backtrolling under some conditions and progress to a faster forward trolling approach. In a big wind, drift or troll forward.

BLADE COLOR

Color can be very important. There are myriad blade colors that produce, so the only mistake you can make is not being versatile enough to try them. While we've not encountered a color that won't catch fish, there are certain colors that seem to be better than others.

Our five favorite colors for fishing reservoirs are fluorescent red, chartreuse, and green, standard nickel, and gold. Expect to find definite preferences on certain reservoirs. However, don't let yourself get locked into one color unless you know it's definitely the best color that day. Tuesday's fish may hit chartreuse like they haven't fed in a week. But Wednesday's walleyes may snub their noses at chartreuse and want nothing but nickel. At the outset of each fishing day, every angler in the boat should put on a different color. Keep switching colors until someone finds the hot number for that particular day.

Having said those things, keep this in mind: While one color may entice many fish from a given school, it's probably not the only color. Keep working a school with the primary color until you've made several passes without turning a fish. Then switch to other colors and see if you can pick up another fish or two.

BLADE SIZE

Blade size can also be an important consideration. Many of our biggest fish have come on a No. 4 blade, which is slightly larger than the standard No. 3 blade found on most commercially tied spinners. Again, however, the walleyes' day-to-day preference will be unpredictable, and the road to success may come through experimentation.

While many fishermen prefer Indiana or Colorado blades, some also like the willow leaf design. The Indiana blade seems to spin somewhat easier than a Colorado and big blades spin easier than small ones. On those rare days when the fish are finicky and a slower trolling speed is necessary, you're best off going with a No. 4 Indiana blade to get the maximum action at the reduced speed.

Spinning gear is certainly adequate, but bait casting gear filled with 12-17 pound monofilament line is perfect. The baitcaster gives you more flexibility for forward spinner trolling than spinning gear. Leave the free-spool button depressed and hold the line with your thumb. If you snag up at a fast trolling speed, you can easily give line. Set the drag loosely, and pump the fish to the boat using your thumb to maintain constant pressure on the fish. Walleyes are tenacious fighters, and a big fish will make several quick runs at the boat, so you must be able to give line in a hurry.

Why use such heavy line? Because most reservoir fish don't seem to care one bit. Under normal conditions, six pound line will not catch more fish than 17 pound line. Of course, there are exceptions, and you must be able to recognize them.

For weight, use bottom bumping rigs such as the Gapen Bait Walker, Meter Bottom Walker, Blakemore Lure Doctor or Lindy/Little Joe Bottom Cruiser. The Bottom Cruiser is handy because you can control how fast it will dive by

Blade Size & Type
actual size

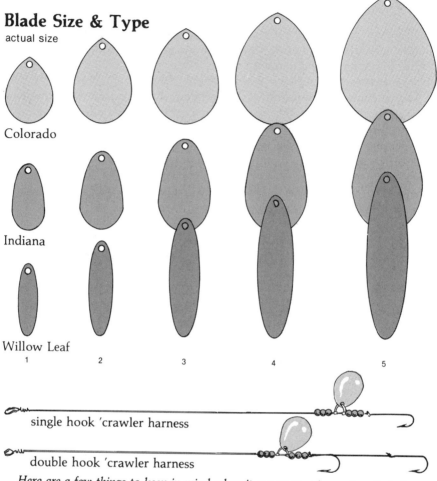

Colorado

Indiana

Willow Leaf

| 1 | 2 | 3 | 4 | 5 |

single hook 'crawler harness

double hook 'crawler harness

Here are a few things to keep in mind when it comes to spinner rigs. First, be willing to experiment with different blade sizes and colors. Although fluorescent orange, red or chartreuse are favorite colors, nickel and gold produce better on some occasions. And even though a No. 3 blade is the standard on most commercial rigs, we've taken a lot of big fish on the larger No. 4 blade, especially during low light periods.

Indiana, Colorado or willow leaf blade types are all excellent. However, the Indiana blade seems to spin easier than a Colorado and big blades spin easier than small ones. On those days when slow trolling is necessary, a No. 4 Indiana blade seems to work best.

When the fish are really popping, a single hook rig is excellent. Still, there are advantages to the two hook harness. It increases your hooking capabilities under most conditions, and the long, strung-out 'crawler probably has more fish appeal. These rigs are available commercially or can be homemade.

adjusting the Cruiser's lead head. By closing the V-shaped upper arm, you can make the 1-1/2 ounce model dive to 20 or 30 feet with no problem. By opening the V, you can run the same sinker through five feet of water without having it dig up the bottom.

Finicky fish can be a problem anywhere you fish; you will encounter days when the walleyes just seem to pick at their food. When that happens, nine times out of ten it means you're trolling too slow. Pick up the speed and they'll attack your bait. Or it could mean that you haven't found the best blade color for that particular day. Or perhaps you should be dressing your spinner with a different bait.

In most instances, nightcrawlers are the No. 1 producer. But we've seen minnows or leeches outfish them on certain reservoirs or on certain days. The moral is: Never assume what the fish want. Let them tell you. It gets expensive hauling leeches, minnows and 'crawlers along on every trip. But if the guy in the next boat is ripping seven pounders on minnows and you have a cooler full of 'crawlers, you'd probably pay $10.00 a dozen for some fatheads.

There'll be days when no matter what you throw, you get back half a bait—even with nightcrawler harnesses! The best way to overcome this problem is by teasing the fish. When you get a strike, maintain steady pressure. You'll feel the walleye swimming along with your bait, but don't give in to the temptation and set the hook. Drop the rod tip slowly back toward the fish and wait for the next tug. The tug means the fish has chomped up another inch on the bait. Now set the hook!

OTHER BAITS

Sure, there are a lot of baits that will produce fish for you. There are some days when you'd swear you could take a limit of nice fish on jerkbaits or buzz baits. But those days are rare.

With a weight-forward spinner, we prefer to hook the 'crawler in the middle, trailing it behind the lure in a V. The 5/8 ounce size works best at faster trolling speeds. And on those days when the fish are shallow, it's great for casting.

Crankbaits are also sensational at times. Like the weight-forward spinner, cranks produce more fish and bigger fish on given days. When you encounter active fish, tie on a crankbait and either cast it to the shallows or quickly troll it along the break. But don't overdo it; if they're not hitting plugs, put them away.

Jigs? You can't beat jigs in the spring when you're working pre-spawn fish. And we've taken some good walleyes in the middle of summer as well.

Like the jig, standard live bait rigs like the Lindy Rig produce best on a seasonal basis. During the fall you just can't beat a rig and a minnow. Rigs will take some fish during summer, too.

Thus, while you shouldn't be on the water without a supply of crankbaits, weight-forward spinners, jigs and rigs, expect to catch most of your summer plateau and hill-land reservoir walleyes trolling a spinner and live bait. Of course, this will probably change in the future as these bodies of water receive more sophisticated fishing pressure. It's common for anglers fishing a large population of competitive and rather naive fish to take them with relatively unsophisticated techniques. Indeed, when dealing with a large and aggressive fish population, location is usually the major factor. Once you find fish, catching them is usually relatively easy. As time progresses and fishing pressure in-

Bottom Cruiser

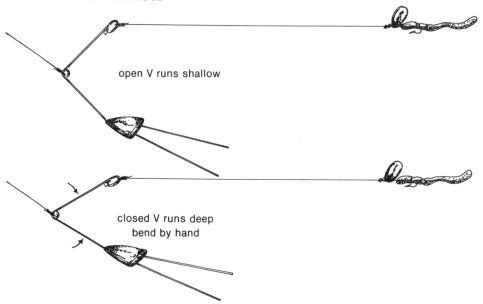

open V runs shallow

closed V runs deep
bend by hand

Although any bottom-bumping sinker will take a spinner/live bait combo down to the walleyes, Dan Nelson favors the Lindy/Little Joe Bottom Cruiser. The Bottom Cruiser, complete with two wire feelers to keep the bait riding off the bottom and over snags, can be altered to run deep or shallow. With an open V as illustrated here, the Cruiser will run shallow. Close the V to obtain depth. Using this option, the 1½ ounce model can be fished in 20-30 feet of water.

tensifies, the fish susceptible to easy presentations are often plucked from the population, leaving both fewer and warier fish. Refined presentation and a measure of versatility becomes necessary in such instances. Expect this when it comes to walleyes in plateau and hill-land reservoirs, too.

Super spots, super walleyes? You betcha! There are millions of acres of reservoir water spread all across the U.S. chock-full of walleyes just waiting to be caught.

Spot Versus Super Spot

A high percentage area has a variety of features likely to attract and hold walleyes. While the island pictured in Figure 1 will attract some fish, the more complex "super island" offers more options for the fish. The same principle applies to the points in Figure 2.

Spot Versus Super Spot

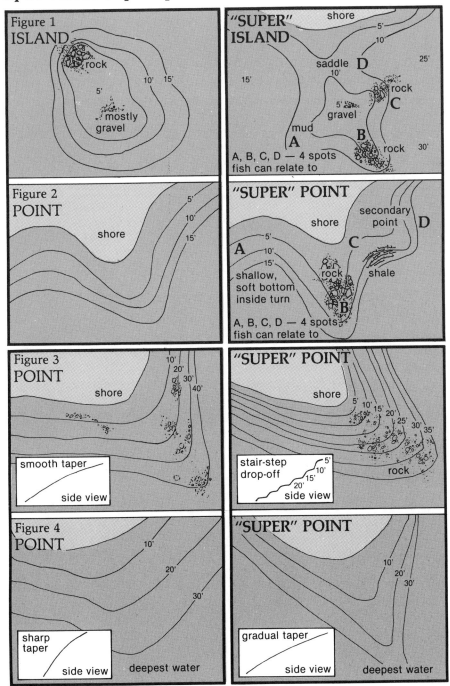

Another type of spot versus "super spot" point condition is illustrated in Figure 3. Points which break steadily into deep water don't offer the variety of a stairstep drop-off. Relative size can also be important. All other things being equal, exceptionally long, gradual points reaching directly into deep water attract and hold more fish than short steep points (Figure 4).

Chapter 14

THE POST-SUMMER PERIOD

"A Time of Impending Change"

Hot days with dead-calm periods, followed by cool nights, are typical during this period. This is the cosmic signal to the ecosystem that things are going to slow down. The time of plenty is about to give way to reduced quantities of the food chain.

The key factor is the slowing of the food chain. Fish activity is rated active. Patterns from the Summer Period carry into the Post-Summer Period. One major location change is found in lakes where walleyes are using the weeds.

During this Post-summer Period large northern pike become active in the weeds and sometimes drive the walleyes out into deeper areas.

The following body of water type is very productive for walleyes during the summer and Post-summer Periods.

THE LOWLAND AND FLATLAND RESERVOIR WALLEYE

Lowland and flatland reservoirs are sprinkled all across the country. On a day-to-day basis, these waters offers some of the most consistent walleye fishing anywhere.

Let's lay everything right on the line! Some of the country's most consistent walleye fishing exists in lowland and flatland reservoirs. (They're also called *flowages* in some parts of the country.) Indeed, although most fishermen probably take walleyes on many different types of water, when the chips are really down—when crisp, clear, cold front days roll in three times a week—there's no better place to be than a lowland or flatland reservoir. Obviously, if that's true under tough conditions, these reservoirs are also a good bet under optimum conditions—that is, of course, if you understand how to fish them.

Most lowland and flatland impoundments are unique in comparison to what might be termed "classic" walleye water. Although the bottom configuration is hardly uniform, the huge flats typically found on these systems often makes it appear that way. Add stained water, or water with heavy particle suspension, and further problems arise. If the water doesn't look like clear, classic walleye water, it can completely blow an angler's confidence. Yet perhaps this water color-caused trauma is somewhat justified; water clarity has a definite bearing on fish location, and you need to temper your location and presentation tactics.

Finally, let's add one last factor—*wood!* Wood? In walleye water? You bet! It's a common feature on many, although not all, lowland and flatland reservoirs, and you'd better believe it can have a critical bearing on fish location—as well as presentation.

A BIT OF HISTORY

Lowland and flatland reservoirs are born of the need for electrical power and/or water storage. Although many of these impoundments date back to the early 1900's, many were recently constructed.

The time period reservoirs were built in has a bearing on their finished structure. While early reservoirs were allowed to fill without the timber and other obstructions first being cleared, recent Army Corp of Engineers' procedure has called for the clearing of obstructions. The resulting amount of fish-holding habitat has a bearing on the total fish population. Although both "cleared" and "uncleared" reservoirs hold fish, uncleared (cover-filled) reservoirs are usually more productive.

Most lowland and flatland reservoirs are eutrophic in nature, and fish production is very good. In most cases, strong year classes are produced either naturally or through stocking, and the fish quickly grow to catchable size. Yet while these reservoirs are known to produce *numbers* of fish—the key to consistent fish—they are not known for producing *large* fish. However, many studies show that large fish are available, but simply not tapped into by anglers.

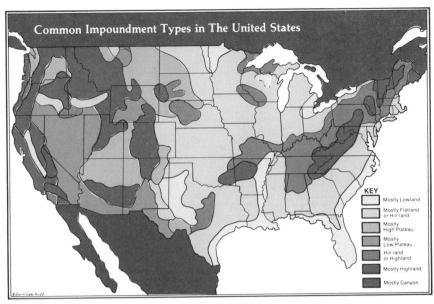

Common Impoundment Types in The United States

KEY

Mostly Lowland

Mostly Flatland or Hill-land

Mostly High Plateau

Mostly Low Plateau

Hill-land or Highland

Mostly Highland

Mostly Canyon

Common Impoundment Types in The United States

Flatland and lowland reservoirs are spread across much of the United States and eastern Ontario. Of course, some southern lowland or flatland impoundments don't have walleyes. However, you'll find good lowland or flatland reservoir walleye fishing in Nebraska, Kansas, and the Dakotas, and every state east into Pennsylvania.

Flatland reservoirs typically have a distinctive river channel, although the upper end commonly silts in with age and may resemble a lowland reservoir. Lowland reservoirs often lack a distinctive channel because they are usually formed by impounding small rivers or swamps, rather than flat farmland and larger rivers. Still, when it comes to walleyes, the fish behave much the same in both kinds of impoundments.

THE SUMMER/POST-SUMMER PERIOD

As early season progresses, reservoir conditions change. Although shallow bays and classic lake areas always attract some fish, most of the fish begin scattering after the Summer Peak. It's vitally important to realize that rock and rubble *may* be important during the early season, but that *sand, clay and/or wood are more important during the Summer/Post-summer Periods.*

To put it very simply, lowland and flatland reservoir walleyes are wanderers during this period. However, most of the fish wander on *particular* flats. While fish generally scatter individually or in small groups across any extensive flat adjacent to a channel, the *tongue areas* produced by the meandering river channel are especially important. In most shallow reservoirs these tongues (flats) range from 6-12 feet deep and are common in the middle or upper reservoir section.

With fish ranging far and wide on the flats, you must look for something that attracts and holds fish—at least for a short time. Because the fish are flat-oriented, the sharper-breaking edges of the flat adjacent to the channel are not particularly attractive to the fish. That's not to say, however, that distinct in-

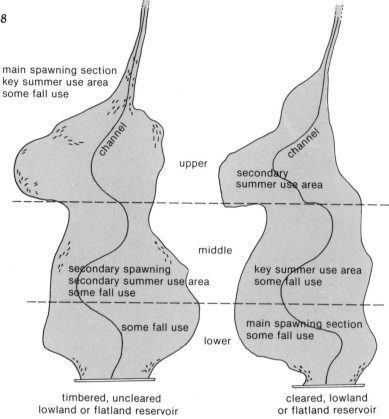

main spawning section
key summer use area
some fall use

channel

upper

secondary
summer use area

channel

middle

secondary spawning
secondary summer use area
some fall use

key summer use area
some fall use

some fall use

lower

main spawning section
some fall use

timbered, uncleared
lowland or flatland reservoir

cleared, lowland
or flatland reservoir

Basic Yearly Migration in Two Types of Lowland/Flatland Reservoirs

Although it's not as simple as we make it seem here, there are basic differences in walleye migration and use patterns in the two types (cleared or uncleared) of lowland or flatland reservoirs. By dividing each reservoir into three sections, we think we can deliver the thrust of what's happening.

The walleyes in an "uncleared" lowland reservoir typically migrate to the upper reservoir during the late Cold Water and Pre-spawn Calendar Periods. Intense spawning takes place in the upper 1/3 of the reservoir—especially if the proper bottom composition exists. If proper bottom conditions are also present in the middle 1/3 of the reservoir, this section will receive secondary spawning use.

After spawning, the fish begin to migrate back towards the main reservoir. However, the 4-12 foot deep flat conditions the fish desire during the Summer Period/Post-summer Period are immediately available in the same upper and middle reservoir sections; there's no need for them to progress farther. The only time any amount of walleyes use the lower 1/3 of the reservoir is during fall.

The situation in a "cleared" reservoir is somewhat different. In most of these reservoirs the only suitable spawning bottom is found on the rocky rip-rap at the face of the dam. Thus, the majority of the walleyes migrate to this section to spawn; it's the complete opposite of what typically happens in an uncleared reservoir.

After spawning, the fish head into the main reservoir, first finding appropriate summer conditions in mid-reservoir. Thus, most of the fish position themselves in mid-reservoir while a secondary, yet important group of fish also moves all the way to the upper reservoir.

Again, the key summer use area in an "uncleared" reservoir is in the upper 1/3 of the reservoir with the middle 1/3 being of secondary importance. In a "cleared" reservoir, the middle 1/3 is usually the most important summer use section, with the upper 1/3 being an area of secondary importance. In both cases, the area near the dam is usually no great shakes for summer and post-summer fish.

side and outside bends in the old channel won't attract fish. They can be especially good if these areas coincide with timber or brush.

What we're really looking for is something *up on the flats* that attracts and holds fish. Unfortunately, in reservoirs that have been cleared before filling, very little cover may exist. The name-of-the-game in such reservoirs is fish constantly moving across these flats. Consequently, you will have to modify your presentation strategy on such reservoirs.

One good option for fishing the flats on both cleared and uncleared reservoirs is fishing areas of slightly firmer bottom content. No matter how small such areas are, a sand area on an otherwise muck flat (just one example) can attract fish!

A second possible holding area is a bit unusual and applies only to those reservoirs in bog country. Chunks of bog, complete with brush and even trees, often break loose and float around. Although they look like islands, they aren't attached to the bottom and the water beneath them is attractively shaded. When these bogs blow onto a 6-12 foot deep flat they definitely attract fish.

A third option for attracting and concentrating fish—wood—is perhaps your best bet for taking fish consistently. Before these reservoirs filled, the flats were often covered with brush and trees. Depending on the age of the reservoir, these cover options probably still exist. At the very least, there should be: (1) logs scattered across the bottom. You may also find (2) standing (vertical) timber; (3) perfectly horizontal, floating logs; as well as (4) logs tipped and laying almost horizontally, but with the rooted end still attached to the bottom and the tip slightly protruding from the water. This timber and brush will attract and hold the largest fish, as well as many of the standard "bread-and-butter" fish. As you might imagine, though, all "wood" is not created equal. There are definite fish-holding keys to look for. We'll cover them in detail when we discuss presentation.

Before we proceed, let's finish covering the Calendar Periods and their effect on walleye location. Remember this: Once fish are relating to flats and/or wood, some of them continue to do so until the end of the season. In other words, you can almost always expect to take some fish from the flats and wood if it's available.

As the Summer Period draws to a close and the fish progress through the Post-summer Period and into the Cold Water Period, fish location no longer centers around the flats adjacent to the channel. In fact, with one exception, there often is no focal point for fall fishing. That's the problem. Although summer and fall fishing is usually considered consistent, fall fish are often widely scattered throughout the system; thus there are many patterns to consider.

Quick-breaking, hard-bottom shoreline projections; hard-bottom humps; distinct inside and outside bends in the old river channel; floating bogs; plus timbered or untimbered flats may all attract fish.

There is one exception to this trend. Some reservoirs have old lake basins within the watershed. The drawdowns that often occur during fall trigger fish in any system to head for deeper water; in systems that have old lake basins, the walleyes may migrate en masse to these areas. Walleyes that set up there will normally be deeper and more tightly schooled than at any other time of year. Catching walleyes on classic, deep rock slides in over 20 feet of water is common at this time—and the fishing in these lake basins can be very consistent.

Good Versus Bad Timber

Possible But Not Probable

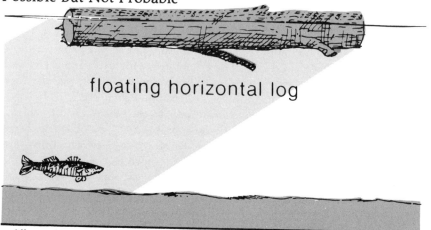

floating horizontal log

All wood is not created equal—at least not in terms of attracting lowland and flatland reservoir walleyes. During the Summer Period the walleyes scatter across the 4-12 foot deep flats often located adjacent to an old channel area. Any wood located on these flats can draw fish, but the kind and quantity of it has a bearing on its fish-holding potential.

Floating horizontal logs provide plenty of shaded cover, but the fact that these logs move is a strike against them. Individual vertical stumps don't move, but they don't

Probable

semi-horizontal log

Very Probable

series of semi-horizontal logs

C. NELSON

provide quite enough cover. Thus, they fall into the same category. Both spots should be considered possible, but not probable, holding areas.

Individual semi-horizontal logs with their root systems still touching the bottom but with the end of the log floating slightly above the water usually attract fish. Although fish may hold up high under the log, expect the bottom 1/3 of the log to attract the most fish.

Here's another rule to keep in mind: Quantity can result in quality! Thus, while an individual vertical stump might not be particularly appealing, a bunch of stumps is a different story. Now fish are likely to be attracted to the area. The same thing's true for a series of semi-horizontal logs. The more the merrier!

THE EFFECTS OF WEATHER

Before discussing presentation, let's again emphasize that the fishing on lowland and flatland reservoirs is usually very consistent. Not only are there a lot of fish available, but of all the body of water types that hold walleyes, these reservoirs are the least affected by changing weather conditions. While the very best summer weather conditions probably occur when the weather is flat, hot and muggy, consistent fishing is also typical even following a cold front.

PRESENTATION

Having discussed the basic locational factors for consistently finding shallow impoundment walleyes, it's time to examine presentation tactics. As always, there is no one presentation method that will fit every situation; a measure of versatility is always a virtue. The following general presentation methods apply to the fishing on most lowland and flatland reservoirs.

CRANKBAITS

Long, thin, shallow-running, floating/diving, minnow-shaped crankbaits such as the Bagley Bang-O-Lure, Rapala, Rebel Minnow, Bomber Long-A-Minnow or the Lindy Baitfish are very well suited for lowland and flatland reservoir walleyes. During Post-summer, they are great fished through stump fields or trolled across open flats. In reservoirs with very dark water, walleyes will take these crankbaits right on through the middle of the day. However, on clearer water reservoirs this presentation is better suited to low-light hours, and even after dark.

TUNING A CRANKBAIT FOR FISHING IN TIMBER

Some extra precaution is necessary to minimize hang-ups when fishing through timber. A simple but effective way to tune your crankbait for running through timber and brush is bending the lower (downward) forward-extending hook on each treble *slightly* in. As the timber gets thicker, bend the hook in farther. This hook usually accounts for the most snags. If the snag area is outrageously thick, you may have to go to a different presentation method, although bending the hook completely shut helps to a point.

Crankbaits work best with a small but strong snap like a size 10 Berkley Crosslock model. Don't tie your line directly to the plug unless you use a loop knot, and certainly don't use a wire leader. These are sensitive little plugs and it doesn't take much to kill their action.

Modifying Crankbaits for Timber Fishing

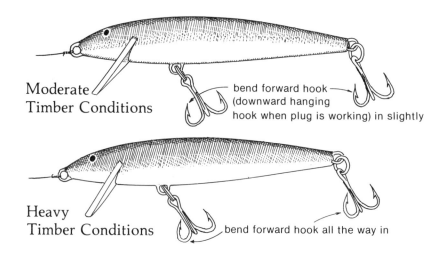

Moderate
Timber Conditions — bend forward hook
(downward hanging
hook when plug is working) in slightly

Heavy
Timber Conditions — bend forward hook all the way in

FISHING A CRANKBAIT THROUGH TIMBER

Providing exposed timber isn't too thick, make a cast of about 75 feet. Crank the plug back with the rod tip pointed low and slightly off to one side. This position allows you to feel the crankbait vibrating and is helpful in working through snags. When you do run into a snag, stop your retrieve and more the rod tip back in a direct line towards the lure. This creates some slack in your line and the crankbait should float up and free itself from the snag. Since most floater/diver crankbaits run nose-down and tail-up, the diving bill usually makes first contact with any obstruction. As long as the lower treble is not wide open, you can usually work the plug through moderate snags.

Here's a little fish-triggering tip that can make a difference. After each six-to-eight cranks of the reel handle, add some extra flash to the bait by twitching the rod tip. Also be willing to try a stop-and-go retrieve. There are times when these additions really make a difference.

Deeper-running crankbait models work best over deeper rocks and through deeper brush and timber. The same basic approach applies, but get the bait running as deep as possible, as soon as possible, by initially cranking hard and fast while lowering your rod tip. After the plug has dived down, ease back slightly and retrieve the plug with a slow to moderate speed, depending upon water temperature and clarity. The basic rule is: dark, cold water, slow retrieve; clear, warm water, moderate retrieve. In clear, cold water or dark, warm water, you might employ a retrieve speed in between those just mentioned.

Working Semi-Horizontal Wood

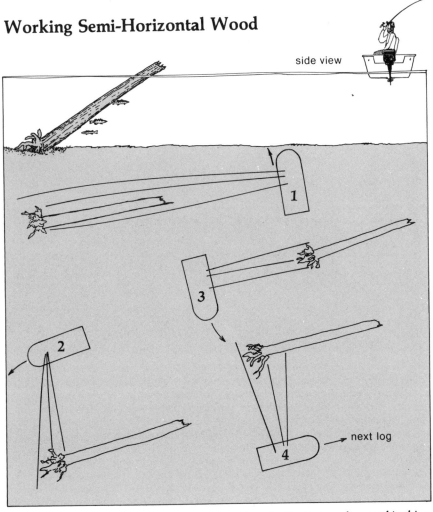

side view

Although we can't quite duplicate the "stump jumping" technique discussed in this article unless we "break out the oars," we can do an admirable job of covering semi-horizontal wood providing we fish with a weedless hook or brush guard jig. Start by positioning the boat perpendicular to, but on either end of, the log (position 1). At least three casts are necessary on each side of the log, preferably to the positions shown. Move around to position 2 and make at least three more casts; do the same for positions 3 and 4. Then it's on to another piece of wood. Are the fish here (on a particular piece of wood) today and gone tomorrow? Nope! Because the flats are full of wandering fish, any fish taken from wood will probably be replaced, perhaps even by the next day. When fishing walleyes relating to wood on a lowland or flatland reservoir, it's more like, "here today, back tomorrow!"

THE SLIDING BOBBER METHOD

When walleyes are deeper or more inactive, sliding (slip) bobbers and live bait are an excellent option. Fishing with a sliding bobber is so easy it's hard to believe it can work. There's no need to be an experienced hand at "feeling" a fish take; and no need to be an expert caster, either. Simple? Yes, but does it

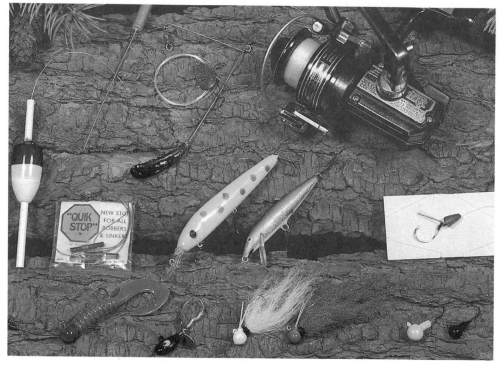

Slip bobbers (left) are outstanding for fishing fallen trees and stumps. Position the sliding bobber stop so your leech or 'crawler is barely inches above the submerged wood. Then simply cast out and let it drift into fish territory.

Bottom walkers at the upper left work well with a variety of lures. Team them with a spinner/'crawler combination at the upper left, or wobbling, minnow-imitating lures in the center. They're excellent for trolling or drifting wooded flats.

Jigs are usually your number one flowage lures. Cast or drift them along the edges or across the tops of the submerged timber. Pictured at the bottom from left to right are: a fluorescent jig with a Mister Twister tail; a slow-sinking jig for casting alongside trees; two weedguard jigs; and 1/4 and 1/8 oz. fluorescent jigheads. These fluorescent and/or noise-making jigs provide that "something extra" that works magic on fish in off-colored water.

Finally, at the far right is a 1/8 oz. slip sinker rig. Peg the sinker against the hook with a toothpick—a weedless rig you can cast right into and through the meanest snags!

catch fish and stay out of snags!

The sliding bobber option is especially applicable for fishing brush and timber stationed at a relatively uniform depth. Many flats with brush piles and scattered timber fit this billing as do many stump fields bordering old river bends. Sliding bobbers are also good options if the rocks you fish during spring and late fall are unusually snaggy and the fish are holding at a particular depth.

While the standard bobber rig works fine, one trick that increases hooking percentage and ups catches is replacing the single hook with a small fluorescent leadhead jig. The jig serves as an attractor, but more importantly, it allows you to hook more fish. You see, when a jig is used, the fish seem to concentrate on, and thus inhale, the jig portion of the bait. This is especially true when 'crawler fishing. Using the standard slip bobber rig, you often miss fish when they grab the 'crawler by the tail and run off into brush before gobbling it down. Consequently, if the hook is set too quickly, you miss the fish. But if you let the fish run a distance before setting the hook, you end up in "snag city." Thus a fluorescent leadhead jig can be a big key to success because it helps focus the fish's attention on the hooking part of the bait.

Decreasing the slack in your line before setting the hook increases hooking success with the sliding bobber rig. When the bobber goes down, don't just rear back immediately! Point the rod tip at the bobber and pick up most of the slack line; actually wait until you feel slight tension or additional weight before you set the hook. The deeper you fish, the more important this hook setting technique becomes.

WEEDLESS HOOKS

When fishing a brush-filled area where the depth is inconsistent, or when fishing neutral walleyes laying in the middle of cover, use a weedless hook. In this instance, the sliding bobber does not work quite so well.

A weedless hook must be both snag-free and able to hook fish well. Admittedly, weedless hooks have gained a bad reputation over the years because of their inability to hook fish.

An unweighted weedless hook rigged with a lively, lip-hooked minnow is effective for working brush shorelines or fallen tree-rimmed shorelines in spring. Slide a colored bead or two in front of the hook as an attractor; it makes a difference.

You'll need to add some weight for summer fishing on timbered flats. Rig a toothpick-pegged bullet sinker on your line. Make sure it's snugged up against the weedless hook. Basically, this rig functions much the same as a weedless jig. We feel, however, that with practice the jig is the easiest to use and most productive option. Remember, with the jig you have an additional positive factor—fluorescence!

Although some anglers prefer to use a jig with an open, light wire hook in thick cover situations, and simply bend themselves out of snag-ups, there are serious drawbacks to this proposition. First, you'll still get snagged, and you must then move around the brush or timber in an effort to free yourself. This disrupts the area and spooks fish! Secondly, if you hit a sizeable fish, it is nearly impossible to rassle it out of the brush without straightening the hook.

Perhaps the most serious problem is your mental attitude! With an open hook, you're going to be more "edge conscious" and not as likely to get that bait right into the snaggy, brushy area where the best fish may be hiding. Plenty of fishing experiences reveal that the largest fish often lie right in the middle of brush or in the root system on a tree. The more numerous and flighty small fish mill around the outside.

BASIC TACKLE

For most lowland or flatland reservoir fishing, we suggest medium spinning tackle since timber and other obstructions are often present. A spinning reel loaded with 6, 8 or even 10 (if the water is dark) pound test line is a good basic outfit. If timber is present, use a line with good abrasion resistance; and retie knots often. The rod should be 5'9" to 6' for fishing crankbaits, weedless hooks and jigs. A longer rod of 6½ or 7 feet is better for bobber fishing because the extra length makes it easier to lob casts, as well as set the hook. And if you fish a cleared reservoir and do a lot of trolling, a medium-action casting rod and reel combo loaded with 10 pound test line is great.

STUMP JUMPING

The "stump jumping" technique originated in the Flambeau Flowage area of Wisconsin. When the fish scatter over the flats during summer, they relate to wood *if* it is present. All wood is not created equal, however. Logs laying very close to horizontal are much more productive than vertical stumps. Apparently, the fish are attracted to the shade-providing cover, and horizontal wood offers more of it. It's not unusual to find three or four fish relating to one horizontal log. Although groups (fields) of vertical stumps may produce fish, individual, vertical standing stumps are usually not productive.

Hardcore stump jumpers practice their art with a 14 foot aluminum boat and a set of oars. (Most of these guys even use ball-bearing oar-locks, which shows you the emphasis they place on rowing.) After running up to the end of the log that is closest to being upwind, they turn off the gas motor. Through expert use of the oars, they position the middle of the boat perpendicular to the log and "walk" the boat down the log while one or two anglers vertically dip 'crawlers on a two-hook worm harness. Care is taken in two respects: (1) They keep the bait about 6 inches off the bottom; and (2) they keep the lines right next to each side of the log as the boat walks down the log. When an old protruding branch is encountered as the boat slides along, the angler gently lifts the bait over the branch and back down again. They rarely miss an inch of possibly productive water.

Stump jumpers always spend extra time at the base of the log where the old roots protrude; the bottom 1/3 of a horizontal log is the most productive. Biters are immediately jerked straight up out of the water. It takes perhaps 2 or 3 minutes to cover a good log, and then it's on to another. A log here and a log there—these guys know every horizontal log position (and there are hundreds of them) by heart—and before long a limit of fish is in the cooler. Fish are scatterd all over the flats, so fish removed from a log are soon replaced by others.

Perhaps this system of fishing sounds crude, but it is one of the most productive systems when fish are scattered on the flats and there is horizontal wood present. Trouble is, without rowing, the system is almost impossible to duplicate. Walking down the log with your electric motor? We've tried it! It just doesn't work as well. The best we can do—and it is still productive—is to position ourselves perpendicular to good logs and cast or flip light, weedless hook rigs, jigs with brush guards, or slip bobber rigs, parallel to the log. Couple these rigs with either a worm or leech *and make sure you work them as close to the log as possible!* Pay special attention to the rooted base of the log.

OTHER POST-SUMMER PATTERNS

Having discussed fishing wooded flats, let's remember that all flats do not have a lot of wood, and some reservoirs are completely void of wood. What options do you use in this case? Keep in mind that fish are widely scattered over the flats, either singly or in small groups. If there is little wood to hold the fish, they will wander, relating only to the flat in general. Making drift patterns across these flats will catch fish. When drifting, use worm-tipped jigs or trail a spinner/worm harness rig behind a bottom bumper. You're dealing with warm water and active fish! Don't just drift; if it's legal in your area, troll! Go ahead; add some speed to the bottom bumper, spinner and nightcrawler harness rig. And don't forget crankbaits; either fish the long, thin baits behind a bottom bumper or go with a diver that runs at the appropriate depth.

INSIDE AND OUTSIDE CHANNEL BENDS

Although they become less productive during Post-summer, always check distinct inside and outside (especially outside) bends of the old channel. This is doubly true if these areas coincide with wood. Float a slip bobber into the corner from an anchored position if you wish; cast crankbaits or leadhead jigs while you position the boat with your motor. All these presentations produce fish. Remember, though, that these areas are primarily early and late season spots!

FLOATING BOGS

Although they're not a widespread phenomenon, let's spend a moment discussing presentation around floating bogs. These bogs are actually self-sustaining, floating platforms made up of soil, brush and even trees. They simply move with the wind, often causing resorts some distress when a larger specimen (perhaps an acre) blows into their swimming area. In most cases, the resorters simply use three or four boats to tow the bog away.

Obviously, bogs provide cover, and cover draws baitfish and walleyes—especially if the bog is located over a fish-holding flat. Generally the side of the bog away from the sun is the most productive. Casting a worm-tipped, leadhead jig up to the bog and letting it sink is one productive option; dropping a slip bobber next to a bog is another.

We also position the boat up next to bogs with the electric motor and fish vertically with a leadhead jig. During midday, it is vitally important to stay next to the bog. During evening or early morning, however, fish may stray out farther from the protective cover of the bog.

IN CONCLUSION

Although we have now covered the basic patterns for fishing walleyes in shallow reservoirs, always be willing to roll with the punches. Successful fishing is a percentage game. Consider all the options and then put together a plan of attack. If the obvious options aren't producing the intended percentages, be willing to try something else.

Remember, consistency is the word for Post-summer, lowland and flatland reservoir walleyes. On these impoundments during good weather and bad, limits are the rule—providing you know what you're doing.

Chapter 15

THE TURNOVER PERIOD

"A Time of Turmoil"

During the summer, many walleye lakes stratify into three layers based on temperature and water density. The upper, warmer, oxygenated layer is called the "epilimnion" and the colder, lower layer, often lacking in oxygen, is called the "hypolimnion." In the middle lies an area of rapid temperature change called the "metalimnion," or more commonly named, the "thermocline."

In late summer or early fall, surface waters cool, setting up mixing currents in the warmer, upper layer. The thermocline layer is slowly compacted as the upper layer nears the temperature and density of the thermocline.

Eventually strong winds cause violent currents, rupturing the thermocline and causing the entire water column to take on the same temperature and oxygen levels.

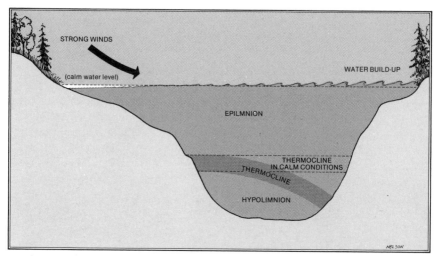

The "Turnover Period" is the short time (a week to two weeks) immediately following actual turnover. This period represents a major change in the walleyes' environment and usually serves to disrupt fish and fishing. Of course, there are bodies of water where turnovers are of little consequence. Rivers are a prime example.

No longer are walleyes restricted to certain depth levels by a summer thermocline or depleted oxygen levels in deep water; nor are they forced under

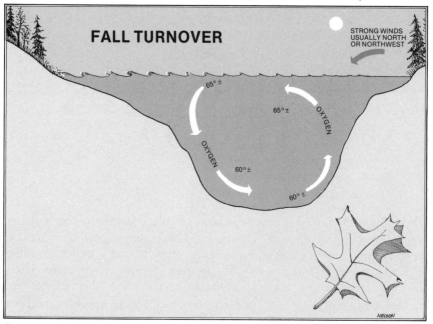

heavy weeds to get out of the sun. The Fall Turnover process mixes the lake's water, breaking up the thermocline and returning oxygen to the depths. And since the sun dips low in the sky in fall, light penetration into the water is minimal. The fish are simply more free to move around.

Deep water structural elements that were "off limits" during summer are now prime feeding zones. Those beautiful deep water points and sunken islands that looked so good but produced poorly in summer might now be dynamite.

Admittedly, the walleyes can be spread out more than in summer because of the many feeding areas now available. You will have to hunt to find them. But they are so much easier to catch once you locate them. You'll find them on easily-located rocky points—feeding—instead of suspended and turned off. Or you'll find them feasting on the weedline instead of tucked away, inactive, under thick weed clumps. And even better, especially in deeper trophy lakes, they'll usually feed all day instead of just during morning and evening.

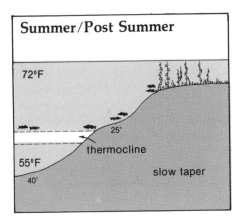 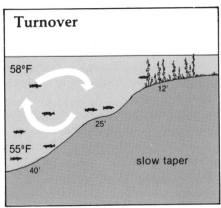

The Changing Season

This illustration shows the tremendous changes in walleye location that occur during the transition from summer to fall in a meso lake. Summer walleyes are usually limited to fairly shallow water (30 feet and shallower) due to the summer thermocline and the oxygen shortage beneath it. Some fish are in the weeds, some on the breaks, others are suspended. In general, the fish prefer a slow tapering area and you can establish a "fish catching" depth that holds pretty consistent throughout the summer.

Then comes the Fall Turnover. The lake is thrown into turmoil and fish scatter like leaves in a strong wind. Fishing is notoriously poor until conditions stabilize.

SHALLOW LAKES

The first lakes to cool down in fall are small, shallow lakes, where most of the water is shallower than 35 feet. They have less water to cool than deep lakes, and their high surface area-to-volume ratio makes them lose heat rapidly once the weather gets colder and the hours of sunlight grow short.

Admittedly, the trophy walleye potential of most small, shallow lakes is limited, although some may have a residual population of big females. Usually, though, they're stocked walleye lakes and few walleyes grow to tremendous size. But they are the first lakes to set up fall fishing patterns, so begin your fall fishing here.

Next to cool are large, shallow lakes. Some have excellent trophy fishing, while others offer basically small to medium-size fish. The size of your catch will depend on what's available in the lake. Check with your local conservation department to find the best lakes in your area.

Regardless of size, shallow lakes have several characteristics in common. On the positive side, they are generally *not* the structural maze deep lakes can be. But, many shallow lakes drive fishermen crazy because they are dishpan-shaped, which can make it hard to narrow down walleye location.

During the day, the best bet is to look for any points, sunken islands or stands of healthy weedgrowth that will concentrate the fish. That's a starting point. But if the lake is a complete dishpan with no obvious areas, or if the weeds have begun to die, you may be faced with a night fishing situation. Then, look for a shoreline area that will draw walleyes into a limited area at night. This gives you a place you can concentrate on rather than running all over the lake.

In most cases, this will be an area with current. A feeder stream entering the lake is usually the best spot. While there are other potential areas, like the mouths of bays, bridge pilings, rocky points, etc., no other spot offers the clear-cut advantages offered by current areas. Current attracts forage, and thereby funnels big walleyes into a small area. Your chances of making fish contact are surprisingly high, even on lakes with only a fair walleye population.

The basic premise of this strategy is, once again, to avoid the Turnover by *finding water that doesn't undergo this phenomenon,* or else fishing waters that either haven't experienced the turnover yet or are recovered from it.

In reservoirs, this means moving into the river sections containing moving water. In most such areas, the current flow is sufficient to cause enough of a mixing effect that the summer conditions (warm water near surface, cooler below) never sets up.

Moving from lakes to rivers, or just changing lakes still works the same for locating walleyes. Find water that isn't being affected by the Turnover Period.

Chapter 16

THE COLD-WATER PERIOD

"A Time of Tranquility"

This entire cycle should be viewed in four stages—the transition, early, mid and late cold water intervals. This is a time of gradual slowing down of the entire ecosystem. It is a preparation for winter and the rigors of the upcoming spring spawn. The big females' eggs will already be fairly well developed. The walleyes will be feeding heavily and this is an excellent fishing period. The key factor is finding the location of available food. Fish activity is medium to active.

The Cold-Water Period is also one of the best trophy fishing periods of the year. Let's look at a special river situation that's great for big walleyes.

Adult river stretches usually have a gradient (their slope or "drop") of about two-to-three feet per mile—not fast-flowing (during normal water levels), nor slow either. The overall depth can be termed shallow; five-to-eight feet is average with intermittent deep and shallow stretches. Most pools which form below rapids are about eight-to-ten feet deep, with occasional isolated washout holes of fifteen-to-twenty-five feet deep occurring in bend areas. These holes, as we shall see, are important in our examination of late fall walleye movement.

Adult stream stretches are found in western Pennsylvania (the Appalachia is one), and in Arkansas (the Buffalo is another). The St. Croix, which borders Minnesota and Wisconsin, has sections of adult stage river, as does the upper reaches of the Mississippi in Minnesota. Parts of Kentucky, Tennessee, Wisconsin, Minnesota, Iowa, Illinois, Montana and New York also boast adult river stages which harbor walleyes.

The *when* part of applying this late fall/early winter pattern is vital. If you're too early (before the walleyes begin to collect in prime spots), you simply won't catch fish—or at least not many of them. The peak for this late fall pattern occurs when the trees have long past turned color. In fact, the leaves, when the time is ripe, will be crumpled, dry and have fallen for the most part. Water temperature is the key to "when." Once it drops to anywhere from the mid-to-low 40°F's, scattered walleye groups will join back together to winter in select areas.

This late fall/early winter pattern starts to emerge at the onset of the Cold Water Period (55°F and below). But don't expect a lot of fish to gather all at once.

With the arrival of fall, waters begin to cool. As they do, more and more scattered walleye groups evacuate the shallower river stretches and assemble in their wintering areas. At first (when the water temperatures are, say, in the low 50°F's), a few fish will arrive. As early winter commences and the water temperature continues to drop to the high, and then low, 40°F's, more and more fish abandon their summer and early fall haunts and head for their wintertime "digs."

Depending upon region, shallow river walleyes "get the bends" sometimes between October and December. In the north, the fish remain assembled in these areas until spring of the next year, when they begin their pre-spawn movements. However, in these cold weather regions, ice cover usually precludes much fishing by late November. Interestingly, some of our best catches have come when there was a small rim of ice along the shore.

HOW TO READ A RIVER IN FALL

During the summer months, walleyes (as well as other fish) spread throughout the length of a river stretch. Small scattered groups of fish seek opportune areas such as: 1) current breaks like rocks or logs, 2) wing dams, 3) log jams, 4) eddies, 5) humps, holes, etc., and 6) rock runs. But come fall, with the subsequent drop in water temperature, walleyes begin abandoning these sites and moving to deeper water.

The natural geography of most rivers is such that holes usually occur in conjection with bends. Fish which utilized the shallow stretch of stream in section B in summer will either move to the bend in section A or section C—or move way upstream to the washout hole under the dam. By the same token, fish which inhabit section D in summer will move to either section C or section E. In all probability, groups of fish which held in the downstream portion of sec-

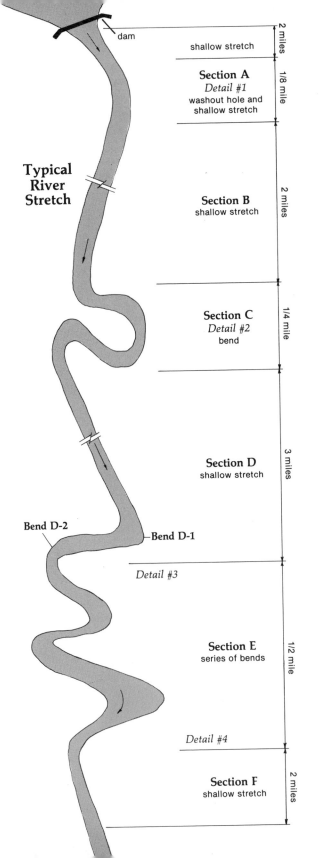

dam

shallow stretch

2 miles

1/8 mile

Section A
Detail #1
washout hole and
shallow stretch

**Typical
River
Stretch**

Section B
shallow stretch

2 miles

Section C
Detail #2
bend

1/4 mile

Section D
shallow stretch

3 miles

Bend D-2

—Bend D-1

Detail #3

Section E
series of bends

1/2 mile

Detail #4

Section F
shallow stretch

2 miles

tion *D* in summer would move to section *E*, while those which utilized the upstream portion of section *D* would move to section *C*.

Summer fish distributed all through a run that is three miles long (section *D*) or two miles long (section *F*) usually collect and concentrate into very confined areas in late fall. Obviously, this situation can make for some fine fishing opportunities.

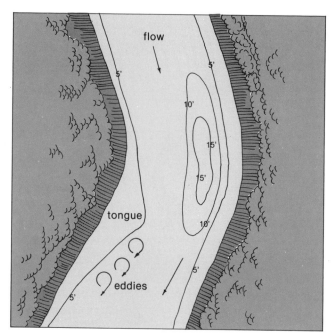

#1

BEND DETAIL #1

Using our good, better, best principle, this particular hole would not be any great shakes. Note that the hole itself is neither large nor deep. It also lacks any prime structural elements. Location-wise also, it is too near the dam area, which is much more inviting to wintering fish. This particular bend also doesn't draw fish from any length of stream stretch. Fish utilizing section *B* in summer would find section *C* and the dam area much more inviting. However, this spot will support a limited amount of fish.

BEND DETAIL #2

This bend, while a particularly fine one, still lacks a few features that would otherwise make it an ultrasuper spot. First off, this saddle-like bend draws fish from five miles of stream—two miles above and three miles below. (Fish appear more likely to move upriver, though, so it would probably pull most of its fish from the adjacent upper mile and the lower 2½ miles or so.) In this respect, it's a lot better than bend #1. The holes, too, are deeper and larger than the one in section *A*. This bend, nonetheless, still lacks one prime ingredient—adjacent flats.

8

187

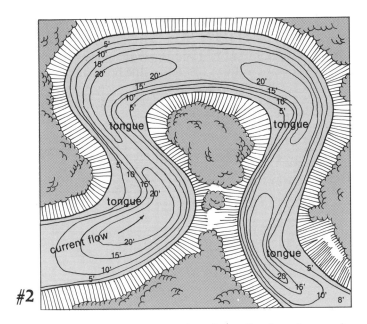

#2

This river section is narrow, quite channelized and cuts through hard materials, so flats do not develop. The "tongue" sections provide some shallow sections and act as current breaks, yet still are not the same kind of fish magnet as flats. All in all, this is a fine bend, and if other nearby bends do not provide better habitat, this bend would attract the lion's share of walleye use.

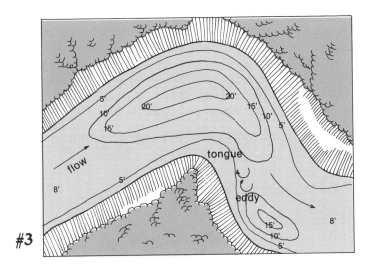

#3

BEND DETAIL #3

This bend is even better than bend #2. Although it doesn't have an adjacent flat, and is about the same size as bend #1, its position in the river makes it a "better" area. First off, it is the first bend with deep water (D-1 and D-2 do not have deep holes) and draws fish from a three-mile stretch of shallow river.

In principle, if you encounter a series of bends which have the proper depth, the one which is first or last in a series is usually better than those in between. The fish appear to drop into the first opportune spot. Only when many fish are present will space limitations force fish to use the holes in between.

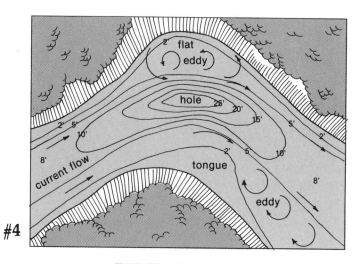

#4

BEND DETAIL #4

Of all the holes depicted here, this one can be termed the best; it has the best combination of all elements. First off, the bend draws from two miles of shallow downstream water and is the first bend downriver fish will encounter. It also has depth in conjunction with flats—not only a flat in the form of a tongue, but also a flat in the small bay. Many current breaks in the form of reverse eddies are formed here and the whole layout is conducive to drawing both predators and prey. This is an ideal situation for walleyes to winter in.

The more structural elements combined in an area, the more fish it will generally draw and hold. If you find a downstream river hole with characteristics like these, make sure you check it out in fall.

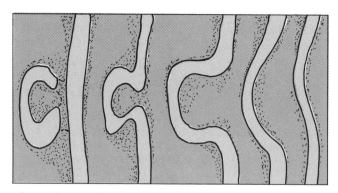

The natural meandering of a river first forms gentle bends, but as the river continues to erode the banks, bends become more and more pronounced until they finally pinch themselves off. When this occurs, the river runs a straight course once again and isolated "oxbow" lakes are formed.

Probable Fish Position by Attitude

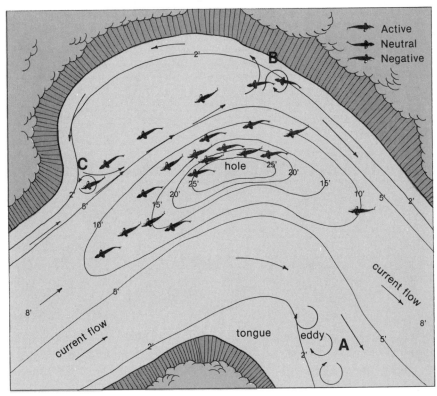

Fish position gives you a pretty good indication of their attitude, and consequently how you should go about fishing them. Using Bend #4 as an example, we find that active fish are often on the shallow flat. The walleyes are not concentrated, so your casts can be less precise. Yet since they are responsive, you can fish a little faster. You will, however, be forced to spread your casts over larger stretches of water.

On the other hand, when the fish are in a neutral mood—not really feeding, but still ready to strike if the lure comes close enough—they will be more concentrated. They will also tend to be at the exact top edge of the hole, rather than spread out on the flat or down the sides of the hole. The fish will be more concentrated than when they were active, and that's good. But the "not so good" part is that you have to be a lot more precise in terms of speed and direction of retrieve than you were when the fish were active.

The third mood the fish display is a negative one. This is when the walleyes are off feed and very slow to respond. When fish are in this mood, they usually move down the sides of the hole to deeper water. While they will be concentrated in a specific area, they are also more difficult to trigger into striking. So, when the fish are in this position, you not only have to lay your lure right where they are sitting (they won't move to grab an offering), but you must also work the lure at just the right speed and action to elicit a strike. You'll also have to make many more casts in a spot before a fish decides to respond than you did when fish were in other, more responsive moods.

It is interesting to note that few fish use the inside bend portion of the bend at this time of the year, despite that enticing-looking back eddy (Area A).

The fish commonly (at certain times of the day) move onto the flat when active, sit at the edge when in a neutral mood and move to the base of the hole when they're "off." They usually leave the hole periodically in morning, feed on that flat at midday and toward evening, and will be either on the edge of the hole or down into it during the late morning and early afternoon hours. Since this is a fairly confined area, first look for fish on the flat. If they aren't there, look for them on the edge. And if they're not there, try the deep hole. It's not a difficult pattern to work.

Spooking can be a factor, and if you pull too many fish out of an area, or make too much commotion, they may move within the general area. *For example, you could be taking fish from eddy B; but spook them, and they could move to eddy C, or to a number of other positions on the flat. By all means, try moving around a bit if the action slows!*

Boat Position

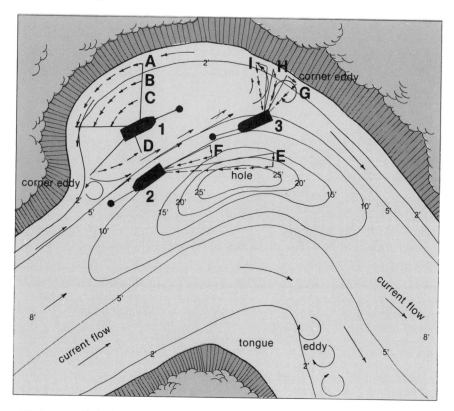

We have trolled, drifted and anchored bends in fall; without question, anchoring is the way to go. In many cases you will direct your casts toward current breaks—those "edges" where calm water meets current—and they're most easily worked from an anchored position.

Make no mistake about it, it takes a number of casts to determine how your lure will "track" (move) in current. This is important, because fish often sit on a knife-edged current break, and if the lure is too far away and tumbled by fast current, they won't move far enough to grab it. But if the lure walks right into position, you'll probably trigger a strike.

In order to fish various areas, you probably need to anchor in a number of different positions. Boat position #1 shows one way to work the flat. Note that a number of sweep retrieves A, B and C are made in the reverse current. This "clears" a portion of the flat. From an anchored position like this, you can also fish the current break on the edge of the river channel itself (cast D). However, you must work to keep your casts within the flow of the reverse current, and not out into the main flow where the jig (and your line) would be swept downstream, instead of in the clockwise direction shown here.

In order to completely fish the flat, simply move and anchor. Each time, cast and retrieve with the sweep of the current flow until you cover the entire area.

If the fish are concentrated on the top rim, in the hole or down into it, move to boat position #2. Use a slightly heavier jig (a 1/4, 3/8 or possibly even a 1/2 ounce size). Because of the flow patterns, you would be forced to cast "down-current" and retrieve "up-current" (casts E and F) at a slight angle. Match your jig size to the force of flow; select a jig that will stay down against the force of the current.

Corner eddies have to be approached in a still different manner. Here the water splits in two directions, and a dead spot forms in between. Therefore, casts have to be directed: 1) for reverse flow (cast G), 2) in the dead water area (cast H), or 3) in a downstream direction (cast I). A number of casts have to be made to determine how the lure will "track." Walleyes can pile into pockets like this at times, using one side or the other, or even the slack water. Thus corner eddies must always be fully checked.

PRESENTATION

Actually, catching late fall walleyes in the bends is quite uncomplicated; well, almost! You do have to take current flow into consideration, and that takes a little presence of mind. First off, remember that water levels are usually at a sustained, low level at this time, so you're not confronted with roaring water. However, current is still present, and fish do make use of current breaks and orient themselves accordingly. Also, you'll most likely be fishing with jigs. While not an immense problem, jigs do hang up and you'll have to learn when and where a jig will roll, tumble or move in current—or when it won't.

As already stated, jigs are the way to go. Of all the various kinds of lures and baits we have tried, day in and day out, jigs were most productive. We have used live bait rigs and caught fish; we have used crankbaits and balsa plugs and caught fish; we have even caught some on spinners. Yet in no case did we catch as many walleyes as we did with jigs—or rather jigs sweetened with minnows.

When choosing and working lures, remember that you are fishing cold water and thus dealing with fish that will not chase very far or exert themselves too much to catch prey. In the low 40°F's, you can expect to be dealing with slow-moving, slow-reacting fish—so *slow* is the key presentation speed. The only lure that allows you to hop a bait, let it lay motionless and then perhaps drag it a bit is a jig.

Our first choice of minnow type is a chub, yet these are not always available since many bait shops close at this time of year; this is an iterim time between late fall fishing and ice fishing, and the vast majority of anglers have simply "hung it up."

Our second choice is a fathead minnow (the bigger ones). If need be, we would even resort to small suckers if nothing else was available. We have tried nightcrawlers and leeches and they didn't work that well. We also used small water dogs and did great until the water got too cold. But the smaller size water dog that works well is also hard to come by this time of year. The same can be said about small frogs; they work, but are very hard to come by. But no matter—minnows like chubs or fatheads are more than sufficient.

We also use plain jigs dressed with twister tails if we are into the fish heavy, and they appear active enough that they don't seem to have any special preference for "meat." We do this by testing; if we are into a lot of fish and they are "snapping" on the minnows, we start using plastic-bodied jigs. If they work as well as a jig and minnow, stick with the plastic. Let's face it, it's easier than messing with minnows. If you can get away with a jig all by itself, by all means do so!

Rod, reel and line-wise, keep one thing in mind—cold weather! On some days, rod guides will freeze up, mono line gets stiff and springy, and even reels (due to thicker grease) work harder. We recommend you use any *good* graphite or boron rod in the 5'6" to 6' length in a fast or moderate action. Hits can be light, and sensitive rods will help you detect them quicker.

Once anchored in place and casting, "feel" will be of paramount importance. A number of things will be working against you. First off, the weather is cold and your hands will not be able to easily sense a light fish "pick-up" so common to the season. Dipping your hands in a minnow bucket doesn't help too much either! When you compound this with current flow putting a bow in your line, it makes concentration imperative.

Put forth the effort to properly position yourself when anchoring. You might anchor but find that you're just too far from or too close to the spot you want to fish. Going through the trouble of moving pays big dividends.

How long do you stay in an area if you don't catch a fish, or if they quit biting? Keep in mind that these fish *will not* vacate the hole, and they only have three possible positions: 1) up on the flats, 2) on the rim of the hole, or 3) down deep in the hole.

The fish might spend some time up on the flat—then move to a corner eddy—then move to the rim of the drop-off—or move down into the hole itself. Then, too, certain groups of fish might be active and up shallow, but at the same time less active fish could be down in the hole. The rule of thumb here is, if you don't catch fish or they stop biting for about 15 minutes, and changing lures or re-anchoring won't trigger them, simply move to another hole. Remember, you can spook fish after catching quite a few of them. Come back in an hour or two and you'll probably catch some more.

LAKES

Natural Lakes provide a combination of approaches during the Cold-Water Period. Presentation varies from shallow to deep water. First, shore casting.

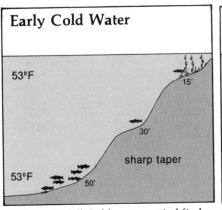

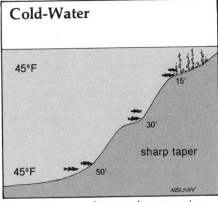

The early fall Cold-water period finds walleyes setting up shop on sharp tapering areas—the opposite of summer. Notice that early fall walleye activity (immediately after the Turnover) seems to be concentrated in deep water, rather than scattered up and down. Pay careful attention to the area where a drop-off bottoms out into the lake's basin.

Once the Cold-water period has become firmly established, you'll find groups of walleyes spread out at different depth levels up and down a sharp tapering area. Perhaps a bit tough to pin down, but they're willing to bite once you find them!

Typical Shallow Walleye Lake
Limited Structural Features

Shallow walleye lakes are often difficult to fish during the day because of the lack of structural elements to concentrate the fish. If you can find a prominent point, hump or weedbed, chances are you can catch walleyes during the day using a standard approach—live bait rigs, jigs, etc. But if the lake is basically a shallow dishpan with no distinct features, you're usually better off fishing at night in a spot that

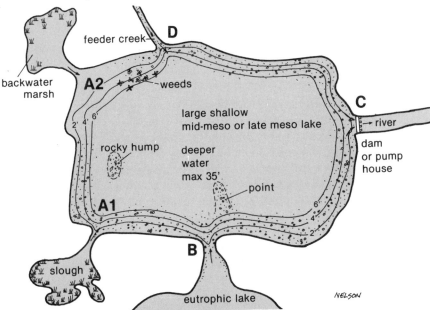

concentrates the fish in a limited area along the shoreline.

In most cases, this will be a current area. It draws both walleyes and baitfish to a small spot where you can get at them effectively. It may not be a classic example of walleye behavior, but on these lakes it's usually an overlooked pattern for catching walleyes—particularly big ones. The big fish will hang somewhere outside these areas in deeper water during the day, and then move right up into the current to feed at night.

All current areas do not have the same potential. It is best if they have classic hard bottoms. Pure sand will produce only if you can verify that there's plenty of forage moving through the area. Of course, as the season progresses and everything else freezes over, almost any open, flowing spot can become a hot spot. The key once again would be the presence of prey.

Through experience, these current areas have been found to draw prey. They are illustrated on the map.

Areas A are shallow back-water areas connected to the main lake. Prey move in and out during the night and big hungry walleyes will be there to ambush them.

Area B is where current flows from one lake to another. It's particularly good where a more fertile, food-rich eutrophic lake is connected to a meso lake. As the season progresses, prey and predator alike usually congregate on the current flow side.

Area C is an example of a lake outlet flowing over a dam and into a river. Fish the river if it's large enough to hold numbers of fish, or the area above the dam. These areas can also be related to a city pumping station or power house. Such areas can really be dynamite later in the season when everything else locks up.

Area D is a small or large feeder creek with good water flow. Although creek mouths entering onto huge flats do produce at times, it is best if all of these current areas drop-off into, or have immediate access to, deeper water. Remember that a drop-off area is a comparative thing. In a shallow lake deeper water might be 6-8 feet. You don't have to reach the deeper water with your casts, but it should be available for the fish to use during the day.

On the map, Area A-1 is superior to A-2 because there is deeper water nearby. It also seems to be better if there's weed remnants in shore casting current areas; they seem to help hold forage.

In some parts of the country you'll know the good areas because they will be fished. However, in most areas no one shorecasts so you'll have to do a bit of experimenting. If you find a decent area and no one's fishing it—who knows what could happen! □

SHORE CASTING THE SHALLOWS

Shore casting has great potential for taking big walleyes. It's quite simple and cheap, and providing that you pick a decent spot, there's very few things you can do wrong. Yet, aside from a few pockets of popularity in northern Iowa, southern Minnesota and eastern South Dakota, few walleye anglers take advantage of this dynamite presentation technique.

This is a shallow water technique and it's almost always necessary to practice it at night. Yes, it can be cold and lonely, so dress warm and perhaps take a friend along. You must have a pair of good insulated waders as well as a hooded, waterproof coat to wear over your clothing and waders. If you have a couple of decent spots in mind, you'd best fish the one which allows you the comfort of having the wind at your back.

Gloves, a snowmobile suit, a stocking hat and so on are all necessary as it gets colder. A long handled net with a hoop diameter of 24 inches should be used to land big fish. It will also double as a wading staff. Attach the net to yourself with a cord and a big snap-swivel tied on the end. Include in this menagerie a small lure box, a flashlight and a rope stringer.

Use the big, size 13 Rapala or the 5 inch Bang-O-Lure as these plugs are easier for fish to see and strike at night. Another lure is a Powrr head jig, usually 3/8 ounce with a heavy hook, dressed with a large 4 inch Sassy Shad. The barbed 1/4 ounce jigs couple nicely with the 4 inch Sassy Shad.

As we've said, if there's no current areas to attract walleyes, location is a bit tougher. Try the shore casting techniques on points, bridge pilings or at the mouths of bays, but if it doesn't pan out, you'll be forced to get out and cover some water.

TROLLING THE SHALLOWS

The best way to effectively work large expanses of shallow water is with stealth, a long line and an electric trolling motor. Pitch a long, thin Rapala, Bang-O-Lure or Rebel 30-40 yards out behind the boat and start slowly trolling across the shallows. Or try a spinner like a Panther Martin, Vibrax or Mepps. Just get out there, troll back and forth and keep checking. It may take a while, but eventually you'll find the fish. Once a general area has been nailed down, you can return to a casting approach if you prefer. Choose whichever suits the conditions. It's not difficult—it just takes time. And remember, both shore casting and trolling the shallows will be most effective at night or just at daybreak and dusk.

DEEP LAKES

A week or two after shallow lakes have cooled down, deep lakes (those with lots of water over 35 or 40 feet deep) will also cool enough to enter their fall Cold Water Period. Again, it's the smaller deep lakes (under 1,000 acres) that cool first.

The attractive part of fishing small, deep lakes is that they are usually quite easy to fish. If there are good current areas, fish shallow at night. If not, fish deep during the day. Because these lakes are small there are usually a limited number of potential deep water congregation areas. Or, if you can't fish during the day and there are no clear-cut shore casting spots, consider using alternate night techniques. Try long-line trolling or anchoring and casting likely areas at night.

The last lakes to cool are large, deep bodies of water. Generally speaking, you can start fishing these large, deep lakes seriously anytime after the Turnover; but they usually do not really turn on for a good month after the small, shallow lakes start popping fish, or at least 2-3 weeks after large, shallow lakes do.

It's in these big, early meso or mid-meso classic walleye waters that you'll find some *big*, hawg-jawed mamas swimming. But, during the day, the fish can be a bit tough to locate because of the large number of potential fishing areas. There always seems to be a multitude of good looking deep water structural elements. If you're tough, you can fish potentially prime spots 24 hours a day! In short, you'll have all sorts of high percentage choices—maybe too many!

The secret to this type of fishing is the same as with shore casting: You must identify a spot or spots on a lake in which most of the fish will be concentrated. In this case, many of the main groups of large fish will be located near the deepest drop-offs, adjacent to the most massive (and probably the deepest) area of the lake. Normally speaking, these areas will also be connected to a shoreline area with a good sized flat. Pick up any lake map and you can usually point out the potential areas in about 5 minutes.

Once again, find the deepest area of the lake or the part of the lake which has the most massive area of really deep water. In large lakes there could be a number of such areas. Look for the fastest breaking spots going into the lake's basin. If these areas are rock or any mixture of rock, gravel or clay, and there's an extensive shallow flat adjacent to this deep area, that's the spot.

Sunken islands with areas fitting the previous billing look great, and they can be just that if they have their *own large shallow flat* on top, or if they are located near a substantial shallow shoreline flat. Small, isolated, deep sunken islands look like potential walleye havens, but in most cases they are a waste of your time because they just can't hold enough forage. Instead, pick an area where your odds are better.

Typical Deep Walleye Lake

In the daytime, look for the fastest breaking spots which have quick access to the shallows yet break into the lake's deepest water. The shallows should consist of a good sized flat.

As you first look at the map, Area B through I *appear to be potential spots. With a bit more time we'd rule out* Area G *because it's too isolated from the very deep area of the lake and the flat on top is too small.* Area I *could hold some fish, but it has low potential because it's not immediately adjacent to the largest area of deep water.* Area F *has the wrong bottom content.*

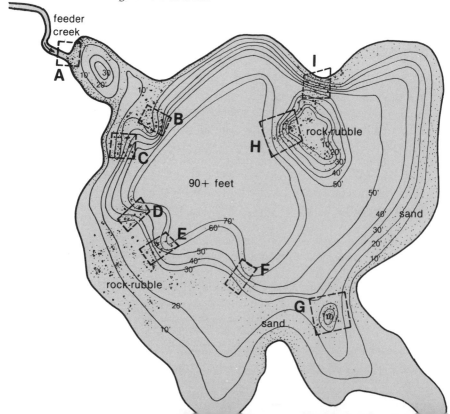

That leaves B, C, D, E and H. *All of these could hold fish, but to narrow things down more we'd eliminate* Areas D and E. *On closer inspection, these areas have more of a gradual slope. Instead of plunging directly into deep water, they break in a sloping stair-step fashion.*

Areas B, C, *and* H *are the best bets. They all plunge from the first drop all the way to deep water and have a hard, rocky bottom.*

These assumptions are made by looking at the map. Of course, you'll have to actually fish them to see if they produce. And further exploration may turn up other good spots.

The prime night spot would be A *if there's current. If not, the shallows adjacent to* B *or* C *and even* H *could hold fish.*

PRESENTATIONS FOR DEEP LAKES

Presentation methods necessary to take fish on deep lakes are divided into two categories: those used in shallow water night fishing, or those used to fish deep during the day. If you fish deep during the day, you'll also have two major choices: You can fish with a live bait rig and a large minnow (red tail chub, creek chub, blue chub or shiner), or you can fish with a jig and minnow. With the live bait rig you'll have to choose a sinker weight that will keep your bait down and allow you to fish almost vertically. In most cases that will be 1/2 ounce from about 25-40 feet down and 3/4 ounce when you fish deeper. Snell lengths should be moderate, say 24-30 inches, and should be made of 8 or 10 pound test line.

Don't be afraid to use big minnows in fall. The average baitfish has grown to a large size this late in the year, and the walleyes are looking for an easy meal. A healthy 4, 5 or 6 inch chub or shiner, hooked lightly up through the lips, is right up their alley. They'll eagerly smack it. Make sure you give them time to swallow that big minnow, though. Don't be overanxious! A 10 pound walleye is well worth a couple of minutes wait.

Big minnows are a big fish bait because they'll tell you if there's fish down there. Pull one near a big walleye and the minnow will go nuts. He'll be down there jumping and struggling—he's no dummy. That's a mouthful of teeth he's staring into. When you suddenly feel him telegraphing this kind of motion up the line, slow down. Work and re-work the area. There are big fish nearby.

Fishing a leadhead jig tipped with a small minnow is also a favored method, because when ol' hawg jaws grabs it you can stick'em right now—there's no waiting around or feeding line. If you've ever fished 40-60 feet deep with a live bait rig, you know that setting the hook after you've let a fish run is no sure thing. You have to be extra careful to minimize the slack when you're trying to set the hook this deep.

In many cases you can fish a 1/2 ounce jig all the way down to 55 feet. However, if you're going to consistently fish very, very deep, a 5/8 or even a 3/4 ounce jig will also be necessary. You must fish with a sturdy rod to be able to set the hook at these depths.

Whether you're fishing the live bait rig or the leadhead jig, you should present these baits by backtrolling the area. By fishing vertically, you'll have less trouble keeping your lures on the bottom and also setting the hook. Snake trolling up and down a breakline is a good idea until you've established the level a group of fish are holding at. Once found, work them over until they spook.

Let's say you've caught several walleyes at 30 feet and suddenly they're gone. Should you leave the area? No. Continue working the area at a different depth. You may encounter another group at 40 or 50 feet, or even up at 15 feet on the weedline. You never know for sure until you cover the area. That's why the zig-zag snake trolling approach is best. You'll cover a variety of depth ranges on a single pass (25-35, 35-45, and so on), and can get on a productive depth more quickly.

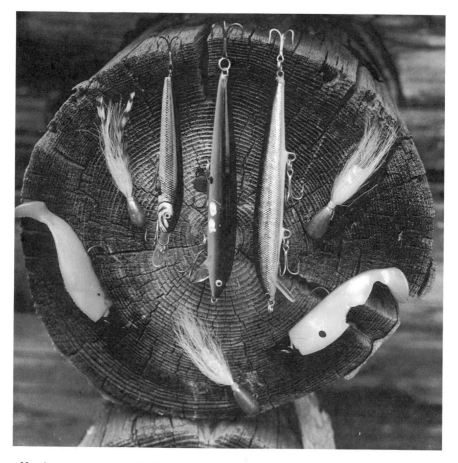

Here's an assortment of walleye lures that'll get you fish from top to bottom. The bucktail jigs are "Rock-a-Roo's," a popular jig in northwest Iowa. Shown are 1/4, 3/8 and 1/2 oz. models. A handful of jigs in this size range lets you cover all depths effectively.

The plastic baits in the bottom corners are Mr. Twister Sassy Shads teamed with a Pow-rr head jighead. They're great for shorecasting or pitching through weeds. Note that the one at the bottom right has a bite out of it. No, old leviathan didn't do that! Taking a small chunk out of these baits makes the tail wiggle more. It's a good trick to remember.

The three imitation minnow lures in the center are an injected foam Lindy Bait-

fish, a Balsa Rapala and a Bang-O-Lure. They're all excellent shorecasting lures. Note that Doug has drilled several holes in the Rapala, inserted split shots, and glued it back up again. That's one of his neutrally buoyant "doctored" Rapalas that's so deadly for shorecasting walleyes.

SHALLOW PRESENTATIONS FOR DEEP LAKES

Although deep water daytime angling is the standard way to approach these kinds of lakes in late fall, you can still catch some fish in the shallows at night. If there are obvious concentration points (like a river mouth), use the shore casting technique we described earlier. If not, here's a few tactics that will allow you to cover a lot of water quickly and efficiently.

First of all, confine your shallow fishing to bars adjacent to the deep water areas we have just talked about. Make no mistake, walleyes will be prowling these shallow bars at night, but the trouble is that they often scatter widely in a search for forage. The fish won't be as confined as when shore casting a current spot, or fishing a deep breakline during the day. However, you can still score.

Trolling a floating plug like a Rebel, Rapala or Hellcat on a long line behind the boat is a good bet. This is effective over very shallow rocks or across the tops of weedbeds. You can also use a three-way swivel or use a slip sinker ahead of a swivel and a 4 foot snell. Walleyes are accustomed to big forage by this time of the year, and indeed prefer it, so you should use a big plug. Troll the plug a foot off the bottom and about 60-100 feet in back of the boat. By using this method you can thoroughly cover an area and hopefully make contact with some nice fish.

If you can find a shallow rock bar next to a good deep water area, you can bet that it's going to get fish use at times. In this case, anchor and cast this shallow area at night with plugs or leadhead jigs.

Long Line Trolling Rigs

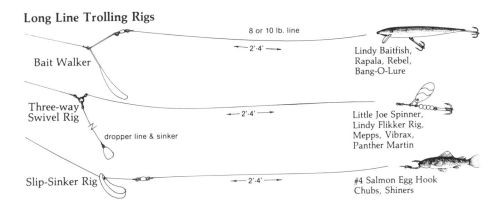

8 or 10 lb. line

Bait Walker

— 2'-4' —

Lindy Baitfish, Rapala, Rebel, Bang-O-Lure

Three-way Swivel Rig

dropper line & sinker

— 2'-4' —

Little Joe Spinner, Lindy Flikker Rig, Mepps, Vibrax, Panther Martin

Slip-Sinker Rig

— 2'-4' —

#4 Salmon Egg Hook Chubs, Shiners

CONCLUSION

If you are completely unfamiliar with these techniques, it might take you a season or two of experimentation. But after that, you'll have a lifetime to enjoy your ability to catch big eye-poppin' walleyes.

Early mesotrophic lakes seem to consistently hold the largest walleyes, but other lakes can also produce some hawgs. Any deeper lake with half a reputation for some larger fish might be considered, as long as you can identify an obvious area which the fish will use. And, be ready for a surprise. Quite often you'll catch big northern pike mixed right in with the larger walleyes. Nothing wrong with that!

Although there are other methods for taking monster fall walleyes, those covered here have proven to be the most consistent. One other thought: These methods incorporate everything you need to know to begin taking walleyes in both deep and shallow lakes. If you learn these techniques, there's no reason you cannot take a trophy walleye this fall. . .and maybe a bunch!

Presentation By Lake Types After Turnover

Lake	Start Fishing*	Main Presentations	Alternate Presentation
Small Shallow	1st	Shore Cast Current (N)** Live Bait Rig or Jig on Rock Piles, Points (D) and Weedlines	Shore Cast Rock-Rubble Points (N) Long Line Shallows (N)
Large Shallow	2nd (1-2 wks. later)	Shore Cast Current (N) Live Bait Rig or Jig on Rock Piles, Points (D) and Weedlines	Shore Cast Rock-Rubble Points (N) Long Line Shallows (N)
Small Deep	3rd (1½-2½ wks. later)	Shore Cast Current (N) Live Bait Rig or Jig (D) in Deep Water	Shore Cast Rock-Rubble Points (N) Long Line Shallows (N)
Large Deep	4th (3-4 wks. later)	Shore Cast Current (N) Live Bait Rig or Jig (D) in Deep Water	Shore Cast Rock-Rubble Points (N) Long Line Shallows (N)

*Typically, the Turnover lasts from a week to 10 days. The first lakes to stabilize are small, shallow lakes. Begin your fishing and jump to the large trophy lakes as conditions stabilize.

**(N) = Night fishing - 1st ½ hr. before sunset until 1st ½ hr. after sunrise.

(D) = Daytime fishing.

Chapter 17
COLD/FROZEN WATER

Most bodies of water which contain reproducing populations of walleyes experience ice cover at some time during the year. Depending upon latitude, the Frozen Water Period could last six months, a few days—or not at all.

Rivers may freeze over completely, but most normally have some ice-free sections. These open sections usually occur under dams or near warm water discharges. On some reservoirs, ice cover may briefly occur in coves and wind-protected bays, while the main lake never ices up. The point is, the Frozen Water Period occurs when a body of water is at its coldest range for an extended period.

During this time span, the entire ecosystem of a lake, river or reservoir slows. Yet walleye feeding does take place. Indeed, female fish must feed regularly to maintain their eggs and bodies. On some bodies of water, the biggest walleyes of the year are taken ice fishing.

RIVERS

As summer turns to fall, the water level in rivers typically drops way, way down. By late fall, it's merely a trickle compared to the spring torrent. Under these conditions, walleyes begin moving upstream, eventually winding up in the deeper pool areas immediately below power dams. By early winter, massive concentrations of fish are not only possible—they're commonplace. And, in addition to being bunched up and easily located, they're easy to catch as well.

These massive concentrations of fish continue building all winter long. Walleyes, anticipating the distant spawning ordeal, feed and build up strength for the struggle to come. They'll stay put in one general area, remain fairly aggressive, and provide a great resource to the angler who knows how to take advantage of it.

DAM BASICS

Virtually all of the major rivers in the United States have been dammed. Whether built for flood control, power, recreation, irrigation or navigation, there are approximately 50,000 dams spread across the country. And many of them have been constructed on top-notch walleye waters.

Cross-Section of Typical Dam Area

Here's a look at a typical dam area under the two extremes of water level. During the spring melt, the tremendous amount of water cascading through the dam digs out a deep washout hole. At low water level, however, there's usually very little water crossing the dam. Winter usually sees minimum water flow, and thus a virtual lack of current below the dam. Walleyes are free to roam most of the area.

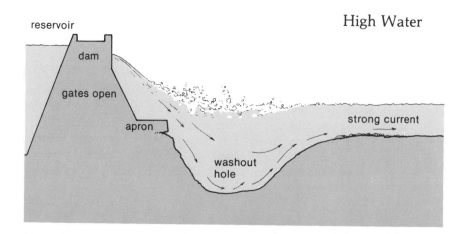

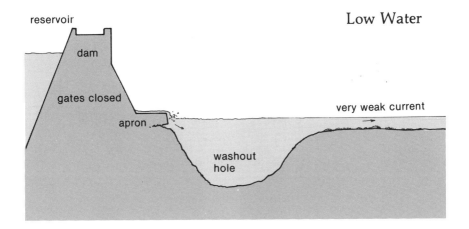

reservoir   Low Water

dam

gates closed   very weak current

apron

washout
hole

Dams not only maintain desired water levels; they regulate the flow as well. At times, a mere trickle of water escapes over, under or through them. Others are a miniature Niagara Falls, with millions of tons of pounding water pouring across the dams that gouge out deep holes directly beneath. Called washout holes, they might be 30, 40, 50 or more feet in depth. Just downstream from them, the river bottom escapes the pounding force of the water's plunge and returns to a normal, shallower depth.

The dam area, then, includes the face of the dam itself, the deep washout hole, and the immediately adjacent downstream water that retains the basic characteristics of the normal river. It's somewhere within this short stretch that our target, the walleye, will be found.

RULES OF THUMB

Although current will seldom be overpowering at this time of year (winter), it is still an extremely important element. The water will be very cold (32°F—33°F), so the walleyes will be sluggish and physically unable to remain in current for any length of time. As a result, they stay in the quiet water out of the main flow.

Depth is your next locational concern. River walleyes are generally found quite shallow in comparison to their lake counterparts. Even though there's a 40 foot hole available, chances are they won't be found in its depths. In fact, the *12 to 20 foot* depth range is consistently the most productive depth in the dam area on most good walleye rivers.

The third consideration is the type of area that attracts walleyes, such as drop-offs or bottom content. It's an easy one to get fooled on. Most folks have been programmed to think "structure" in their lake fishing, but on a river, that's simply not the case. It may be important, or it may not mean a darn thing. Here's the way to decide.

During high water, the crushing force of the current blows the fish out of the

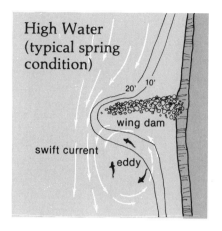 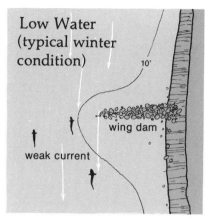

Here's a clear example of how water level and current flow affects fish position in rivers. Under high water conditions, walleyes are forced to move in close to and behind objects, like wing dams, in order to evade the roaring current. But with low water conditions, walleyes are much more free to move about. The most favorable location might even be completely out and away from the wing dam. The walleyes could be a long distance from any major change in depth—as long as there's no current to push them around.

open, exposed areas in the center of the river. Fishing the calm areas formed behind objects is the key to catching fish in high water conditions.

That's high water. The walleyes might be hiding behind those areas, but when the water level is down and there's little current flow, the walleyes are *much more free to roam.*

Think of it this way. The walleyes' existence revolves around remaining in a non-current area at an attractive depth. When the water level is low, perhaps the middle of the channel is fine!

If you've been over-programmed on the "structure" concept, it's probably a hard thought to accept. Not fishing next to an object or depth change seems to go against the rules. But, in rivers, *current* is the rule.

FISHING THE DAM AREA

Take a look at the composite drawing of a typical dam located on one of the Midwest's major river systems. It could be on the Wisconsin, Mississippi, Missouri, or Tennessee Rivers. The water level is low, with little current flow. It is a typical winter condition.

You've got all the ingredients: a dam, washout hole, lock, power house, wing dams and a dredged channel in the center of the river. The channel is dredged by the Corps of Engineers to allow barge traffic. The white buoys mark the right side of the channel, the black buoys the left (as you face upstream).

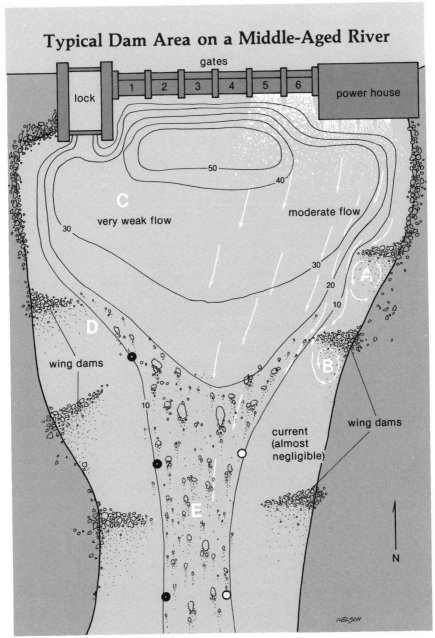

Typical Dam Area on a Middle-Aged River

gates

lock

1 2 3 4 5 6

power house

50

40

C

very weak flow

moderate flow

30

30

20

A

10

D

wing dams

B

10

current
(almost
negligible)

wing dams

E

N

NELSON

Notice that there's just a trickle of water escaping through the dam. Gates 1-4 are closed, as is the lock. Gates 5 and 6, and the power house, are passing a little bit of water—enough to set up a slight current and form a few eddies up near the dam.

There are two small eddies formed behind the wing dams on the east side of the river (A and B). These rocky, man-made objects divert the flow back toward the center of the river to prevent shoreline erosion. Are they good spots?

Probably not. During high water, they'd make super hiding places. But with low water, they're not. The calm water in them is quite shallow (less than ten feet), and not very expansive. They'd put up a couple of fish, but not much more.

The opposite side of the river, the western shore, is far more attractive to walleyes under these conditions. There's virtually no current present. The huge reverse current at C, caused by the adjacent moving water on the opposite side of the river, is a very mild flow. You can just barely see the circular pattern of a few bubbles on the surface.

In short, the western side of the river is out of the current and is by far the most attractive to walleyes. Their exact position, however, will take a little exploration to pin down. Remember, we're looking for calm or near-calm water at the proper depth. Usually, that is 12-20 feet. Let's start narrowing down our options.

First off, there are a few more wing dams on the west side, but once again they're shallow. They're basically high water spots.

Next, there are calm or nearly calm areas all along gates 1, 2, 3, 4 and in front of the lock entrance itself. Under some conditions, they'll pull in some fish. But they're not very *large* areas and they drop pretty fast into the deep hole. You'll see some scattered walleyes along the edge, but still no major concentrations.

Let's turn our search slightly downstream on the downstream edge of the hole. Here there are larger areas of 10-20 foot water with little current flow. Sure, there's some current, but by the time it's this far down the river it's so dispersed that it's hardly noticeable at the present low water levels.

Wide areas of 10-20 foot water, scattered rocks for hiding places, little current flow—starts to sound pretty good, doesn't it? In fact, it's the single most attractive low water area for numbers of fish. Walleyes could be scattered all through the area from D to E, one here, one there, across the center of the river. . .no real concentrations. There's really little depth change, but so what. The walleyes don't care—neither should you.

EVENING ACTIVITY PERIODS

As the sun dips down in the sky and sunset approaches, you'll often see a sudden increase in walleye feeding activity. The diminished sunlight penetration triggers walleyes into a late afternoon feeding spree. You'll catch scattered fish during the day, then suddenly pop a bunch of them, one after the other. *Don't* leave the river early! Make sure to stay for the prime evening fishing.

Walleyes that were lying in the center of the river during the day often move much shallower at this time. You might find them in four to ten feet of water, right up against the river bank. So next time it gets dark enough that you have to take your sunglasses off, try hitting the shallows. It's definitely prime time for taking those cold weather river walleyes.

PRESENTATION

If you like to fish a jig, you'll love fishing the river. It's hard to envision any presentation that's more suited to river fishing than a jig.

Here's a typical line-up of river jigs. At the upper left is a marabou-bodied jig that features a slow breathing action—even at rest. Continuing across the top row is Knight's Tiny Tube, with its multiple rubber legs. And at the upper right is Gapen's Ugly Bug. It has a ton of rubber legs and a fulcrum-style jighead, designed to hug the bottom in current.

At the left in the second row is Mr. Twister's Shiner Minnow jig. Northland Tackle's Whistler jig (center) sports a tiny propellor that spins in current. And at the far right is the old standby—Lindy's Fuzz-E-Grub. All of the jigs pictured here are great for river fishing.

Most of your winter river fishing can be done with light to medium-sized jigs—1/8, 1/4 or 3/8 ounce. You don't have to fight deep water or heavy springtime current.

The style of jighead doesn't make much difference under low water conditions. It's only when the current is strong enough to tumble the jig that head shape starts to make a difference. Round heads, fulcrum heads, wedge heads, keel heads—they're all fine.

The best river jigs have very little bulk to them. Those with thin hair or small plastic tails have the least water resistance and perform the best in current.

When walleyes are active, they'll hit a plain jig as well as one tipped with a minnow. But the vast majority of the time you'll do much better with a small minnow placed on the back of the jig. Simply hook a 2½ inch fathead minnow up through the head and you've got a dynamite rig.

In cold water, walleyes can be incredibly fussy. Sometimes they'll simply tap the tail of the minnow, instead of striking the jig. Under these conditions, you'll miss virtually every walleye *unless* you add a stinger hook.

Most stingers we've seen are comprised of a small treble hook (#6, #8 or #10) attached to the bend of the jig hook by a short piece of ten pound monofilament line. This works pretty well, except that it's very difficult to tie short. The treble hook winds up too far behind the jig.

A super stinger technique developed by Brant Danielsen of Round Lake, Illinois, involves attaching the stinger to the *eye* of the jig hook. Brant carries pre-tied stingers so he doesn't have to try tying them with cold fingers. Slip it right over the jig eye, pull it tight, and you're all set. The treble winds up right at the minnow's tail, in perfect hooking position. You don't even have to hook the treble into the minnow's tail, unless the walleyes are only hitting the jig on a slow drag. Then, hook the treble into the minnow's tail to avoid snagging the bottom.

Color is always a topic of discussion. Experience shows that brown, yellow, orange and green are perhaps the top color choices for river walleyes. Always carry a selection.

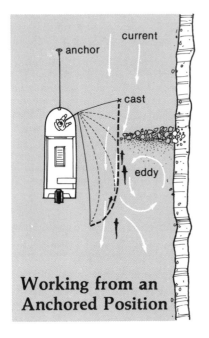

Working from an Anchored Position

Don't be afraid to anchor if you think there's a concentration of fish present. Anchor to the side of and slightly upstream of the suspected holding area. Cast your jig upstream of the fish, let it hit the bottom, and then use a series of lifts and pauses to move the lure downstream. The current will move the jig a few feet each time you lift it.

WORKING THE JIG

Cast it, troll it, drift it—it's impossible to work a jig wrong. Yet there's a time and a place for each approach. Let's look at each.

Say you're working the face of the dam (gates 1-4). A super way to check the area out would be to cast an 1/8 ounce jig up onto the apron and slide it down the face of the dam. Watch for a slight twitch in the line to indicate a strike. Your sense of touch is *crucial*. Cold water walleyes strike so light you've got to pay close attention.

Let's say you want to work the flat from D to E. You can either troll it or drift it. Simply lower the jig down and let out enough line so it can be lifted on and off the bottom, in a slow, six or eight inch motion. This way, you'll remain near the bottom without snagging too often. Walleyes almost always hit as the jig *falls*, not as it rises. So watch carefully for any change in feel. Strikes

Backtrolling the Jig

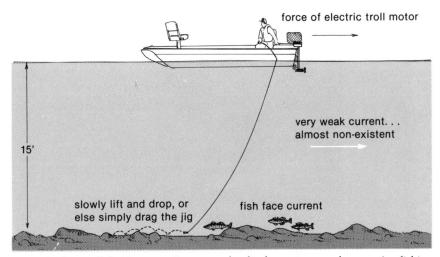

force of electric troll motor

very weak current. . .
almost non-existent

15'

slowly lift and drop, or
else simply drag the jig

fish face current

You're best off having you jig move slowly downstream when you're fishing winter river walleyes. Either drift or use an electric trolling motor to move you very slowly downstream. This gives the fish plenty of opportunity to eyeball the jig. Move too fast—and you'll come up empty.

can be difficult to detect.

Sometimes the walleyes are so lethargic that you can't even bounce the jig up and down. Larry Bollig, Mississippi River expert, catches a ton of walleyes every winter by simply dragging the jig. Bollig prefers to use his electric motor to pull the boat downstream slightly faster than the slow current. Trolling upstream is seldom as productive. *The walleyes face the current*, and by trolling upstream you bring the jig up behind and past them before they have a chance to strike. A simple drag catches them when they don't respond to a retrieve.

If you get on a concentration of fish, don't be afraid to anchor. Select a jig size that is heavy enough to get to the bottom but which will drift downstream a little when you lift it. Cast the jig upstream from the walleyes, let it sink to the bottom, and then lift it momentarily. The current will drift the jig a few feet before it comes to rest. Repeat the procedure. You can walk or "roll" a jig through the area and catch a ton of fish from an anchored position.

SURVIVAL

Keep in mind that it is winter. It can get pretty darn cold out on the river. Dress plenty warm. Bring extra gloves in case one pair gets wet (it always does). A catalytic heater is great for warming frozen fingers and drying out gloves. Bring plenty of coffee or hot chocolate and lots of munchies to nibble on.

Watch the weather. Don't risk going out if there's the chance of a storm.

Winter fishing under dams can be fantastic. Poke around for a few hours. If nothing's happening, don't fight it. Come back another time. Chances are next time it'll be great.

Chapter 18
WEATHER AND WALLEYES

Imagine for a moment, a large, late-stage mesotrophic lake somewhere in northern Wisconsin. Picture two anglers fishing this body of water during the middle of the Summer Peak Calendar Period. After half a day on the water, the pair leave the lake at dusk carrying a beautiful stringer of walleyes, some bonus largemouth bass and an 11 pound northern pike.

These two guys had the time of their lives. The fish were deep in the weeds, just outside of them, and everywhere in between—all feeding like crazy. For a while, both fishermen felt that just maybe the entire fish population was on one massive feeding spree. It was one of those memorable fishing experiences that provide great fuel for those long, late-night, winter bull sessions.

The day had been hot, the sky hazy and the winds calm, just as it had been the previous day—and the day before that. For that matter, the entire week had been a summer ideal: water skiers, humid bed sheets, the sweet scent of sun-drenched evenings and swarms of insects.

Back at the resort, as our heroes are showing off their catch to the "oh's" and "ahh's" of the admiring folk, a few big, dark, anvil-shaped clouds appear on the distant horizon and the wind begins blowing ever-so-slightly. But in the excitement, no one seems to notice. Then, even before the polaroid picture mementoes are dry, the disturbed atmosphere begins growing increasingly humid and a brief lightning flash brightens the far northwestern sky. But the storm is still so far away that the two anglers fail to hear the rumbling thunder. Someone at the resort dock absently mentions that a storm is way out there, but will probably miss the area.

Later that evening, however, as our duo return to their cabin, the wind, which had been blowing gently from the south for the last few days, suddenly shifts and begins gusting from the north, bringing with it a major summer storm. Still later, a rain squall batters the roof of the cabin and briefly disturbs one of our anglers' sleep. By midnight, however, it all ceases. The storm has passed.

The next morning, the two fishermen awaken with great expectations. This time they're certain they've finally discovered the magic formula. Outdoors, there is a mile-high blue sky and the sun is bright as a fireball. Although it's far from cold, the air is fresh—no longer humid or muggy. It feels crisp and dry. In fact, it is *very* dry. Most of the water from last night's storm is already gone. Since the moisture is removed from the atmosphere, light now bombards the earth in increased measure.

Once again on the lake, our pair of fishermen find a steady chop on the water with an occasional whitecap. But, otherwise, they are oblivious to the profound changes that took place overnight. So, they immediately return to the same weedbeds that produced for them yesterday and employ the same baits, techniques and patterns.

But, an hour goes by, and our boys have yet to experience a pickup, peck or pounce. In fact, hours later, these two anglers can't even "buy" a fish. It appears that the fish are totally gone!

The remainder of the day is just as fruitless. So, the pair of once-successful fishermen return to the dock beaten men, just two more victims of angling's arch foe: *drastic weather change!*

What happened to these two fishermen has happened to all of us at one time or another. More time spent on the water will only increase the numbers of experiences like these. What happens? Is it the wind, fronts, pressure or what? What in the world happened to affect the fish in such an adverse manner?

WHY

Much has been written about the impact of things like cold fronts, barometric pressure, magnetic variation, solunar influence, wind and light (radiation) on walleyes' movements and activity. But no one knows for sure what really happens. We know, for example, that all living things are calibrated to a mind-boggling series of related and interrelated events. But so vast is the scope, and so complex the web we are dealing with, that modern science, even with the most sophisticated equipment, can only isolate some of

the more obvious working of the mechanism. However, we know something happens, and that something is somehow transmitted to the fish through some kind of complex rhythm.

While barometric pressure may be a measure of something happening to the environment, exactly *how* that something relates to fish is not known. We also know the passing of a cold front usually affects fish feeding mood and activity patterns. But just *why* it does is still a mystery. We know wind (or lack of it) can have a profound effect on fish mood and activity. Many guesses can be ventured, but definitive answers are lacking. Moon phases also appear to affect fish, but again, exactly *why* is guesswork.

Anyone who has spent a great deal of time on the water can cite certain cases where they caught lots of walleyes under what most folks consider adverse weather circumstances. Many walleyes have been caught on bright sunny, hot, glass-calm waters at mid-afternoon. And, oh yes, good catches of walleyes are taken (occasionally) under even post-cold frontal conditions. And, of course, there are days when all the signs might *appear* perfect, yet the fishing can be slow or even very tough.

To say a thing like barometric pressure turns the fish on or off is also overly simplistic, because many walleyes have been caught at every inch of the mercury movement on the barometer. While barometric pressure can be a contributing cause, it is highly unlikely that it is *the prime cause*. And, really, if you get into it and try to isolate this or that particular item, like cold fronts, humidity, wind velocity, available light, etc., etc., you always find exceptions.

If you start analyzing the many varied aspects of cosmic, global and local weather and its effect on fish, and attempt to isolate definitive causes, you find yourself ultimately trying to crack the code of creation—and that's tough. For we anglers, it would be nice to know exactly *why* this or that happens. But knowing *why* something happens is not absolutely essential to catch fish! A small child may not know exactly why a light goes on when he flips a switch —or be able to explain the intricate mechanism of electricity. But that child quickly learns that if the wall switch is up, a light will probably go on, and if it's flipped down, the light will probably go off. And so it is with the ability to recognize nature's signs and figure with a fair degree of accuracy how fish will probably react.

This ability is called empirical knowledge. It is the product of experience and observation. We are surely interested in scientific *cause* and *effect*, but in the absence of fully understanding the causes, *"signs"* and probable *effects* still allow us to accomplish much the same end: catch fish with more consistency.

NATURE'S SIGNS

In our opinion, there are two natural signs the average angler can consider to consistently catch more walleyes:

1) *The degree of light intensity*

and

2) *The relative stability of a local weather pattern.*

In our experience, the degree of light intensity is the *synchronizer* which determines basic walleye *feeding times*. It also seems to determine how *long* and *how intensely* walleyes will feed. On the other hand, the relative stability of a local weather pattern usually determines *how many* walleyes out of a given number will be inclined to feed when those prime feeding periods arrive.

With these two easy-to-identify signs, you can predict with a fair degree of accuracy if it will be a good, bad or just a so-so fishing day. You can also predict (within rough time frames) when the most walleyes will be active and feeding.

First, let's examine a few things about light. Each plant or animal responds (based on its genetic make-up) to celestial control. Yes, there is a universal timekeeper that affects the behavior of living things. As the earth moves about the sun, and the moon moves about the earth, a cadence is set up that gives terrestrial life seasonal, as well as daily, rhythm. Just as some fish primarily feed during the day, at night or at twilight, plants also have their own biological rhythm; so the phenomenon is observable. This phenomenon of control by light, like everything else involved with this subject, is very complex. But again, we don't have to know all the answers in order to see that light affects fish.

Unlike man-made timepieces, the natural order is not that geared to specific hours, minutes and seconds, but instead, to *changing degrees of light intensity.* Fish do not eat their dinner meal at 6:00 p.m. each evening—regardless of season. Birds and bees begin their day and return to their roosting places or hives at particular times—times governed, in part, by available light, not by set hours on a clock.

Some animals are active all day long; others, for only short periods. Oysters may feed as long as 20 hours per day. But they appear to be least active in early morning and most active in late afternoon. Some species of bats fly about all night; others are active only just after sunset and before dawn.

Walleyes also have their own rhythm based on light. In the temperate zone, where the duration of daylight in summer is much longer than in winter, and vice versa, fish like walleyes (which are primarily, but not exclusively, crepuscular [twilight] feeders) respond by regulating their activities by the length of daylight; they are active or inactive for longer or shorter periods of time, accordingly.

For example, on consecutive dark, overcast days, the walleyes' activity periods tend to be longer in duration than on consecutive, very bright, cloudless days. In both instances, the fish feed. But in one circumstance (the bright day condition), they may be active for a very short period of time at dawn and again at dusk. Under special circumstances, many of the very large fish might activate at twilight and feed slowly through the night, or simply make very short-lived, late-night movements.

Bright light doesn't *halt* feeding activity; however, it usually shortens or intensifies it, or moves it to periods of lesser light, or of darkness. However, even if a number of consecutive days are bright and the water calm, you can encounter mid-summer, mid-afternoon walleye feeding sprees. But like feeding activity at the twilight times, during bright days it is usually short-lived. Again, the brightness of light appears to *accelerate* the feeding activity.

On the other hand, on dark, overcast days the fish appear to be less hurried to feed. You may catch fish all day long, but never experience an intense feeding spree as such. Instead, you catch a few fish here, a few there. The action may be steady, but never intense; even the strikes tend to be less vicious.

OTHER FACTORS

There can be many mitigating factors, but a very obvious one is the availability of prey! The aforementioned bright day, mid-afternoon, mid-summer feeding spree situation was probably triggered by the passing of a mass of baitfish—a surprised arrival of targets of opportunity.

A group of walleyes might be laying down the side of some reef during the bright part of the day, and if the pattern of the previous day's activity were a guide, they would move up on the reef at dusk to forage and feed. But all of a sudden, a mass of bait (say shiners) appears at noon. Many times numbers of neutral attitude fish (but probably not negative fish) will be triggered, activate and feed even if light conditions are not that opportune.

In this case, the pickings are so easy that fish which were inclined to feed later opt to do it now. Interestingly, that night, even if all the conditions were "go," probably less fish than normal would be active up on the reef, since many fish have already fed.

Mitigating factors like these are often the reasons why fishing can be slow, even when all the other signs look perfect. The fish simply took advantage of some surprise opportunity at an off-time. This phenomenon can also explain why, on an otherwise slow day, one spot is productive while all others remain slow. This target of opportunity phenomenon probably also accounts for fish caught during off-beat time periods. The fish are in a neutral attitude, and if a bait is presented correctly, every once in a while a fish will grab it!

Consider another ramification of light. In the far Canadian North, where the length of day can be as long as 20 hours and only 4 hours can be considered dark, walleyes may feed in slight flurries at various intervals all day long—even in summer and even on bright days. However, while the length of day is longer, the intensity of the sunlight (because of the roundness of the earth and the obliqueness of the sun's rays) is markedly less than on waters to the south.

Also, the dark periods arrive much more gradually in these far northern climes than they do further south, so the rapid lowering of the light levels is never as abrupt. Consequently, the feeding times are more spread out. However, even in these far north waters, the overcast or lower-light situations will usually spell more prolonged walleye activity than during the brighter midday times.

While light is the fish's synchronizer, and thus our measuring tool of the timing of probable fish activity, we must, nonetheless, weigh the circumstances in which the walleyes will be affected by light. For example, say a summer group of walleyes are holding on a deep sunken island that tops off at 25 feet. These walleyes may feed during late afternoon. But a group of walleyes in the same lake using a shallow reef that tops off at 5 feet might not become active and feed until dusk. However, if you were to backtrack at dusk to the deep sunken island, where the fish were active earlier, chances are you couldn't buy a strike down deep.

In this case, the trigger of rapidly-decreasing light affected one depth sooner than another. Remember, walleyes are by nature crepuscular (twilight) predators. They have the most advantage, and thus feed most efficiently and effectively, when the light is simultaneously at favorable levels for them and at an unfavorable level for preyfish like perch.

The effect of water on light rays (refraction) creates a difference in when we experience twilight and how it appears to the fish under the water. Basically, sunset occurs about 1/2 hour earlier below the water than it does above the water. Likewise, sunrise occurs 1/2 hour later below water than it does above. When you experience sunset, it has already been dark for 1/2 hour below. On very dark, cloudy days, twilight may occur hours before sundown or after sunrise. Thus, light conditions must always be viewed from the fish's perspective as well as our own.

Wind produces a chop, thus diffusing the light coming into the water and serving to lower the level of light. Therefore, under most conditions, especially during the summer on clear lakes, a chop on the water generally produces more opportune feeding conditions than on calm days. Under conditions like these, just a moderate amount of cloud cover or thick haze can further reduce the light near the walleye's most advantageous level, and the chop will cut down the incidence of light all the more. This produces a condition where walleyes in a neutral attitude (which will become positive a little later in the day) can be coaxed into striking during an off-time. However, if it was very bright and the water calm, they would forego the opportunity to feed until the light condition appeared a little more opportune.

Early in the year, bright sunlight can warm a stream or a shallow bay or a rocky shoreline, starting food chain activity which also draws the predatory walleyes. However, just because they come in shallow during the day does not necessarily mean they are feeding. Most times, actual feeding will occur under lower light conditions. The angle of the sun at this time of the year is not very direct—even at noon. It might not adversely affect them in the shallow water like it does when the sun is more direct in summer.

Again, being twilight activists, walleyes usually feed longer and at a slower pace under low light conditions. Conversely, walleyes tend to feed more intensely, and therefore at shorter intervals, when it is bright out, or when the light is changing rapidly as it does at dusk and dawn.

Low light also allows walleyes to spread out over wider areas, and they'll roam the outside edges of cover or cruise along a few feet off the bottom. Bright light tends to keep fish bunched up, and can push them toward the bottom, tight to cover or cause them to suspend off the edge of a structural element.

Walleyes, at least in clear water, seem to chase baits further during low light conditions. So, light not only acts as a timing device; it also serves to influence the intensity of their feeding behavior, how they move about and how they tend to attack their prey.

One final example of how a rapid change of light can affect walleye activity occurs on very bright days. A patch of cloud cover can pass through an area for say, 45 minutes, trigger a slight feeding spree for 15 minutes or so, and then cease as soon as the cloud cover passes. If the cloud cover did not pass through, in all probability they would not have been activated and fed.

In all these examples, we have established that low light periods, and periods when the light is changing rapidly (dusk, dawn, approaching storms or at night), are times when walleyes may have a distinct vision advantage over their prey, and they will likely be active and feed. Light is the controlling factor that signals to the fish that it is to their advantage to feed. However, light does not necessarily tell them they *must* feed. Low light levels trigger fish already inclined to feed. However, light does not seem to trigger fish which *are not* so inclined to feed. In other words, fish in a positive or neutral feeding mood may be triggered to feed by changing light levels. Rarely, however, will negative fish be completely turned on by such changes.

WEATHER

In order to measure what motivates increasing numbers of fish to feed, we must look to another natural sign: *weather stability*. In short, the more stable the weather has been, the more likely large numbers of fish are to be active and feed. *How many* fish in a given group will be predisposed to feed on any given day appears to be governed by this force. Just as we look to light as a "sign" as to when the *majority* of fish feeding will occur, we look to the local prevailing weather conditions to give us a clue to *how many* fish we can expect to be in an active mood during a given feeding period.

From what we can deduce from observation and experience, it appears that at the point of a drastic weather change, the majority of fish from a given walleye group *switch* from a positive or neutral to primarily a negative mood. Dogs, cats, goldfish—all sorts of creatures—seem to be indicators of an impending earthquake; it's amazing how accurate some of these predictors appear to be. Without doubt, changing weather also affects fish behavior. Why this is so we cannot be sure, but there is little question that animals can sense impending change.

When this change is drastic, you can expect fish like walleyes to respond by slowing down all activity, including feeding. It's no secret that many times large numbers of fish feed very intensely at the end of a long period of stable weather. Those periods just before, or even during the passing of a front, herald a great change. So, we can assume fish sense impending change and feed more vigorously prior to a period of potential slow down.

Regardless of weather conditions, all fish in a given group usually *do not all* feed at the same time. Some fish from a group will be active, others neutral and still others in a negative mood. How many fish of a given group will be in an active, neutral or negative mood can be roughly gauged by how many consecutive stable days of weather there have been.

This means that a walleye feeding movement can occur at dusk, and the fish that do feed can even be aggressive. But it does not necessarily mean that lots of fish *must* feed at that interval. Remember, the more consecutive days the weather is stable, the more likely larger numbers of fish will be inclined to feed—sometime.

By the same token, an overcast day is not always a signal that lots of fish will feed leisurely throughout the day. This sign only means that what fish are already prone to feed will *tend* to feed leisurely. Only if that overcast day was, say, the third or fourth one in a consistent progression of warm stable days could you expect *lots* of fish to be active.

Nor does the light intensity factor by itself mean that just because it's bright out, very few fish will be prone to feed. Again, what fish are inclined to feed will feed in short bursts during the low light periods, or feed more leisurely into the dark of the night. If that bright day was one of a succession of stable weather days, the evening feeding movement could be attended by lots of fish. In fact, these are those days when fishermen all over a good walleye lake will experience good (if short-lived) walleye action at sundown.

Apparently, the number of fish from a given group which are inclined to feed is at its lowest number right after the passing of a front. As the weather stabilizes, the number of fish inclined to feed steadily increases up until the end of the stable weather period, just before the weather changes once again.

So, the first day after a drastic weather change we can expect a very low number of fish to be active and inclined to feed. On the second day, we can expect a slightly larger number to be in a positive feeding attitude; on the third day, still more. And on the fourth day, a still higher number of fish will be responsive to feeding stimuli. In our experience, after the fourth day, if stable conditions persist, fish activity kind of levels out. So if stable weather lasts 5, 6 or 7 days, you can pretty much expect what happened on day 4 to continue.

You'll seldom experience more than 4 days or so of stable weather, however. In fact, in some years, 2 or 3 days of stable weather between changes is more the rule than the exception in the upper portion of the North American continent where most walleye fisheries exist.

You must also consider the severity of a weather change. As a general rule, the more drastic the change, the more fish will switch from a positive/neutral attitude to a negative one. But the less drastic the change, the less fish will become inactive.

For example, let's say the weather has been stable and typified by warm temperatures, moderate southern breezes and a partly cloudy, hazy sky for a couple of days. Then a front switches the wind to the north, clears the sky a little and drops temperatures a few degrees without kicking up the wind. The sky, except for the passing of the front, remains cloudy. In all probability few fish will shut off. Instead, a day or so later the fishing might perk right up again if the incoming weather stabilizes—or if the weather pattern immediately swings back to the weather pattern that was consistent before. In fact, during most of the summer, most of the weather you encounter will be of this swing-around, so-so type of change.

The main principle to keep in mind is that the shorter the span between days of drastic weather change, the less fish you can expect to be in a positive feeding attitude. If we get two warm, calm days; followed by two cold, windy days; followed by two warm, calm days, etc.; the fishing will never get real good. By the same token, if the change isn't that severe, the fishing won't be too bad, either.

This doesn't mean you can't catch fish during times of change; it simply means you must usually work harder or longer for less return. If you were on the water each and every day throughout the summer season, you might only experience 8 or 10 of the real "great" days. More often than not, you're dealing with the poor or moderate kinds of situations—not the prime conditions.

More than this, we must view stability relative to the season and the Calendar Period. Look at it this way: In a broad sense, 2 or 3 stable days in spring or fall may bring about the same peak response as 4 or 5 days of consistent weather in summer. (By a peak, we mean the largest potential number of fish that can be turned on for that *specific* period of time.)

With everything being equal in terms of stability, more fish will be triggered to feed in the Summer Peak Period than in the fall Cold Water Period. Why? Because more walleyes of a given group of fish will respond positively during periods of the year when a lot of food is consumed than at times when less food is being eaten. So, good days are relative—relative to the Calendar Periods. A slow day during the Summer Peak (or any other prime period) may equal a good day in some other (less prime) Calendar Period.

PUTTING IT ALL IN PERSPECTIVE

The preceding information is in the form of principles and trends—*not* in clear-cut situations—because clear-cut situations are relative to specific circumstances only. But with principles, you can apply them to most any situation. Here is a recap of the principles we discussed:

1) Walleyes are most active in the low light periods—or in conditions they perceive as low light (overcast days, windy days, etc.).
2) The low light periods which entertain the *most* walleye feeding activity are dusk and dawn. However, the largest fish may feed at the dark of night.
3) The dark, night hours can be a great equalizer for adverse weather conditions. Whether there be a cold front, or a long bright light day, as a rule you will catch many more walleyes fishing *from dusk to dawn* than from dawn to dusk.
4) If few walleyes are being caught during the day or at dusk and dawn, try night fishing. This is especially true on clear water lakes. There is also evidence to suggest that many lunker walleyes are exclusively night feeders, regardless of season or available light.
5) While you can catch walleyes in the midday hours, without cloud cover or lots of wind, in most cases these will be: (1) deep water fish where light is already reduced, or (2) fish in very murky waters.
6) Weather stability increases the number of fish which will be in a positive/ neutral feeding mood. However, stability must be viewed in relation to season and Calendar Period.
7) In spite of all this knowledge, you still must know the location of the fish. A guide who is out on a lake every day, and a man who has been in an office for the last 10 days, can both look out and read the signs. But the guide is in better touch with where the fish were last located (deep vs shallow; in cover or out of it, etc.). So, regardless of other knowledge, you still must locate the greater mass of walleyes—and use lures, baits and methods that are most conducive to the current situation.
8) During daylight, if you can't fish during perfect conditions, it's usually better to concentrate on deep fish (if they exist) than try to catch fish that are shallow. You can also work known fish-holding areas where the wind is driving in, rather than where it is calm. Further, if you must fish during the day after a frontal change, you can (if available) try to go to dark-water lakes, or try to stay with high-percentage spots (areas known to recently have held walleyes), as opposed to fishing helter-skelter. Surprisingly, some dark or murky bodies of water host their best fishing on bright days! The extra light penetration helps trigger a feeding response by *increasing* the light to a more favorable level.
9) Whenever you must fish during any adverse time (high light or changing

weather), it's best to either fish very slow with live bait and light line, or go to the other extreme and fish fast with a lure and try to *trigger* a response. The "in between" methods which produce during the more conducive times usually won't be that productive.

We have attempted to familiarize you with some of the things that years of experience, the school of hard knocks and trial and error, have taught us. We are not claiming any of this with scientific certainty. But we have learned that if you click a light switch up, most times you can expect a light will go on.

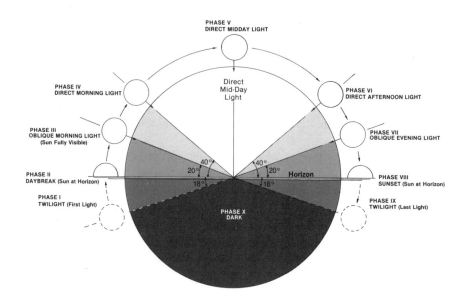

Chapter 19

BOAT CONTROL

(Making Your Boat Work For You.)

Correct presentation is more than just casting well, retrieving right, or having a good sense of "feel." These things are simply the finer points of technique —only parts of a whole. Total presentation is much broader. It results from the successful combination of two elements—namely *boat control* and *lure delivery*. One without the other is often a waste of time. Properly combined, however, they can be true angling artistry.

Although you can "book learn" things about fish behavior and the way lakes, reservoirs or rivers function, sooner or later you still have to put a bait in the water and coax a fish to strike. Make no mistake about it, catchin' fish is an acquired mechanical skill.

In the beginning, finding fish is the big problem for most people. If they find their way into a few fish, they feel they have really accomplished something. But for an experienced hand, 50% of angling success often depends upon how he handles his equipment—the boat as well as the lures. No matter how bad the conditions are, a good angler will eventually find some water that holds fish.

Proper combinations of lure delivery and boat control assume great importance. Handling a boat well takes experience—lots of it! Like playing a piano, you must have a theoretical knowledge of music. But to play the instrument smoothly, you must put that knowledge to a practical test.

The sages of old tell us that everything has its time and place. This proverb surely applies to the boat control part of total presentation. First of all, there are a lot of ways to move a boat on the water. You can drift, move about with oars, or use either an electric or outboard motor to go frontwards, backwards, sideways, move up and back, spin in a circle or even sit still. The secret is to match the proper boat control technique to the lure delivery system best suited to the situation you are faced with.

Today we know that shallow-water fish relate more to available cover than precise depth. Generally—in the shallows—a difference of 6 inches, 1 foot, or even 3 feet will not always be of primary importance. But in deeper, open water, a specific depth level assumes a much greater significance. Light penetration, water temperature, oxygen levels and prey position all play a significant role. A tapering flat may hold walleyes—but it's still a pile of rocks, a small ledge, or a trench on a flat that will hold the *major* concentrations.

Along such deep breaks, precision backtrolling comes into its own. Presentation now becomes more vertical. It makes little difference if a deep "break" is a weedline, a creek channel, the top of the thermocline, or a ledge of rocks; the same principles of presentation apply.

Backtrolling in deep water is much more than just moving in reverse gear. Too many folks have this mistaken impression. Instead, it's a full-fledged system of boat control whereby the movement of the boat does the work of presenting the bait.

There is no need to cast to an object in deep water, nor even retrieve. The forward, reverse, or drifting passes accomplish all this work for you. When casting and retrieving a bait, the offering is in the water less than two-thirds of the time, and even then it's usually only in a given fish zone for a short period of time. In backtrolling, the bait is *constantly* in the water and *always* working for you. On a pure percentage basis, this gives you an edge.

Although backtrolling is based on backing the boat into the wind, it obviously involves other movements. While backtrolling can be used to cast the edge of a weedline or even a shallow flat, the concept is best understood first as a deep water operation.

The major objective of any backtrolling run is to use your motor (either outboard or electric) in conjunction with the wind to move along a given depth at a given rate of speed. It may sound easy, but there are many little things that work to confound the process.

The variable speed and direction of the wind must be constantly taken into account—and corrected for. As the cover, depth or the bottom content changes, so must the direction of the troll. Each set of combining circumstances at any given moment calls for different procedures.

Pinpoint spots can be immediately retraced by simply placing the motor in neutral and letting the wind carry you back, or by adjusting (slowing) your speed so the force of the wind "slips" you right back over a specific spot. In short, proper backtrolling offers a multiplicity of options designed to keep your bait where it belongs—*in the fish zone!*

The various combinations of maneuvers are the product of three basic motions:

Movement #1 — MOVING INTO THE WIND

Movement #2 — HOLDING IN PLACE

Movement #3 — BEING CARRIED BACK BY THE WIND

In order to better visualize the total process, we will briefly look at each of these directional movements. No attempt will be made to explain the fine points of boat or motor handling, which are really best perfected on the water through experience. At this time, only the pure objectives of each of the movements will be explained. One final tip: Before backtrolling an area, it is always a good idea to "run" over it first with your depth finder to visualize what it looks like. Then, when you actually fish it, you can anticipate necessary adjustments in speed and direction.

MOVEMENT 1
MOVING INTO THE WIND

The basic movement is accomplished by simply placing the motor (either the outboard or electric) into reverse and backing into the wind (see Fig. #1). Although there are times when you might have to backtroll *with* the wind, this option should be avoided whenever possible. The idea is to use the wind and the motor together to slow or push the boat in one direction or another. The driver (assuming he is right handed) keeps his left hand on the tiller as much as possible. This allows for easy and quick adjustments of speed and/or direction. To move along at a given rate of speed, the boat operator seeks the correct amount of backward motor thrust to compensate for the prevailing force of the wind.

In the case of a strong wind, the motor is revved up to overcome it. With a very light wind, however, an outboard may have too much power—even at its slowest speed. In this case, the operator must continually shift from reverse to neutral (or even forward) in order to slow the boat down. An easy answer on glass-slick water is to use a less powerful electric motor. The options depend upon the equipment you have available. But remember, any change in speed also causes different angles of "slide." This phenomenon is one of the principles used in following a contour (see Fig. #2).

226

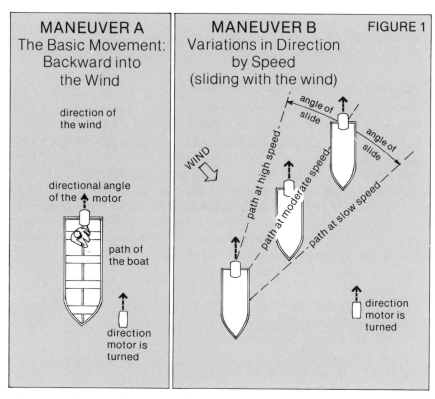

Maneuver A shows the basic backward movement. If the wind is directly *perpen-dicular* to the transom, the boat will move backward in a straight path as long as the motor is facing directly into the wind. But that will seldom be the case. More than likely the wind will play on the boat more from one direction than the other (See Maneuver B).

When this occurs, the force of the wind will make the boat "slide off" at an angle, even though the motor is still pointed in a given direction. This sliding effect, as we shall see, works to your advantage when following a bend in a contour. The slower the back speed, the more the angle of the "slide"; the faster the speed, the more direct the path.

MOVEMENT 2
HOLDING IN PLACE

There are a lot of times when you don't want to stop to anchor because it would be too much trouble. But for any number of reasons, a spot might have to be fished slower, vertically, or checked more thoroughly. Maybe you had a light pick-up or felt an odd tug, or saw some fish on the flasher, and you feel the area should be covered a little more slowly and thoroughly. Here's a simple alternative for staying in place and thoroughly fishing an area with a minimum of set-up time and effort.

The *hovering maneuver* is the most simple of the backtrolling tactics. It involves placing the motor in reverse gear, turning the back of the boat *directly* into the wind, and adjusting the speed of the motor to *exactly* neutralize the force of the wind. There's nothing hard or fancy about it. You can very easily

By combining maneuvers A & B (as in Figure #1), it's a simple matter to tightly follow a contour. Let's assume we want to track the 20 foot contour. Once a path of movement is set up, no adjustment in either speed or direction is necessary to move from Point A to Point B. The motor's direction remains the same. The driver simply holds his course and the wind will carry him in the desired direction. But, at Point B the 20 foot contour begins to bend slightly— but not enough to require a major directional movement with the motor. Instead the driver simply increases his speed. This added thrust will carry the boat to Point C. During the entire pass the boat has hugged the 20 foot contour. But, at this point the contour starts to bend sharply upwind, so the motor (for the first time) must be turned into the wind, thus bringing the boat around the bend to Point D. Once the turn is completed, however, the motor is once again turned to center transom and a straight back movement (with no wind slide) will move the boat to Position E.

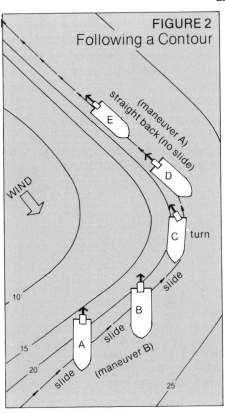

FIGURE 2
Following a Contour

FIGURE 3
Hovering in Place

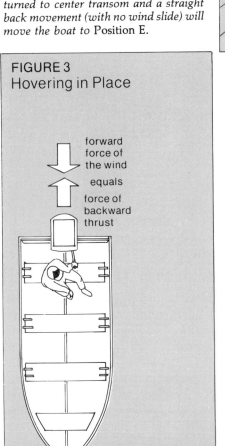

forward force of the wind

equals

force of backward thrust

Stalemate! — wind force and back thrust of the boat are counterbalanced. A boat can stay on a spot with suprisingly little movement. It's almost like being anchored. The trick is to keep the motor's direction and the boat's transom as directly into the wind as possible. Remember, as soon as the boat is turned sideways too much, "slide" will start taking place. If the boat cannot be positioned to buck directly into the wind, or if winds are so light that a balance of forces cannot be achieved, then you are much better off switching to the rocking method (see Fig. #4).

sit in one spot for several minutes—allowing you to cast, change lures, vertically jig up and down, let your bait sit still—whatever you want (see Fig. #3).

A variation of this hovering maneuver enables you to cover a slightly larger area, yet accomplish much the same thing. It's called *rocking-in-place*. Instead of *exactly* neutralizing the wind, the backward thrust of the motor is either slowed down or placed in neutral, allowing the boat to drift downwind a short distance. Once the desired area has been backtracked, the motor is given enough reverse speed to proceed back upwind again. This backtroll/drift combination is very effective for thoroughly covering a limited area that is larger than the length of the boat.

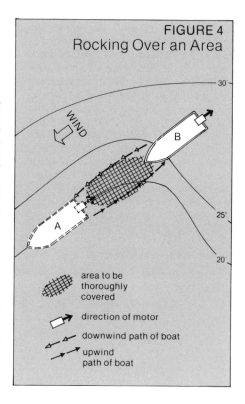

Let's assume you want to check out the cross-hatched area. But not enough fish contact has been made to go to the trouble of anchoring. Or, possibly, the wind is such that anchoring is a problem and it's better to just keep "rocking" over the fish. Note that backtrolls are made from Positions A to B, *then the boat is allowed to slip back to* Position A. *By repeating this process continually, a small (or any given area) can be saturated. Variations in depth can also be employed. On a downwind slip the 20 foot contour could be covered. . . then on the upwind backtroll 22 feet worked. . .then on the downwind slip maybe 25 feet could be checked. . .and so on and so forth until the best depth range is established. Also, if fish are scattered throughout the various depths, the staggered, depthrocking process would simply be continued.*

MOVEMENT 3
BEING CARRIED FORWARD BY THE WIND

While the "rocking" maneuver has its place in small specific areas, its main flaw is that your line winds up under the boat on the downwind pass, and may become tangled in the propeller of the motor. To avoid this and other line tangle mishaps, it's best to employ a "controlled" drift maneuver whenever you want to move any great distance.

On a controlled drift, the boat is simply turned perpendicular to the wind, and the motor left in neutral. As soon as it is determined that the wind will blow the boat off the proposed course (usually a predetermined contour), the motor is then placed in either forward or reverse to correct for any deviations (see Fig. #5).

A variation of the controlled drift is called "wind-slipping." (This is not to be confused with river slipping.) There are times when the wind is too strong and the boat will travel too fast by simply letting the wind carry it. The "slip" maneuver is much like hovering in place—except the backward thrust of the motor is geared so the power will neither stalemate or overtake the force of the wind. Instead, the boat loses a little ground and thus "slips" downwind.

Let's assume we have backtrolled into the wind up to Boat Position A, *along the 25 foot contour. On the way we found walleyes loosely strung out all along this section and feel the area should be reworked. You can run all the way back to* Boat Position H *and backtroll up again, but if the winds are moderate and you can maintain a correct speed, it's not necessary. Simply backtrack by using a controlled drift maneuver. Note that at* Point A *the boat is positioned perpendicular to the wind and the motor is pointing out to deep water. Remember the wind plays least on the transom, so maximum control is maintained by positioning the boat in this manner. At* Positions B & C, *the boat is edged out by alternating between reverse and neutral, allowing the boat to hold tight on the 25 foot contour. At* Position D *(the apex of the point) the boat is allowed to drift again until the contour turns shoreward. Then, at* Position E *the boat is placed in forward to follow the 25 foot contour. By combinations of drifting in neutral and various reverse or forward movements, the boat can be made to follow any given contour like it's on rails.*

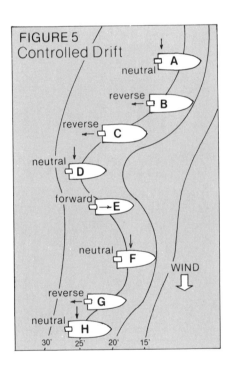

FIGURE 5
Controlled Drift

Because slipping involves the force of strong winds, it's much more difficult to execute, and cannot be used on jagged contours that run long distances. Instead, it's best when the contour is mostly straight without a lot of sharp bends.

COMBINATIONS OF MANEUVERS

The backtrolling system is not difficult, but it does take practice. Being able to know how and when to apply it can make a tremendous difference in your ability to catch fish.

Remember, the *wind is your ally*—not your enemy. Always use it to your advantage. If you fight it, you defeat the purpose.

Now that we are briefly acquainted with the various maneuvers using our three basic movements, let's see how we would combine a few of them to make a complete, sustained run around an extended, deep underwater point (see Fig. #6).

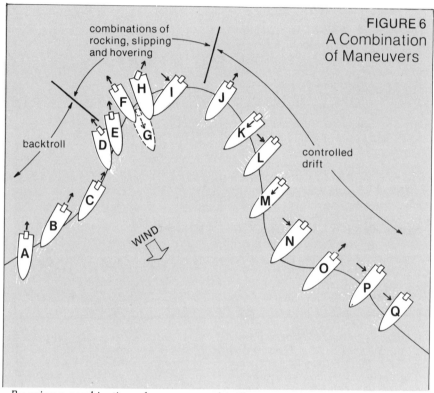

By using a combination of maneuvers, this illustration shows how an underwater point can be reworked without having to backtrack to the original starting point.

Let's assume the entire section from Boat Position Q to A had been backtrolled and enough walleyes were taken on the run to justify that it be fished again.

Starting at Boat Position A, a backtrolling sequence using the wind to "slide" the boat along the contour is used to carry the boat up the first leg of the run. At Position D, however, a directional correction is necessary, otherwise the boat would be carried to shallow water. The change is made by turning the handle of the motor out and swinging the transom toward the wind. Once in this position it is easier to negotiate the complex bend by a series of maneuvers that entail rocking, slipping and even hovering. In this manner, the boat is brought to Position I — where a controlled drift, along with a few minor adjustments, will carry the boat along the remainder of the run.

Boat handling during some of the maneuvers, particularly in Positions E thru I, must be viewed with respect to the lines in the water, and how they might cross or tangle. Some of the movements are shown here without explanation, but they do illustrate the boat positions necessary to navigate the corner, and at the same time, fish it correctly. The rationale for each move must be experienced with lines actually in the water to be fully understood. In short, there is no substitute for on-the-water experience.

ANCHORING

Boat anchoring is one of the oldest forms of boat control. Even today, anchoring can play an important part in special conditions.

We are not going to get into the different types of anchors, but instead simply show two ideal situations for this form of boat control.

The first example is a small river during the Cold Water Period. Walleyes are holding in holes in a neutral attitude. Note how the proper anchor position puts you right on the fish.

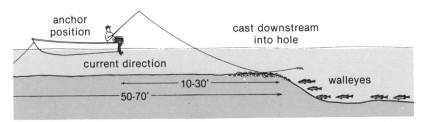

The second example depicts anchoring on reefs, rock points or rock piles, and using the wind to your advantage. In this instance, active walleyes move up on small, specific spots, and anchoring and casting is the best approach.

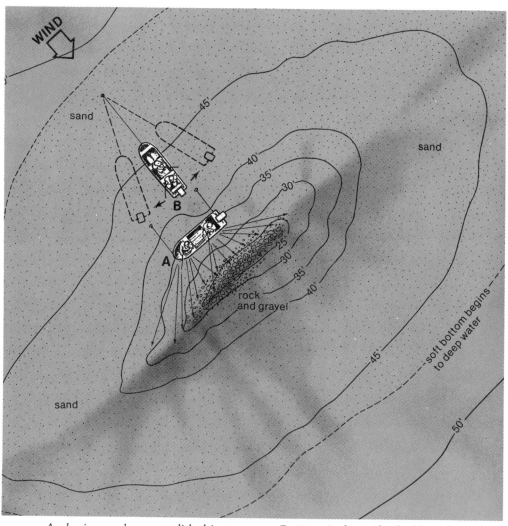

Anchoring can be accomplished in two ways. **Position A** *shows the double-anchor setup. If the wind permits, this is the way to go. Note the boat is upwind, enabling the anglers to "swing cast" cumbersome live bait rigs. During post-frontal conditions, the bait can be allowed to remain more or less in place with occasional slight movements or slowly retrieved with periodic rests.*

Position B *shows a single-anchor setup used when the wind is very strong and would cause waves to slap the boat too hard if it were double-anchored. For the single-anchor setup, however, plenty of anchor line is required. Once anchored, the boat will swing from side to side. Care must be taken to keep a tight line because, as the boat swings, bows may develop in the line, not only making hook setting difficult but possibly putting undue pressure on the line and making fish reject the bait after a pickup.*

SEA ANCHORS

One of the latest devices used for boat control is the sea anchor. These are mainly used on larger bodies of waters like the Dakota Reservoirs, the Great Lakes or Lake Winnebago in Wisconsin.

Sea anchors are basically large bags dragged through the water on the end of a rope. The main purpose is to aid controlling your drift or slowing your boat speed. They work best on long stretches of reefs, uniform drop-offs or flats.

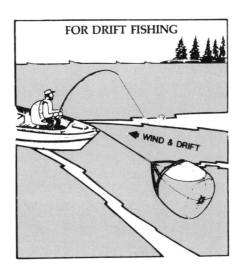

DRAG VOLUME	RECOMMENDED FOR:
31 Gal.	Canoes, Cartop Boats, Etc., up to 14 Feet in Length
63 Gal.	Small Fishing Boats, Canoes, Etc., up to 16 Feet
114 Gal.	Large Fishing Boats, Pike Boats, Bass Boats, Etc., up to 18 Feet in Length
276 Gal.	Charter Launches, Cruisers, Pontoon Boats, Etc., 18 Feet & Over in Length

THE RIVER SLIPPING METHOD

"River slipping" is similar to backtrolling—a system of exact boat control. It is particularly effective in the faster water of young to mature rivers. Slipping allows you to correctly position your rig to make the most efficient use of each cast or troll. There are few wasted pitches. In the course of a day, this can add up.

Just like backtrolling, the secret of slipping is keeping your bait right in the fish zone as long as possible on each cast or trolling run. And like backtrolling, you can hold your boat virtually motionless without anchoring, or move with precision as the occasion calls for it. Mobility is the key; it is easy to use the force of the current as an aid to lateral movement.

This photo illustrates what the basics of slipping are all about. Arrow #1 symbolizes the force of the downstream current. Arrow #2 is the speed of the motor. Note that the motor's forward thrust is less than the force of the current. This means that although the boat is facing the current and the motor is running in forward, the boat is actually losing ground. Arrow #3 is the difference between the current and the thrust of the motor. With a little practice you can hold a boat virtually motionless by balancing the forward speed of the motor with the downstream speed of the current.

Slipping results when the forward speed is reduced to a point where the forward thrust of the motor can not overtake the speed of the current. But be careful! Once you begin to slip and start casting, your lure will travel much faster than the amount of slip (arrow #4), so your lure will come back to you faster than you are slipping. You must always keep a tight line to maintain proper "feel." You steadily retrieve and keep a high rod tip to reduce slack and bows in your line. This is very important because with too much bow the current will tend to lift your lure off bottom. In a nutshell, this is the secret to slipping.

There are many other benefits, too. You can follow the current path of an eddy with the same ease as a leaf on the water's surface, but just as easily change direction and pull out. One of the primary strengths of this method, along with its speed and mobility, is that all-precious commodity, versatility. You can jig, cast plugs, or troll live bait—all effectively.

Slipping An Eddy (illustration on next page)

The simple ease with which the boat follows the current is the strongest recommendation for the "slipping" system. The fish relate to these flow patterns; the boat follows them perfectly, allowing for precise lure delivery, placement and retrieve. What can be more simple or precise than to take full advantage of the current instead of fighting it?

We like to use jigs while "slipping." Most of the time we cast jigs, but sometimes we drag them behind the boat. This is a versatile system that allows for many variations in presentation. In this case we are using an 1/8 oz. jig with a plastic body (tipped with a piece of a nightcrawler or a leech) because we are fishing a shallow eddy no deeper than 6 feet. In strong current running to depths of 8-12 feet, a 1/4 oz. or maybe even a 3/8 oz. jig would be necessary. The idea is to use the lightest possible jig that will sink to the bottom in the current.

BOAT POSITION #1 shows the boat approaching the eddy formed by a finger of land and shallow rocks that breaks the current flow.

BOAT POSITION #2 - Now we began to "slip" the eddy. We make a few casts to the slower water behind the rocks (notice the angle of the cast). Big fish are seldom taken here, yet once in a while a straggler might come in looking for a crawfish or frog.

BOAT POSITION #3 - Note how we cast at a 20°-30° angle upstream, and watch for that telltale line of rippled water that identifies the current break. The edge of this line is our target because the majority of the fish will hold right on this break. Occasionally we have to slow down or swing in or out to properly position the boat for the upstream casts. If BOAT POSITION #3 fails to produce we drop back to BOAT POSITION #4. Now we aim our casts farther into the eddy. This allows our lures to drag closer to the bottom than in BOAT POSITION #3, where there was more lift due to current.

So far we have worked the outside face of the eddy. At this point we swing our boat along the downstream side of the eddy as in BOAT POSITION #5. We fire a few more casts into the outside current break, and resist the temptation to make a cast downstream across to the rock. At this point we start backing into the reverse current.

BOAT POSITION #6 - From here we can fish both the shoreline and the outside of the eddy. While walleyes tend to hold on the current break on the outside of the eddy, smallmouth might be feeding on frogs near the shoreline timber falls.

BOAT POSITION #7 - Now we'll thoroughly cover the upper portion of the eddy. We take care to present the jig from different angles. The angle of approach to the fish can spell the difference between a take and a pass. Once we have thoroughly fished the area, we maneuver the boat back into the downstream flow to. . .

BOAT POSITION #8 - With the bow facing back upstream, we are right back on the current break and have two options: If the water is fast, a cast and retrieve is best. In slower water, the lures could be cast and dragged right down the slot of the current break, giving the fish a long time to look at the bait. At this point we could finish working the eddy by moving to. . .

BOAT POSITION #9 - This area is often ignored as anglers hurry downstream to another spot. But hold on: The big smallmouths in this stretch could be in this arm of the eddy, so it should be worked thoroughly.

Once you learn to work an eddy like this, you'll be amazed at both the fish you catch and the complete ease with which you float through it. There is no question, "slipping" is the way to fish an eddy!

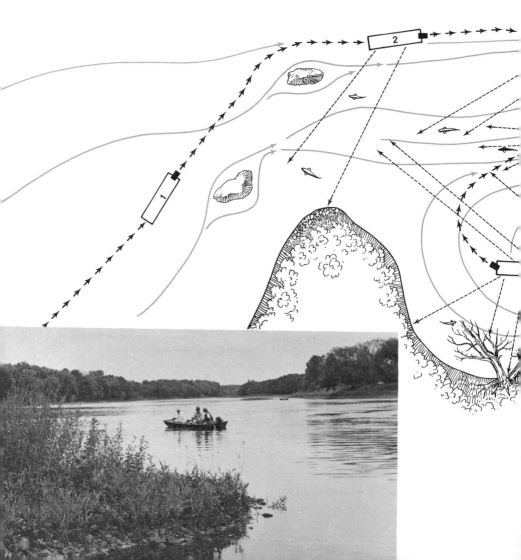

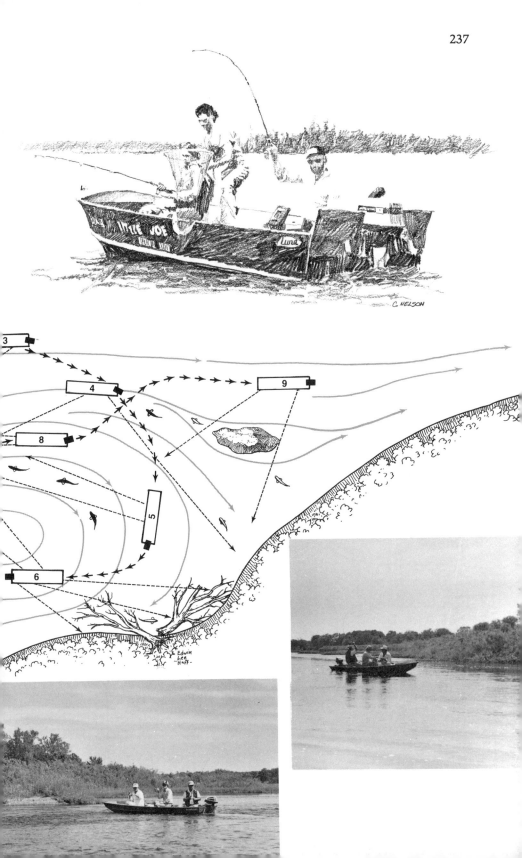

Bow or Transom

Electric motors have been a solid addition to fishing. Bow mounts are used the most by bass fisherman. But, for walleye fishing, our choice is the transom mount.
This allows you the alternate use of the outboard and electric for backtrolling. If it's windy, use the outboard. When it's calm, drop in the electric.
Following are instructions for making your electric work in your favor.

The Backtroller's Problem

standard electric motor has weak thrust in reverse because the thrust is deflected by the motor housing

The Backtroller's Solution

electric motor with reversed head... thrust is powerful and unobstructed in reverse

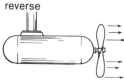

How to Modify an Electric Motor for Backtrolling

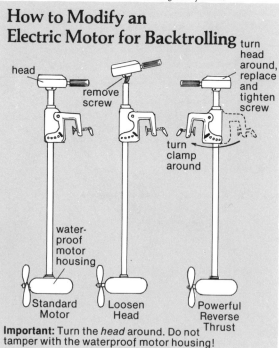

head

remove screw

turn head around, replace and tighten screw

turn clamp around

water-proof motor housing

Standard Motor

Loosen Head

Powerful Reverse Thrust

Important: Turn the *head* around. Do not tamper with the waterproof motor housing!

What is a trophy walleye? In some areas, a 5-pounder is mighty big. In others, a wall-hanger is much larger. We'd say a 10-pounder is a true trophy just about anywhere you go. Bet you'd like to catch one, wouldn't ya'? Who wouldn't?

Trouble is, a walleye of that size is usually a pretty rare catch. However, what would you say if we said we could put you in the right place, at the right time, with the right lure, to maximize your odds of catching a big fish? Well, here it is—our guide to lunker walleyes.

Chapter 20
TROPHY WALLEYES

It was a mid-March night in 1982, not unlike others in central Arkansas. Sporadic cool rains had ended, and air temperatures were in the high 40°F's. Greer's Ferry Reservoir had risen 4 feet from the rains, the water temperature had warmed, and conditions were perfect for pre-spawn walleye movements up Greer's tributary rivers.

Al Nelson of Higden, Arkansas had an appointment with destiny. Al was trolling a 6-inch gray Bomber Long "A" minnow along a stretch of creek arm when he hit something solid. After a 10 minute fight, Nelson brought a walleye up and couldn't believe his eyes. His trophy tipped the scales at an incredible 22 lbs. 11 oz. for a new Arkansas state record.

Some luck was involved in this extraordinary catch, but the truth is, Nelson had better odds going for him than most anglers. First, he's a pretty good walleye fisherman. Second, he understood the significance of the water levels and temperature. And third, he was fishing a reservoir containing *huge* wall-eyes. In short, he was *fishing in the right place at the right time with the right presentation to maximize his chances of catching a big fish.*

Al Nelson cruises South Fork in his sneak boat.

An optimist once said, "I'd rather be lucky than good." Trouble is, luck comes in many forms, ranging from very good (rare) to downright horrible (common). Any fisherman who relies on "good luck" is in a world of hurt. But a good fisherman—and especially a successful *lunker hunter—makes* his own luck. Once you see how it's done, you can do it, too!

Glen Runge, a friend of Dave Csanda, used to drive people crazy with the numbers of *big* bass and walleyes he caught. Although he fished long and hard and very well, half the time he caught 'em on heavy line, or hadn't retied his knot for two days or had performed some similar "unthinkable" horror. Yet many of his friends who paid meticulous attention to every little mechnical detail still caught far fewer big fish than Glen.

One night Glen revealed his secret to success. "It's really very simple," he said. "Just *fish big fish lakes, and fish 'em when they're hittin.*" His friends nearly laughed at his obvious simplification, but then it dawned on them how profound that simple philosophy was.

Many anglers place *all* their faith in catching big fish on *pure technique*— light line, sensitive feel, weed interpretation, etc.—thinking that they are bound to catch a bunch of big fish every now and then on raw talent alone. They do—*every now and then.* But *consistency* eludes them. However, once they realize that mechanical skill is certainly important, but skill applied in the *right place* at the *right time* is *deadly*, their trophy catches skyrocket.

Runge's Rules—(1) fish big fish lakes and (2) fish 'em when they're hittin'—are a big step toward lunker success. Pay attention to which lakes, which species, what time of year, etc., *before* you apply the "how." It works! Your big fish consistency will increase dramatically.

PEAK PERIODS

Most anglers would agree that the best fishing—for any species—occurs when you find *large numbers of fairly active and aggressive fish concentrated in specific areas.*

For walleyes, these conditions typically occur at three main times of the year: the Cold Water, Pre-spawn and Summer Peak Periods. Re-read our chapters explaining these Calendar Periods before advancing further and you'll see why these are prime trophy times.

After checking the Calendar periods, your next task is picking out prime bodies of water to concentrate on. After all, experience shows that all bodies of water do not have the same capacity to produce big fish. In fact, the more "homework" you do, the more you find the same waters continually producing the majority of big fish, year after year. Talk to fisheries biologists, check big fish contests, visit bait shops, etc., and the same lake names keep popping up. *There is a reason!*

While big walleyes occur in a variety of waters, they all have several characteristics in common. First off, walleyes are generally *native* to the system and reproduce fairly well without stocking. Stocking often indicates: (1) walleyes being placed in a non-native environment, or else (2) a lake "in trouble" that can no longer maintain its walleye population by natural means. The first case indicates potential walleye *numbers*, but seldom *size*. The second case may have *some* big fish present, but usually not a *strong population* of big fish. Thus it would not be a prime candidate, and would only be your #1 trophy option if it was the only trophy lake in your area.

In short, the best trophy waters usually have fishable numbers of walleyes, and provide a suitable environment to grow big fish. That generally means a plentiful and varied food supply that provides walleyes with easy meals all year long.

For instance, rather than scrounging on insects and a few tiny minnows all year long, the walleyes instead have easy access to perch, shiners, etc., and preferably high-protein forage like ciscoes or shad. In short, food supply makes a world of difference. Given such a favorable habitat, and no excessive competition from other large predators like northern pike, chances are walleyes can grow very large.

The following examples are all situations where these conditions occur. Obviously, space prevents us from going into lengthy detail on each situation. However, in each case we've combined a "big fish" body of water with one of the three peak Calendar Periods, and listed a prime presentation to use.

COLD WATER—MESO LAKES DURING THE DAY
Time Period: Mid-September thru November

This pattern applies on clear water meso lakes and small bodies of water connected to the Great Lakes. Fall brings a general shift of walleyes away from the shoreline flats toward structural elements in the deeper portions of the lake. The steep-dropping, firm-bottomed portions of long shoreline bars and humps are very attractive to cold water walleyes, and host the most consistent daytime fishing. Walleyes typically school in depths anywhere from 15-50 feet.

Live bait rigging with a hefty, 4-6-inch chub, shiner or water dog and a 3/8-3/4 oz. slip sinker is outstanding under these conditions. Backtroll likely areas as slowly and vertically as possible to maximize your sense of feel. Pay particular attention to any changes in bottom composition (rock to clay, etc.) that might concentrate fish. If you feel the minnow panic, miss a fish or spot fish on your depth finder, re-work the area several times before leaving. You can tease neutral fish into striking if you give them enough opportunity.

This pattern will hold up all the way until ice-up. First ice (2-4 inches) generally spurs good ice fishing action in the same areas. Once again, use fairly large, lively minnows, vertically jigging or using a tip-up arrangement.

COLD WATER—MESO LAKES AT NIGHT
Time Period: Mid-September thru November

This pattern also applies to stocked, shallow prairie lakes with big walleyes. However, it is a classic big walleye pattern on deep meso lakes as well.

Inflowing creeks, or narrows between lakes that constrict water flow and set up a current, induce big walleyes to move shallow at night. The best current areas are near a steep drop to deep water where walleyes can rest during the day. These are prime feeding grounds, and walleyes move right up into the very shallow current at night. The best big fish movements occur during the full and new moon phases, all other factors being equal.

Shore casting is the easiest and most effective method for fishing these areas. Or better yet, pull on a set of insulated waders and move out a bit deeper after the fish. Cast either: (1) large, wobbling, minnow-imitating lures like Rapalas or Bang-O-Lures—preferably the sinking or neutrally buoyant models; or (2) large, action-tailed, plastic-bodied jigs like a Pow-rr head jighead and Mister Twister Sassy Shad. Retrieve the lures slowly with frequent pauses.

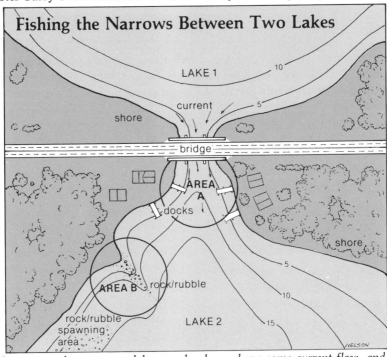

Fishing the Narrows Between Two Lakes

The narrows between two lakes nearly always have some current flow, and are a prime walleye attractor after dark. They are particularly good if deep water resting areas are nearby. The down-current side (AREA A) typically attracts the most fish, although nearby rocky points like AREA B could draw walleyes, too. Cast a neutrally buoyant or countdown minnow imitator at night.

COLD WATER AND PRE-SPAWN— MIDDLE-AGED RIVERS
Time Period: October thru April

This same basic pattern holds up during two Calendar Periods on middle-aged walleye rivers like the Missouri, Mississippi and Wisconsin Rivers. Walleyes begin gathering below the dams on these rivers in early fall, and continue accumulating in the general tailwater areas all winter. The walleyes will eventually spawn in this vicinity once the water temperature reaches the upper 40°F's in spring.

The best walleye attractors are moderately deep areas (8-25 feet) where current is *minimized*, though not necessarily absent. These generally occur on the back sides of wing dams or mid-river humps that break the force of the current. However, mid-river holes, and even mid-river, rubble-bottomed flats at these depths can also be excellent. The key to consistent fishing success is adapting to varying water levels by finding areas with the proper combination of depth and current.

Jig and minnow fishing is the #1 producer. Use jigs in the 1/8-3/8 oz. range and ever-so-slowly drag-lift-drag them across the bottom while the boat drifts with the current. Keep the motion of the jig to a minimum for these cold water fish.

PRE-SPAWN—HIGHLAND RESERVOIRS
Time period: Late February thru Early April

The mountain reservoirs of the South boast the largest walleyes in the United States. However, walleyes are often low in number, so the best time to fish them is when they concentrate in limited areas, such as during their spring spawning run.

Melting snow and spring rains raise both the water level and water temperature of the narrow, winding rivers that feed these reservoirs. This triggers an upriver spawning run from the main body of the impoundments. Pre-spawn walleyes will swim miles up these rivers until they locate rocky rapids at the proper depth for spawning.

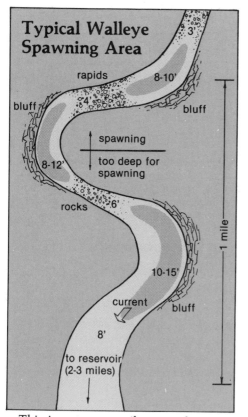

Typical Walleye Spawning Area

rapids
8-10'
bluff
4'
bluff
spawning
8-12'
too deep for spawning
rocks 6'
1 mile
10-15'
current
bluff
8'
to reservoir (2-3 miles)

Highland reservoir walleyes run up the feeder rivers to spawn in 2-4 foot deep rapids. They'll linger in holes during the day, and you might catch a few on a jig and minnow. However, the best way to nail a big 'un is trolling a deep-diving crankbait through the holes and up to the edges of the rapids at night.

Fishing the pools beneath these rapids with a jig and minnow during the day will produce some fish. However, the largest fish are typically caught trolling crankbaits or casting at night.

This is not necessarily a numbers pattern, but it is a true trophy pattern. Greers Ferry Reservoir in Arkansas has produced several 20 pound plus walleyes on this method the last few years, and is the best bet for a new world record in the near future.

PRE-SPAWN—MESO LAKES
Time Period: April thru May

This pattern applies on meso lakes with year-'round open fishing seasons, and on northern U.S. lakes when a late spring season prevents walleyes from spawning until after the fishing season opens. Big pre-spawn walleyes will still be congregated in the general vicinity of the spawning sites.

Rocky inlet streams, windswept rocky shorelines or very shallow (1-3 foot) offshore rocky humps are key pre-spawn spots. Slowly backtroll the drop-off areas directly adjacent to these spawning sites during the day. Use a live bait rig with a medium-sized, 3-4 inch chub or shiner, or else a jig and minnow combination.

Some of the best pre-spawn fishing occurs at night. Cruise the shallows after sundown, shining a Q-Beam spotlight in the water. When you spot the reflections of the walleyes' eyes, turn off the light and fish the general area. Cast a shallow-running minnow imitator like a Rebel, retrieving it slowly with frequent pauses. A small jig scraped across the bottom is also a good bet.

PRE-SPAWN—CANADIAN SHIELD LAKES
Time Period: May thru June

Most Canadian Shield lakes are fed or connected by rivers, and this is where walleyes spawn. Pre-spawn walleyes congregate near river mouths or rocky narrows even before the ice fully leaves the lakes, and pre-spawn walleyes run up the rivers as soon as possible. Good pre-spawn fishing occurs in years where a cold spring delays the walleye spawn until after the fishing season opens.

Jig and minnow fishing is excellent in the pools below rocky rapids or waterfalls. Unlike southern reservoirs, however, the pool areas may be too small and shallow to troll crankbaits in at night. You might be better off anchoring and casting a split shot/hook/shiner rig, and letting it "soak."

There is a distinct parallel between walleye behavior in Canadian Shield lakes and in the Great lakes. Bays and connected waters often have localized populations of big Great Lakes walleyes that run upriver to spawn in small rocky rivers. The fish are typically in the rivers for about a week, and the same techniques work very well. This is a very underfished trophy pattern.

SUMMER PEAK—MESO LAKES
Time Period: June

This is the first real "red hot" fishing of the summer season. Groups of large walleyes set up on classic structural elements. The edges of weedbeds, tips of points and hard bottomed humps all attract fish. The best fishing typically occurs in the 12-30 foot depth range.

Live bait rigging with nightcrawlers or jumbo leeches is deadly. If you spot fish up off the bottom on your depth finder, use an air-injected 'crawler or floating jighead and a long snell to raise the bait up off the bottom. Slowly backtroll, meticulously working and re-working known big fish areas. Concentrate your efforts at early morning and late evening when the lunkers are most active.

Offshore humps are key big fish areas on lakes where big walleyes feed on ciscoes. Ciscoes encounter these areas in their open water wanderings, and big walleyes will relate to them in force during the 10-20 day Summer Peak. Try backtrolling 4-6 inch water dogs for big fish. After the Summer Peak, the action slows down to a more normal pace.

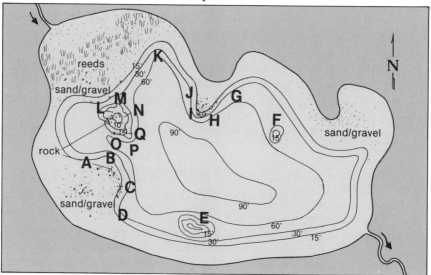

Summer Peak walleye hotspots are remarkably similar to good fall spots on meso lakes. Sharp-breaking, main lake, inside corners in the breakline are best for big fish. AREAS E, N, O and Q have best "on-paper" potential. However, you could backtroll the other spots listed here if you had time to check them out.
AREAS L thru Q are key trophy spots during the Summer Peak.

SUMMER PEAK—CANADIAN SHIELD LAKES
Time Period: July

When the first fast and furious summer fishing begins on Canadian Shield lakes, some of the best big fish activity takes place on offshore humps. As soon as the main body of the lake warms sufficiently, some big walleyes will leave the shoreline areas and feed heavily on these mid-lake feeding grounds.

In extremely clear lakes, the best fishing typically occurs at night. On hard-bottomed humps, cast a deep-diving crankbait right across the top and retrieve it fast enough to occasionally smack the rocky bottom. On slightly off-colored waters like Lake of the Woods, the same pattern works during the day. Or, if the hump has weedgrowth, backtroll a nightcrawler/spinner harness along the edges of the weeds.

Once again, strikingly similar walleyes behavior takes place on bays of the Great Lakes. Pitch crankbaits along rocky shores, over weeds, or along man-made docks and slab piles at night. The prime summer trophy fishing occurs during the Summer Peak, although you can catch some fish all summer long.

THE TROPHY HUNTER

These are some of the best and most widespread big walleye patterns in North America. Are these the *only* big walleye patterns? Of course not. You'll probably encounter other situations where local conditions combine to give you a good shot at big walleyes. However, the ones we've listed here are real classics, and will revolutionize your big walleye catches.

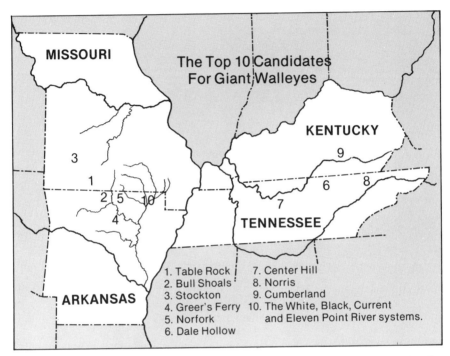

If we had to select the top ten places in the South to go for a giant walleye, they would be the areas indicated on the accompanying map. They are not necessarily listed in order of preference. Nine of them are reservoirs, while the tenth is a river system. Within this relatively small portion of the country are the largest walleyes to be found anywhere.

Chapter 21
GREAT LAKES WALLEYE

With the exception of the shallow western basin of Lake Erie, most of the deep, open water of the Great Lakes is salmon or trout country. However, there are many localized walleye populations in the shallower waters of the connecting rivers, canals, bays and adjacent small lakes. These areas function as small warm water environments connected to huge cold water ones. Some of these sections are small and provide only a limited walleye fishery. Others are quite large, such as: the St. Louis River estuary of Lake Superior; portions of Green Bay and Sturgeon Bay in Lake Michigan; huge Lake St. Clair, and the Detroit and St. Clair Rivers between Lake Huron and Lake Erie; and The Thousand Islands/Bay of Quinte region of Lake Ontario.

The fishing potential of each Great Lakes walleye area must be judged on a case-by-case basis. The local habitat (or environment) determines how numerous the walleye population can become. Keep in mind that you must also deal with the wild card of commercial gillnetting, which can be either of a tribal or commercial nature. Pollution and commercial gillnetting have

decimated many of these formerly fabulous fisheries. However, if care is taken of the environment, and if commercial netting is controlled, the various fisheries manage to bounce back with amazing resiliency, as has been proven in a number of incidences in the last decade.

One characteristic most Great Lakes walleyes share is their excellent growth rate. The variety and wealth of baitfish enables walleyes to grow very large, very fast. In fact, some of these Great Lakes spots are among the best places in the country to hunt for trophy fish.

Perhaps the best advice to fishing Great Lakes walleyes is *not* to become intimidated by what at first may appear to be "unusual" conditions. The fact is, besides the huge waters, there is nothing very much out of the ordinary involved. Walleyes relate to humps, points, weed beds, etc., just like they do in smaller inland waters. The fishing methods, except where very fast current or suspension is involved, are much the same as in inland waters. True, the larger bays are *large,* yet they're no more imposing than fishing big waters like Mille Lacs Lake in Minnesota or Lake Winnebago in Wisconsin. In most areas (except perhaps the western basin of Lake Erie) you can usually use the same types of boats you use on inland waters.

Great Lakes walleyes congregate in and around hard-bottomed rivers in early spring. These are the prime spawning sites. The fish run up the rivers to spawn in rocky rapids, and they may remain in the river for some time, then filter back out into the main lake; or they might simply spawn and move out quite quickly. If the season is open when the fish are still in the rivers, you can catch some nice fish using the same tactics you use on any inland river. There are also fall runs to many of these rivers as well. It appears that some populations of fish spawn in the rivers in spring, move out to the big lakes in summer and return to the mouths or go back into rivers themselves in the fall. So, basically, many of these are twice-a-year fisheries.

In small lakes connected directly to the "big water" by rivers or canals, fish relate to weeds, points, humps and man-made structural elements like rock or wood slab piles in the summer and fall. In fact, it's virtually identical to fishing an inland lake. Many times fish in these small lakes will move out in the summer to the big waters only to return again in the fall. In larger bays, they use long rocky points, offshore humps and the shallow sections around strings of islands. It's much the same as fishing a rocky Canadian lake for walleyes.

When you encounter suspended fish, as you can in summer in some shallow areas which are located out in one of the Great Lakes itself, try the weight-forward spinner system that's so popular on Lake Erie. But be willing to do a lot more experimenting, too. Try backtrolling live-bait rigs with 3-6 inch chubs, or even waterdogs (we've caught big Great Lakes walleyes on 'em) down the edges of drop-offs. Cast a jig and minnow across the tops of rocky reefs or troll with plugs. In short, don't get hung up on one system.

The best tip for catching a huge Great Lakes walleye is to fish prime areas at night. There aren't a whole lot of folks who are doing this yet. In fact, it is fast-becoming apparent that some of the best walleye fishing on the Great Lakes is of the nighttime variety. Crawl a crankbait or Rapala or jig across rocky

points or slab piles in 3-8 feet of water. That's right—the big fish move that shallow! Many of the areas you'll be dealing with have very clear water, and daytime walleye activity can be very spotty to nonexistent. Yet great numbers of fish can be present, but catching them during the day is like pulling teeth. In many cases, big fish appear to be most, if not exclusively, active at night, and going to the extra trouble of fishing after dark could result in opening up a whole new ball game for trophy walleye in the Great Lakes.

The warmer water, inshore fisheries of the Great Lakes are perhaps the most ignored trophy areas for walleyes, pike and smallmouth bass. Remember, the Great Lakes *are not* simply trout and salmon water. If you're adventuresome and want a shot at a big walleye, give some of the coastal waters of the Great Lakes a try.

The accompanying map lists some of the better-known and documented walleye fisheries of the Great Lakes. We've included a brief description of the general area, a note on the general structural condition and some of the more popular methods used. In most cases (except for a few of the specialized methods utilized on the western basin of Lake Erie, Lake St. Clair or the Detroit River), the fishing situations and techniques used in these various areas are commonly used in other waters and are fully described in other chapters of this book.

GREAT LAKES

The areas noted here also are not to be considered all-inclusive. There are many other places where limited fisheries exist. But due to exit and entry problems, distance away from landings, or just difficulties zeroing in on moving fish, these limited fisheries are practically unknown or unexploited. You might contact your state or provincial fisheries department and get additional information on some of these little-known opportunities. You will probably be surprised what you and everyone else have been missing.

After we list some of the better walleye fishing opportunities of the Great Lakes, we'll examine the Lake Erie walleye phenomenon in detail. What happens here will perhaps enlighten you on other situations you can encounter on the Great Lakes.

GREAT LAKES

1. **Georgian Bay (Province of Ontario)**
2. **Bay of Quinte—Hay Bay Areas**
3. **Thousand Islands Area**

1. Georgian Bay (Province of Ontario): This area produces some real lunker walleyes; but don't expect to bring in great stringers. Most of the lake fishing is done in the general vicinity of the mouths of the principal walleye rivers in spring and then again in fall. In summer, the fish are out in the lake—primarily suspended and scattered over great areas.

Some of the major walleye river mouths are the Nottawasaga, Port Severn, Moon, Point au Baril, Key French and Pickerel Rivers. There are also other seldom-fished areas along the north bank of the North Channel. In areas like Port Severn and the Moon River, fish in the 12-15 pound class can be and are taken. Most serious fishing is done at dusk and at night. Trolling with Rapalas is a very popular method.

2. Bay of Quinte—Hay Bay Areas: Probably Ontario's best developing walleye area—this fishery has bounded back with incredible energy since the restrictions placed on commercial fishing. Walleyes in the 3-5 pound class are common. May and August are the best months and fishermen gather at the mouths of the various incoming rivers like the Trent, Moira, Salmon and Napanee Rivers. The Hay Bay area is also coming back strong.

Most fishing is done shallow in less than 15 feet around the various humps, reefs and edges of weedlines. While the locals troll Mepps spinners, many fish can be taken on weight-forward spinner methods. They can also be taken on crankbaits like Fat Raps, jigs and nightcrawlers, plus a host of other common walleye methods.

3. Thousand Islands Area: This stretch is actually the outlet of Lake Ontario where it becomes the St. Lawrence River. While various groups of walleyes can be taken downriver as far down as Ogdensburg, the best area appears to be the Cape Vincent run. There are a number of shoals here where the walleyes concentrate in late August and September.

Some of the more productive fishing is done in 20-35 feet of water on jigs tipped with nightcrawlers. While live bait rigging is seldom used (because of the current), it can be used to great advantage at certain times behind some of the shoals.

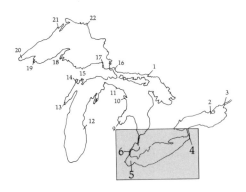

4. The Niagara River:

5. The Western Basin of Lake Erie

6. The Detroit River

4. The Niagara River: Once a good walleye fishery, by 1978 pollution and commercial fishing problems severely depleted the walleye populations of the Niagara River. But, by 1980, cleanup efforts, along with restrictions curtailing commercial fishing, started bearing fruit and the fishing is again coming back. While not a hot fishery yet, it does offer some fair opportunities to folks in the general vicinity. Fish run up to 10 pounds and are taken by either drifting with jigs, or trolling with worm harnesses or lures like a Flatfish. Because of swift current problems, heavy weights like Gapen Bottom Walkers in conjunction with plugs, live bait or bait harnesses are sometimes used.

5. The Western Basin of Lake Erie: This is the most famous of the Great Lakes walleye fisheries. A full examination of this phenomenon follows in the next chapter.

6. The Detroit River: In early spring, fish from Lake Erie move up through the Detroit River into Lake St. Clair and up to the Thames River on the Canadian side to spawn. After spawning, these fish move back into Lake St. Clair—and then move back to Lake Erie again by way of the Detroit River. Therefore, there are fish groups moving through the Detroit River waterway spring, summer and fall.

However, because of the fast drop between the water levels of Lake St. Clair and Lake Erie in less than 20 miles, a current of up to 10 miles per hour can set up, and flows of 5 miles per hour are common. In these conditions, a unique kind of fishing system, utilizing heavy weights and hand lines, has been established. By using 1 or 1-1/2 pound weights, lures like Rapalas, Ray's pencil plugs, Kwikfishes, Flatfish F-5's and F-7's, or fluorescent-bladed nightcrawler harnesses are worked with 3-way swivel rigs and straight hand lines (no rods are used). These rigs are trolled by hand in this fast current in depths to 30 feet. Hand lining gives better feel under these conditions. Anchoring systems utilizing 1/2 ounce jigs and casting upstream and following the lure back are also used.

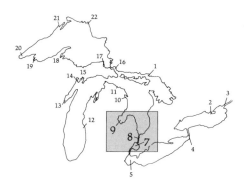

7. Lake St. Clair
8. The St. Clair River
9. Saginaw Bay

7. Lake St. Clair: There are resident populations of walleyes in Lake St. Clair itself, but in early spring, fish from Lake Erie and Lake Huron converge on some of the prime spawning areas like the Thames and Clinton rivers. So, the lake hosts both stable and migrating populations of fish.

Walleyes are trolled for on various flats, on reef and shoal areas or along dredged areas with nightcrawler harnesses or plugs like Flatfishes, Kwikfishes or Rapalas. In the summer months, walleyes are usually fished for during the day, but in late August, or around Labor Day, night fishing becomes more productive. Small boats are used in this fishery but care must be taken if going far out. The lake can get rough and tough.

8. The St. Clair River: This is primarily an early spring to early summer fishery. It appears that a number of groups of walleyes which filter out into the shoal areas of Lake Huron near Sarnia in summer move into the river to reach spawning grounds (maybe the Thames), and then filter back to Lake Huron. Certain resident fish might also be present, and scattered populations from Lake St. Clair might utilize this area. There is considerable current in this area plus a warm water discharge. A dredged channel of 27 feet deep is maintained, but depths of 35-50 feet or more may occur.

Most angling takes place along the banks or on the various flat areas and extended lips which run offshore. Many of the more standard trolling, anchoring and jigging procedures used in the Detroit River and Lake St. Clair are used here. One unique system is called chugging. This is the same type of hand-lined rig used on the Detroit River, except that here they anchor the boat and drop the heavy weights to the bottom, allowing the current to work the lures while they lift and drop (chug) the rig more or less in place.

9. Saginaw Bay: This once-famous and fabulous fishery was depleted primarily by commercial overharvest. But due to fisheries efforts, the conditions look good for a strong comeback. This was once a natural fishery and it appears that self-sustaining populations are being reestablished.

Because of the environmental conditions, this area is a year-'round fishery. In spring, walleyes run into the Saginaw River. Then, in summer, fish filter out into the shallow shoal areas on the eastern side of the bay from the town of Bay City to Sandpoint. Most of these waters are shallow; most of it is under 30 feet and peppered with various humps, holes, reefs, trenches and finger-like extended bars.

This is primarily a small boat fishery and a host of techniques from still-fishing to trolling are regularly employed, with trolling being the most popular method used. It is possible that bobber fishing could be used here at night to great advantage. If things like poaching, commercial fishing and pollution are kept to a minimum, this could develop into one of the Great Lakes' better walleye fisheries.

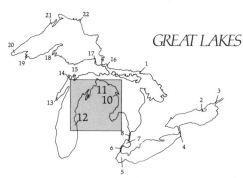

GREAT LAKES

10. Thunder Bay/Alpena

11. Cheboygan

12. The Muskegon River and various small lakes directly connected to Lake Michigan

10. Thunder Bay/Alpena: A marginal population of walleyes exists in this area. This section has an extended shallow shelf and numerous reef areas that jut out into Lake Huron's deeper waters. Whether limited self-sustaining populations have reestablished themselves here is not clear at this time. Since there is not a lot of fishing for walleyes here (most are caught accidentally by trout fishermen), an overall local reliable method has not evolved. Trolling with plugs, nightcrawler harnesses and jigs comprise the majority of the methods used.

11. Cheboygan: A limited fishery has developed here. If netting does not cut into the stocks, this area offers some potential. The walleyes are in fishable numbers and are, for practical purposes, virtually unexploited. A number of large, extensive shoals (30 feet and shallower) bound the narrow channel that runs between Bols Blank Island and the mainland near the town of Cheboygan. Some fish move into the Cheboygan River in early spring, but tend to utilize the shallower shoal areas in late spring and summer. Methods vary, and many inland systems will work here. It appears that trolling is one of the more popular methods. More night fishing might bring about better success.

12. The Muskegon River and various small lakes directly connected to Lake Michigan: A minor population of walleyes (many are very good-sized) has long existed in the Muskegon River. In fact, with the majority of interest now being focused on salmonids, the walleye population has grown in both numbers and overall size. However, as of late, renewed interest by certain walleye groups has skimmed off some of the easy-to-take fish. While actually fish of connected lakes and not of the Great Lakes as such, some walleyes might, if the conditions permit, poke their noses out in the big lake in summer to chow down on the bonanza of smelt and alewife. Since a lake (a widening of the Muskegon River) occurs just as the river meets the lake, there is both a river and lake fishery.

The same conditions pretty much occur on many of the small connecting lakes that dot the upper portion of Michigan's western side, although the streams that feed these lakes are generally very, very small. Lakes like Manistee and others hold populations of walleyes—many times monsters. The walleyes of these waters appear to be resident populations which utilize the small lake most of the time. But they can venture out to the mouths of these waterways where they connect with Lake Michigan, and feed on smelt when these prey are in close enough and the water temperature is correct.

While most of these small lakes at least have walleyes present, some hold fair numbers of big fish. It appears that the walleyes in these waters (especially larger ones) are almost exclusively night feeders, and in some areas the walleyes have not been fished much—at least not fished at the right time of day.

Methods like trolling Rapalas, casting crankbaits or working jigs tipped with live bait have all taken fish. Since all these lakes have at least a few walleyes, we leave it to adventurous anglers to discover just which ones have the fair-sized populations of big fish.

GREAT LAKES

13. Green Bay

14. & 15. Little and Big Bay De Noc

13. Green Bay: This once famous walleye fishery fell victim to commercial overharvest, poaching and pollution. But a number of years ago a program was instituted to reestablish the fishery, and it appears that it is coming back. Good-sized spring runs into the Fox River, as well as other runs into rivers like the Menominee, are regularly-occuring events once again.

While small scattered groups of walleyes are found here and all through Green Bay, the major fishery itself is concentrated in the southern end of Green Bay from about Sturgeon Bay southward where there is a considerable-sized shoal area—most of it under 30 feet deep.

Walleye angling begins in spring at the mouths of the various spawning rivers and creeks. Then, as summer arrives, fish tend to move out into the shallow areas of the bay, where water temperatures and availability of food is more opportune. Fishing methods are of the more traditional type: jigs, trolling with plugs, live bait, etc.

While the walleye spawning runs are fairly well attended by anglers, summer fishing out in the bay itself is still the province of a small band of devotees. A lot is still being learned about these bay-run fish and how to catch them consistently.

If commercial fishing continues to be banned or is strictly regulated, clean-up efforts in main streams like the Fox River are continued, and a total rehabilitative program is put forth, the area holds great promise.

14. & 15. Little and Big Bay De Noc: Like all the other better walleye fisheries of the Great Lakes, the Bay De Noc area has suffered the plague of unrestricted gillnetting and some amount of ecological degradation. Interestingly, this once famous fishery even had a walleye lure named after it, but until the recent stocking effort things looked grim. In fact, today the fishing is still in jeopardy despite the fact that it's up to about 1/8 or 1/4 of its potential. Natural reproduction is taking place, and if gillnetting does not take too much of a toll, it's possible that a fair, self-sustaining walleye population may be developed.

In the old days, a considerable winter (through the ice) walleye fishery flourished here. Perhaps, besides the spring runs, more fish were harvested at this time than any other. However, with the expansion of the salmonid fishery and the consequent adaptation of methods and equipment to fish big water, a summertime walleye fishery can be developed in the shallow shoal areas of both bays where there is a great deal of water under 30 feet deep.

Runs of fish into the Whitefish, Sturgeon and other streams draw the spawning fish in spring. After that they tend to filter back into the shoal areas of the bays where they spend the rest of the year.

Methods vary with season, with the late spring and summer bringing out the trollers, who use both plugs and nightcrawler harnesses. Fishing at night is not extremely popular, but will probably grow as the fishing grows (if it does). There is nothing unique in terms of current or structure here, and methods that work in like kinds of situations in other areas will work equally well here.

16. St. Mary's River

17. Whitefish Bay

18. Keewenaw Ship Canal

16. St. Mary's River: A river and bay environment, these shallow connecting waters between Lake Superior and Lake Huron provide conditions conducive to walleyes. Locks along the river allow ship traffic to pass from one lake level to another—a drop of about 24 feet at the Soo Canal locks—and the rapids sets up quite a current flow at the head of the river. However, at the lower end it has a moderate flow. At present, the fishing can be termed only fair; again, tampering with the environment, as well as unrestricted commercial gillnetting have taken their usual toll.

This is a year-'round fishery. The 30 plus mile long river and the adjacent bays are a shallow water environment—much of the water is 40 feet and shallower. Interestingly, spawning runs take place at the lower end of the river. Later, the various walleye groups break up and scatter on the many reefs, shoals, trenches and flats.

Fishing methods are tailored to fit individual situations, with trolling and bank fishing being the most popular. Other methods that work in other areas can be adapted here. While walleyes are fished at night, the river-like conditions do not produce strong night movements like out in the big lakes themselves.

17. Whitefish Bay: A minor residual fishery still exists in Whitefish Bay of Lake Superior. In spring the fish move to the Tahquamenon River and falls, but filter out in the shoal lake areas that bound the mouth of the river in summer. This is principally a local fishery and local methods like trolling are popular. Since some of these fish stick their noses out into Lake Superior itself when the water temperatures and availability of baitfish allow, night fishing might be the answer during the summer months.

18. Keweenaw Ship Canal: The cutting through of the Keweenaw Peninsula produced a warm/cool water environment between the frigid waters of Lake Superior, and a small walleye fishery which boasts some real lunkers has developed. While technically these fish are not critters of the big lake as such, this fishery more or less, because of its direct access, is like the connecting lakes of Lake Michigan included in this study. While some of the fish may venture to the mouth of the canal where it meets the big lake to take advantage of forage like smelt, the fishing is limited.

This section, like most of the others of the Great Lakes, is a small boat fishery and is fished with all the methods common to different individual structural situations that occur on any inland walleye lake. Lures like tipped jigs, trolled Rapala-type plugs and live bait rigs all have their moments. Night fishing here might open more new vistas.

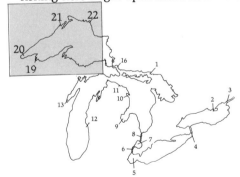

19. Chequamegon Bay

20. St. Louis River

21. Thunder Bay

22. Heron Bay/White River

19. Chequamegon Bay: At one time, numerous northern pike and walleyes plied this area. Although the majority of these fish have been depleted, scattered populations remain. Changes and development of shorelines, altering of streams, gillnetting, plus the introduction of exotic fish like salmon, rainbow and brown trout have altered the entire ecosystem.

Since the walleye population is at low levels and groups are widely scattered, about the only time they are concentrated is during the spawning period. Active fishing for them by anyone except a local, who can constantly stay with the fish, would be a wasted effort. The fishing, nonetheless, is mentioned here to round out those places where walleyes once ranged and could range again if corrective measures were implanted.

20. St. Louis River: A unique walleye fishery that has, even with just a slight clean-up effort, already "bounced back" with considerable energy. In this once highly polluted river, oxygen levels used to drop so low in summer that walleyes either had to leave or face attrition. Because of the contaminants, the flavor of the fish flesh was also very bad, and standards were set on how many walleyes could be consumed in a given period of time.

In spring, fish move into the upper river section to spawn, and then drop back down toward the Duluth Harbor entranceway. Some fish (particularly the smaller ones) are apparently able to summer over in portions of the river itself. Other fish groups move out in to the bays that bound Lake Superior, while still other fish move out into the big lake itself. Some fish are known to run down the south shore of Lake Superior towards the Apostle Islands. However, gillnetting has reduced some of these fish stocks. Other fish groups apparently move up Lake Superior's north shore, but these appear to be very few in number. Most fish appear to summer and winter over just outside Duluth Harbor on some of the shallower shoals.

Depending on season, and position in the river or lake, a number of fishing methods are used. Trolling with Rapala-like lures is popular. But so is trolling with nightcrawler harnesses and various other kinds of rigs. Jigs and live bait are also popular. Fish may suspend at the lower (deeper end of the river), but they also utilize structural elements. Early in the year, daytime fishing is popular. As the season progresses and the majority of fish leave the river, very little angling is done for the fish which move out into the lake and beyond the harbor entrance.

As they move eastward along Lake Superior's south shore, it's hard to stay with these migrating fish groups. Due to the small numbers of fish in relation to the immense size of the lake, it's just tough to find enough of a concentration of fish sitting in an area long enough to work them. Nonetheless, trollers working for salmon and trout "accidentally" pick up big walleyes every now and again. We also know that walleyes will get up on some of the sand beach areas at night along this stretch, but finding them is like looking for a needle in a haystack.

21. Thunder Bay: This bay, along with nearby Black Bay and others, at one time hosted a lot of walleyes. But today there simply isn't anywhere near the number of fish there used to be. In fact, Black Bay is pretty well drained of any real numbers of fish. Degradation of the environment is cited as one cause. Commercial gillnetting overharvest almost certainly played a role in this fishery's demise. Still, a walleye fishery of sorts remains. It's primarily located along the western end of Thunder Bay.

In spring, spawning fish move to the better suited rivers and streams, but appear to move out to the shoal areas of the lake in summer. While not enough fishing is done in summer so that definite patterns emerge, it looks like night fishing in the shallow areas could be very promising. More work would have to be done here, however, before any clear-cut consistent methods may develop.

22. Heron Bay/White River: Again, a declining to almost "pooped out" walleye fishery, this area still harbors some hold-out fish. In spring there is a slight run of leftover fish, and in summer some of these might poke their noses out into the shoal areas of the lake when the water temperature and baitfish situation are opportune. So little is known of this fishery, however, that while there isn't a mass of fish, there might be some pickings for those who are willing to work and give it an honest try. As far as best method is concerned, that would be anybody's guess, and someone who works something new or works at night just might come up with the answer.

The Great Lakes are obviously large; yet small, definitely fishable populations of fish exist in these waters—some of them practically untouched. Big walleyes are the rule, and fish which relate to smelt are another notable pattern. So are night movements in summer in shallow, clear waters. For those adventurous souls who like to explore and experiment, there is a vast opportunity waiting to be tapped.

Chapter 22

LAKE ERIE PHENOMENON

Back in the 1950's and '60's, walleye anglers fished Lake Erie's reefs and shallow water shoreline areas in small boats and runabouts, much the same way walleyes were fished in other parts of the country. During the summer the local folks, along with wealthy members of exclusive fishing clubs, trolled plugs, casted spinners, or drifted with egg sinker slip-rigs and minnows along the rocky reefs and shoals surrounding Pelee and the Bass Islands. Today, many fish are still taken "around the islands" in this manner.

But, in the last few decades, the ecosystem of Lake Erie has been markedly altered. Today there is an oxygen reduction problem in certain inshore and reef sections during the months of July and August. There is also a buildup of sediment in the shallower southwestern section of the lake, and turbidity still remains a problem despite recent cleanup efforts. And the once abundant bottom-dwelling mayfly larvae—a favorite food of the walleye—have to a large extent disappeared since the early 1960's. So, the Lake Erie of today is not nearly the ecosystem it was a score of years ago. These changes have all had a marked effect on the way walleyes function in the lake.

Then, too, a more recent occurrence has had tremendous impact on the walleyes' lifestyle. The 1970 ban on commercial fishing was the primary factor that allowed the once-depleted walleye population to blossom to incredible proportions. As a consequence, the existing reef areas which formerly provided room and board for most of the walleyes during the low population era could not now possibly house all the surviving fish. These overflow populations obviously had to go somewhere.

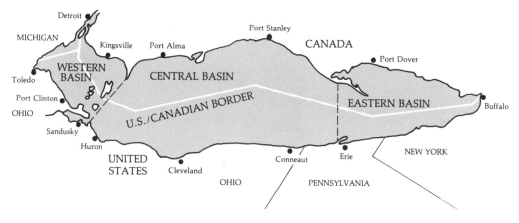

The only abundant food source available to the growing walleye population was the mass of emerald shiners, small alewives, shad, ciscoes and other young-of-the-year fish. All of these forage sources spend much of the year suspended in open water. So when these forage fish moved to open water, huge schools of walleyes did too.

It's a new ballgame—or at least a different one. As the majority of walleyes began to rely more and more on baitfish that related to open water in summer, the methods used to catch walleyes obviously had to change. Suddenly the main task of the Lake Erie angler was not only to figure out *where* the walleyes were at any particular moment, but to discern what *specific depth* they might be suspended at—something anglers in the days of reef fishing didn't have to contend with.

Seasonal Location
of Lake Erie Walleyes
in the Western Basin

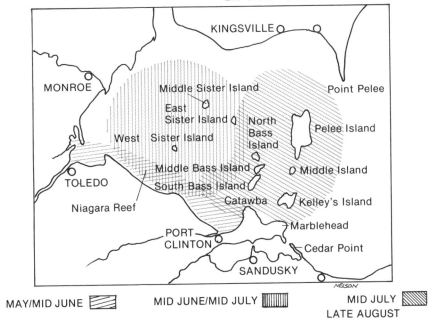

MAY/MID JUNE ▨   MID JUNE/MID JULY ▥   MID JULY ▧
LATE AUGUST

Lake Erie is in reality 3 lakes—or at least 3 different environments. Biologists divide the lake into the western, central and eastern basins. The eastern part of the lake is the deepest and cleanest, while the western portion is the shallowest and most eutrophicated. The central basin, meanwhile, is a huge transition area from a deep, clear habitat to a shallow, dirty one. A little-known fact is that the eastern basin of Lake Erie still supports lake trout, as well as other assorted cold water fish.

The western basin covers 1265 square miles (809,600 acres), and comprises 13% of Lake Erie's total surface area. But because of its overall shallowness, it only amounts to 5% of the lake's volume. At any rate, as far as walleye fishing is concerned today, the western basin is "where it's at." While isolated fisheries exist in other parts of the lake, the makeup of the central and eastern section of the lake is not conducive to supporting the huge amounts of walleyes that the western basin does.

Although the reefs that bound Point Pelee, Kingsville and Colchester on the Canadian side of the western basin could very well abound with walleyes, the population has been ravaged by intensive commercial netting. So, in effect, the American side and the nearby Canadian islands are what sustain the current walleye fishery.

Lake Erie walleyes tend to congregate in certain areas of the western basin at times. While resident fish and other autonomous groups often "do their own thing", the mass of adult fish make fairly predictable seasonal movements. The accompanying map is so small—and the zones of use so sprawling—that individual spots are impossible to depict. Instead, generalized areas are shown. Many of these sections include reefs and shoals, as well as open water. There are also seasonal overlaps. For example, if the water does not become too turbid, Niagara reef can be used by fish from May through August. But by and large, the majority of the walleyes will use the areas shown. □

DEPTH

As Lake Erie anglers began to catch suspended fish, they noted that the depth level the walleyes used often varied. For example, one portion of a massive group of walleyes might be foraging actively on a school of shiners and driving them up to about the 5 foot level. At the same time, however, another group of walleyes located a mile away, but part of the same "mega school," may have just fed and dropped down under or off to the side of a mass of baitfish, hovering at about 15 or 20 feet. Therefore, at any given time,

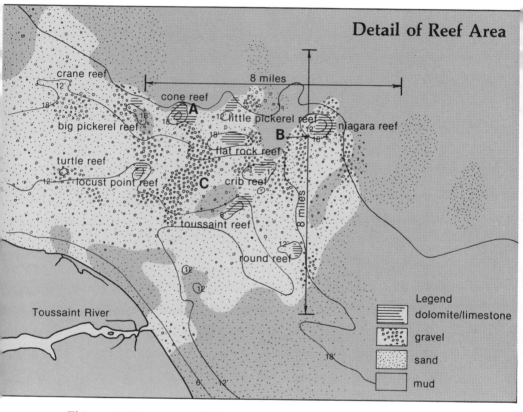

Detail of Reef Area

crane reef
cone reef
A
big pickerel reef
little pickerel reef
niagara reef
B
flat rock reef
turtle reef
locust point reef
C
crib reef
toussaint reef
round reef
Toussaint River
8 miles
8 miles

Legend
dolomite/limestone
gravel
sand
mud

This map indicates some of the structural elements you can expect to encounter on Lake Erie. It also gives you an idea of the expanse of the conditions. For example, the section from Crane to Niagara and from Niagara to Round Reef alone is 64 square miles—or 41,000 acres. All of this is seasonally fishable water!

Because of the vast scope of the structural elements, the number of walleyes present and the way most people fish (drifting), it's easy to lose sight of the fact that the walleyes do indeed tend to relate to bottom content, especially early and late in the summer season. The fish also tend to move toward the shallower reef areas at dusk.

Sharp-eyed observers, in fact, have noted that Lake Erie walleyes will pack into some areas more than others. Spots like Area A—a funnel area in the rock; Area B—a drop-off that changes from rock to gravel; or Area C—a bend where rock fades into sand, are all prime spots.

While fish can and do use this entire area, concentrations of fish are more likely to be found in spots where there is some kind of break in an otherwise constant terrain. Not all the time—but more times than not.

various walleye groups can be right at the surface or suspended 5, 10, 15 or 20 feet below it. This vertical positioning not only changes from day to day, but from hour to hour as well. Consequently, if a lure runs too high, or too low, it will be out of the fish zone. And if a lure is used that only runs at a certain depth, or has to constantly be adjusted in order to change depth—overall angler efficiency suffers tremendously.

The problem of staying on the fish, however, is more complicated than simply working depth. While there is a great deal of vertical movement of fish, there is almost constant horizontal movement as well.

WALLEYE MOVEMENT AND POSITION ACCORDING TO SEASON

The majority of the walleyes in Lake Erie's western basin make very predictable seasonal migrations, based principally on water temperature and available food. Granted, there are small resident populations of fish in some areas, as well as maverick packs that react contrary to the greater mass of fish. These walleye groups "ride out" adverse conditions like low oxygen, high temperatures and turbidity. However, if you follow the prevailing seasonal movements, you're bound to catch fish most of the time.

FIGURE 1

May to the first week of June: *Surface water temperature at this time will generally be between 62°F and 66°F. Most of the walleye activity will be concentrated within the first 3 miles of shore, along the south shore of the western basin in water shallower than 20 feet. On most days the water will have a steady, moderate-sized chop.*

Baitfish will usually be in the upper 10 to 12 feet of water with the walleyes hovering slightly below this level, except when feeding. Active walleyes will move right in among the baitfish. Rough fish like sheepshead will generally be down along the bottom.

FIGURE 2

The first week of June to the second week of July: *By this time the surface water temperature will climb to about 66°F to 68°F. This is the period when the open water fishing begins, and is located primarily between East, West and Middle Sister Islands. During this period the prevailing winds are unpredictable and the lake can vacillate from roaring seas to glass-clam.*

Much of the plankton will be found in the top 6 feet of water. Consequently, many baitfish will be riding high, particularly the smaller ones and the young-of-the-year fish. The larger-sized baitfish and perch, however, might be slightly deeper—perhaps in the 10 foot range. The walleye groups can be found—depending upon the local weather conditions, the positions of forage and the intensity of water traffic—anywhere from 5 to 25 feet deep. As a rule, rough fish like sheepshead and catfish will be found deeper than the walleye schools. Day-by-day, and even hour-by-hour checks are necessary to stay on the fish.

FIGURE 3

Mid-July through August: *During this period the water temperature will reach its peak—somewhere between 69°F and 72°F. When this happens, oxygen depletion can occur in the shallow shoreline reef sections along the American side, particularly during periods of calm. Although certain resident fish remain on the outer shoreline reefs, they become quite lethargic during periods of oxygen reduction and when the water becomes turbid from storms. Much of the open water fishing also begins to dissipate.*

At this time of year most of the fish move to the deeper reefs that bound the Canadian and Bass Islands, particularly in areas where current flow is active. Once on the reefs, the walleyes tend to relate to structural elements—although suspension outside of or between reefs is not uncommon. □

268

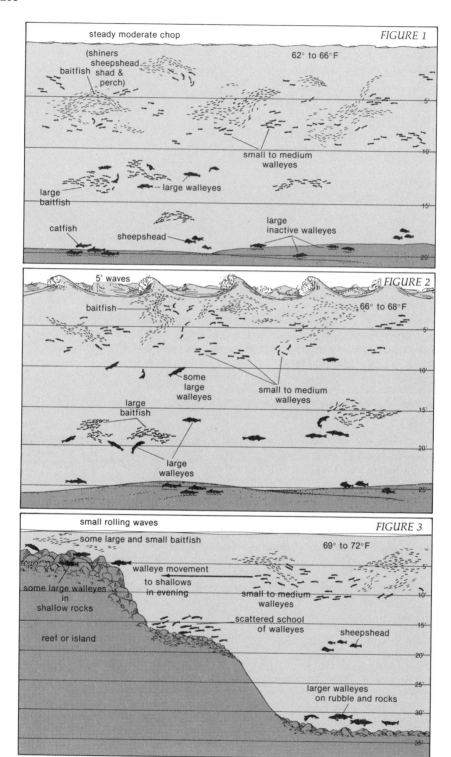

FIGURE 1

steady moderate chop

62° to 66°F

(shiners
sheepshead
baitfish shad &
perch)

small to medium
walleyes

large
baitfish

large walleyes

catfish

sheepshead

large
inactive walleyes

5'

10'

15'

20'

FIGURE 2

5' waves

66° to 68°F

baitfish

some
large
walleyes

small to medium
walleyes

large
baitfish

large
walleyes

5'

10'

15'

20'

25'

FIGURE 3

small rolling waves

some large and small baitfish

69° to 72°F

walleye movement
to shallows
in evening

some large walleyes
in
shallow rocks

small to medium
walleyes

scattered school
of walleyes

sheepshead

reef or island

larger walleyes
on rubble and rocks

5'

10'

15'

20'

25'

30'

35'

SEASONAL LOCATION

Tagging studies indicate the walleyes of Lake Erie's western basin make very predictable seasonal migrations. The fish display definite homing instincts and return to particular reefs and rivers year after year to spawn. Pre-spawn walleyes assemble along the southwest shore of Lake Erie in late February and March. Spawning itself usually takes place in rivers in late March and early April, and in mid-April on the offshore reefs. After spawning is complete and the water begins to warm, the fish make a slow but steady retreat from the shallows to deeper water.

The western basin of Lake Erie is quite shallow, averaging perhaps 27 feet. Thus the shallow water runs perhaps 5-10 feet and the deep water about 15-30 feet or so. By June and July many of the gargantuan walleye schools are operating in the deeper, open-water sections, suspending over 30-35 feet of water.

While the fish will settle in generalized areas for a period of time, Lake Erie fishermen are *never* dealing with stationary populations as such—a situation that is obviously quite different than fishing walleye schools that relate to defined structural elements, such as reefs. So just as the constant vertical fish movements have a bearing on the way a Lake Erie angler fishes, the tendency of the walleyes to constantly mill about also has a dramatic effect on presentation. When faced with this predicament, a lure must not only suit the walleyes, but the fishing method must also take into account the various caprices of walleye behavior.

The problem is further complicated by the fact that Lake Erie is a big water —so large, in fact, that high-powered boats are necessary, not only to cope with the high waves and strong winds, but also to run the distances required to stay with the migrating fish. Since big boats are the order of the day, and 25-30 foot, open-deck cruisers are common, a certain approach to fishing these moving, milling, suspended walleyes has developed.

FISHING THE PACK

Obviously, a school of walleyes that's a half-mile wide and a mile long is pretty tough to keep a secret. Once a boat or two starts catching fish, they quickly draw a crowd. These small armadas, often consisting of 100 boats or more, are referred to as "packs" by Lake Erie anglers, and are a sure tip-off there are walleyes to be caught in the area.

These open water "wolf packs" have fashioned an etiquette of sorts. Experience has shown that running over the fish schools (particularly the shallow-riding ones) with a big whining motor will drive a walleye school off. So as a matter of courtesy, you do not come into the fishing grounds on the run and gun your motor over the fish. This obviously negates trolling as an approach. And under most circumstances, anchoring isn't the answer either. Even if you could anchor, the fish in the midst of all the activity would—in most instances—move off in a short time anyway.

When all things are considered, the easiest, most effective, efficient (and thus the primary) method of presentation is to *cast and drift*. This approach is not without some drawbacks, however. When a big boat passes over a school that is riding high near the surface, the fish will likely move down or slightly off to the side of the drifting boat.

THE MAGIC COMBINATION

While faced with a multitude of presentation problems, the walleye fishermen of Lake Erie have nonetheless learned to deal with all of these contingencies, and have solved the puzzle in a simple and easy manner. They drift, cast and retrieve in a manner called the "count down and swing." After trying all kinds of contraptions, they found that the lure best suited for this type of fishing is an outlandish piece of hardware generically called a "weight-forward spinner." You can drift, cast, let it sink to a specific level, and best of all catch fish like crazy.

In short, a system of fishing walleyes has developed on Lake Erie that, to our knowledge, is unique to a specific lake. However, it also seems that this very productive system is simply the product of how the local anglers adapted their methods to best cope with the prevailing conditions.

Yet when all is said and done, we are still perplexed about certain aspects of the Lake Erie suspended walleye phenomenon. For example, one of the walleyes' favorite foods is the emerald shiner. Yet shiners dressed on the back of the weight-forward spinner don't work as well as a nightcrawler—a bait that's not natural to the environment. A local theory is that the nightcrawler emits a scent trail which the walleyes find irresistible. But, a leech emits a scent, and the walleyes still pick the nightcrawler. We found this hard to accept, since walleyes on most waters love leeches.

Furthermore, a gob of nightcrawlers dangling beneath a slip bobber—usually a good bait under certain conditions—is nowhere near as effective on open water walleyes as a piece of nightcrawler draped on the back of a large, cumbersome spinner. One would think that a plain, lively nightcrawler bobbing up and down (and wiggling around) at just the right depth would be irresistible—but it isn't.

Interestingly, Lake Erie has had a tremendous increase in the number of bloodworms present during the past few years. The bloodworm is a creature that is quite tolerant of low oxygen levels, enabling it to survive in areas that occasionally experience oxygen depletion. Perhaps the walleyes developed a taste for these critters after the mayfly nymphs disappeared. Since nightcrawlers are similar enough in appearance, this fact might have something to do with the nightcrawler preference phenomenon.

Live bait rigs are a top fish catcher on Lake Erie in April and again in late August. But with the exception of catching sheepshead and catfish, they are not very productive for suspended walleyes in June and July. Crankbaits and slip bobber rigs, on the other hand, work quite well toward evening fished near some very shallow reefs. These same lures, however, just don't "cut it" casting for suspended walleyes out in deeper water during the day—even though they run at the exact levels that many of the fish are. However, pioneer captains like Jim Fofrich are beginning to apply the down-rigging system and take walleyes trolling crankbaits. The method is still in its infancy, though.

While we don't have all the answers, the count down system using weight-forward spinners is obviously tailor-made for catching Lake Erie's suspended walleyes. It presents a tempting bait at the proper depth and speed to trigger fish. Only time will tell whether or not the system spreads to become popular in other areas. Initial experiments indicate that it will.

We feel that perhaps this system can be exported and applied on the big, windswept waters of the Triangle area of Lake of the Woods on the Minnesota/Canada border. Commercial fishermen have been known to hang suspended nets for walleyes there, just as they do on Lake Erie. If a sufficient-sized population is present, the count down and drift approach might open up a new realm of fishing on these waters. This system might also work on huge Lake Winnebago in Wisconsin. We've already used it on the Missouri River reservoirs with great success. We're sure it would work on Lakes Winnipeg, Manitoba, and Winnepegosis in the Canadian province of Manitoba, since these lakes have conditions that are very similar to that of Lake Erie. So, even if you don't fish Lake Erie, you should know how it works.

THE COUNT DOWN SYSTEM

No one knows for sure who it was that first discovered the suspended walleyes in the open waters of Lake Erie. Some say it was a group of fishermen from Toledo who used to troll a little-known weedbed beyond Middle Sister Island. As the story goes, they stumbled onto the suspended fish when they unwittingly trolled off into open water in 1975. The wildfire was further spread by a widely-published aerial photo taken a short time later. It showed a "mega school" of walleyes that was several miles long and perhaps 3/4 of a mile wide. It really didn't matter who was first to find the fish, because it wasn't long before everyone knew there was an El Dorado of golden walleyes for the taking out in the open water.

In 1968, a Lake Erie walleye guide named Captain Dan Galbincea designed and marketed a lure called the Erie Dearie. It was not an instant success, to say the least. For seven years he sold some here, some there, supplementing his income during the off-season. The slow sales really didn't bother Dan since he used the lures on his own boat anyway. But in 1975, when walleye anglers discovered (or rediscovered) the suspended walleye phenomenon, everything exploded. Orders came in faster than Dan could fill them! The time for a new "hot lure" had come—and nothing could stop it.

The Erie Dearie, like all lures, however, was not in a class by itself. It was the successor to a long line of forerunners. For years veteran guides Dick Dunlop, Jim Fofrich and Glen Lau had used lures that employed the basic weight-forward/center-spinner concept. Bygone favorites like the Paul Bunyan 66, the June Bug, Lau Lures and Rugheads had long been popular. Nightcrawlers, too, were a historic staple on Lake Erie. Yet these lures and 'crawlers had been used mostly on the reefs, rather than in open water. The open water application, or what is today called the "count down" system, is a product of the last five years.

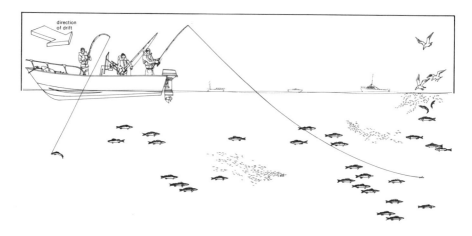

In order to start catching suspended walleyes you must first determine the depth that most of the fish are at. To accomplish this you can, for example, have one fisherman try an 8 count, another a 10 count, another a 12 count, and so on. Then, as soon as fish contact is made, the rest of the fishermen can switch to the count that's most productive.

Here's how it works. Cast out, and as soon as the bait hits the water, count one thousand-one, one thousand-two, etc., up to one thousand-eight if you desire an 8 count. Then begin your retrieve, experimenting a bit with the motion of the lure. You might crank 7 or 8 times, then sweep the rod tip to the side, crank 7 or 8 times and sweep it back again—thus darting the lure from side to side all the way back to the boat. Or you might set up a slow lift-and-drop type of pumping motion throughout the whole retrieve. Naturally, you can try any number of variations.

The initial retrieve speed might be a slow one, and can be increased after a number of casts if you're not taking fish. Sometimes the walleyes want a slow-moving lure, while at other times they prefer one that's moving fast, so it pays to experiment. The other anglers should try much the same thing at their respective depths until fish contact is made. Once you establish a pattern, say, for example, on a 10 count, your fishing partners would then switch over to a 10 count as well.

This is the prime method used to catch suspended walleyes on Lake Erie. The count down system can be used all through the season, but it is most effective in July and August. During June and September, when the walleyes relate more closely to the reefs and use shallow water, you might crawl the bait along just above the bottom.

THE BASIC LURE

The reason the weight-forward spinner concept is so successful is that the depth the lure runs at is not determined by adjusting a lip or adding weight to the lure, but by *varying the length of time the lure is allowed to sink before it is retrieved*. This easy flexibility is the key to the lure's amazing productivity and popularity. If the fish change depth, it's not necessary to change lures, add weight or fiddle with adjustment. Simply let the lure sink a bit longer or shorter before you begin your retrieve. It's that simple!

Most half-ounce models sink about 1 foot for every 1-1/2 seconds of drop time. For example, if you count at one count per second and want the lure to go down 10 feet, you simply count, "one thousand, two thousand. . .etc." until you reach 15 thousand. Thus the term "the count down" system.

Cadence, of course, varies from angler to angler. Some folks count faster than others. But that doesn't matter as long as the angler selects his own *personal* count and lets the lure fall to the depth desired before he starts to retrieve.

Although there are many kinds of weight-forward spinners, they all drop relatively slow and tend to ride on a fairly level plane when retrieved. There are, however, slight variations depending on the individual design, and each spinner has a unique kind of kick or side-to-side wave—or the lack of it. This is caused when the speed of retrieve is suddenly altered. This "kick" or "wave" appears to be one of the secrets of the weight-forward spinner's success.

There are four basic designs of weight-forward spinners: (1) the standard rig, (2) the overhead spinner rig, (3) the twin spin, and (4) a unique new innovation—the flat spinner. Each performs a little differently, and it's important to understand their individual qualities in order to match your lure choice to the conditions.

The standard rig: This lure design features all the weight up front and a spinner blade behind it—hence the designation, "weight-forward spinner." The weight is made of lead and is usually shaped to form a keel of sorts. This is an integral part of the design. The lead body provides the necessary weight to cast and sink the lure, and also acts as a rudder to guide its track and action. The spinner, on the other hand, slows the lure's fall, acts as an attractor, and provides sway, vibration, kick and lift to the lure. Finally, behind the spinner lies a large, long shank, pivoting hook. That's the lure in all its simple glory—a hunk of lead, a spinner and a hook.

The overhead spinner: This lure is no more than a standard weight-forward spinner with a safety pin spinner substituted in place of the wire forearm. This modification allows the lure to drop slower and more level than the standard model. It can be retrieved so slowly that the spinner behind the lead head simply flicks from side-to-side instead of rotating.

One advantage of this set-up is that it allows you to cast a heavier lure into the wind and yet still be able to retrieve it very slowly. It has more lift at a slower rate of retrieve, and rides at a shallower level than a standard rig of the same weight and size.

The overhead spinner has a more distinctive kick action and side-to-side sway than the standard rig. There are times when little peculiarities like these can make a big difference. One other advantage of the overhead spinner is that it can also be crawled along the bottom with fewer hang-ups—a definite advantage when working reefs.

The twin spinner: This lure differs from the standard overhead rigs in that it has a pair of smaller overhead spinners *in front* of the weight instead of behind it. Also, most models sport a single fixed hook instead of a pivoting one. While not technically a weight-forward spinner, these lures nonetheless are classed with them.

Some twin spinners have the eyelet molded directly into the lead head, while others sport a wire forearm. Some are two-piece, hinged affairs, and others are

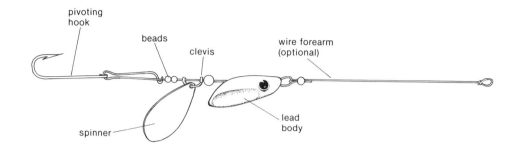

Despite all the different designs, colors and modifications, a weight-forward spinner is composed simply of (1) a lead head, (2) a wire shaft, (3) several beads, a clevis and a blade, and (4) a pivoting hook. While this lure is simple, it is nonetheless a potent fish attractor. With the addition of a nightcrawler this lure has all of the basic triggers that make a fish strike. The lure rides at the right depth and speed, and has built-in action, color, size, sound, shape, scent and even texture with the addition of a nightcrawler. The lure is truly a masterpiece of simplicity, and that's why it works.

single-bodied. Some have nylon or hair skirts, while others simply have a plain fixed hook in the rear.

Twin spin models drop more slowly and helicopter more vertically than all of the other spinner types. They're used mostly in shallow water and near reefs.

Twin spins do not exhibit the pronounced kick or lateral "swing and sway" that the other models do. There are occasional times, although few in number, when the fish are not triggered by a "kick" in the lure. Twin spins are excellent choices for these conditions.

Flat spinners: This model is a new innovation. The lead body is thin and flat and has both an overhead and a central spinner. Of all the spinner types, this design, because of its large, flat, keel-type body, allows for the most conspicuous "kick" when the lure changes speed and direction during what is termed the "swing." This lure, like the twin spin, can also be used quite successfully by inexperienced anglers.

There are many different modifications of these four basic lure types. Today there are perhaps three dozen different manufacturers of weight-forward spinners. Some of these are manufactured by brand name national manufacturers, while others are made in basement operations. Each spinner has its own peculiar functions.

Here's a Lake Erie rule of thumb regarding color and size selection: Start with silver and then start experimenting with hues ranging from bright to dark. The primary lure sizes are 3/8, 1/2 and 5/8 ounce, with the 3/8 ounce size perhaps the most commonly used.

Eight pound test monofilament is the best line for fishing weight-forward spinners. Heavier lines do not cast as far, and since they're more easily seen, they may discourage strikes in the clearer water sections of Lake Erie. If a big fish is played carefully, 8 pound test line is all that's needed. Wire leaders should never be used since they interfere with lure action and show up like a rope even in discolored water.

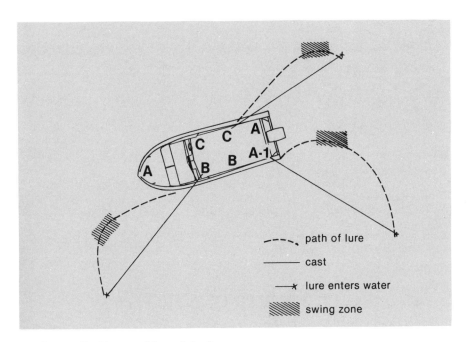

path of lure

cast

lure enters water

swing zone

Casting Positions and Lure Selection

Lake Erie walleye fishing is usually a party effort. Fishermen consequently spread out into casting positions as shown in the accompanying drawing. Some positions, however, are better than others, and can spell the difference between taking plenty of fish, or just a few. Thus it's best to occasionally trade spots to give everyone an equal opportunity to catch fish.

*These best casting positions are labeled **A**. It's easiest to cast forward and out to the sides of the boat from these spots. The walleye schools often shift to either side of the boat as it drifts by, putting the folks at position **A** in perfect location to cast to them. It's also far easier to make a long cast and work the "swing" from these spots.*

*Position **A** on the bow is an excellent spot, but it takes an experienced angler with a good sense of balance to stand up on the front deck in rolling seas. The captain or first mate often occupies this spot. The prime interior position lies at the rear corner at **A-1**, and is definitely the spot to be. The other transom corner at **A** is nearly as good.*

*Positions **B** at the downwind center of the boat are only moderately productive. It's harder to make a long cast and reach fish that have moved to the side. It's also awkward to work the "swing" from this location.*

*Positions **C**, meanwhile, are the most difficult of all to fish from. From **C** you cast to the side, let the lure sink, and then begin the "swing" almost immediately. It only lasts a short time and then you have to reel in and start over. Postion **C** offers the least opportunity to reach the fish before you drift past them.*

There are a wide variety of weight-forward spinners in use on Lake Erie. Yet even with such diversity, they can be classified into four basic groups.

Of the five vertical columns of lures shown here, the two at the left depict several brands of overhead spinners. From top to bottom, the accompanying photo shows a Walleye Princess and a Lindy Tom's Walleye Lure in the 1st column, and a Heddon Jolly Wolly and a Walleye Super Bullet in the 2nd.

The 3rd and 4th columns contain eight of the most popular standard weight-forward spinners. Again from top to bottom, the 3rd column contains Bob Parker's Deep Spin,

THE NIGHTCRAWLER CONTROVERSY

To drape or to thread? A whole 'crawler or only a piece? These are the questions. When only one kind of bait and basically one kind of lure are used, arguments on usage are bound to emerge.

Regardless of the method used, a *well-threaded* 'crawler stays on the hook much better than one that's just hung on. Consequently, you'll save more bait by threading them on.

The walleyes of Lake Erie have a peculiar affinity for nightcrawlers in summer. Why? Well, some speculate that they exude an oily scent trail which is irresistible to the fish. In reality, though, no one knows for sure. Nonetheless, pure experience has shown that the nightcrawler is far and away the number one live bait during the summer.

Lindy's Charter's Choice, an Erie Dearie and a Hildebrandt Whizzo. The 4th features a Mepps Lusox, Lindy's Tom's Walleye Lure, a Bar Bumper and a Parish Lure. The inset shows a West Sister Twister, the newest of the spinners. These are your standard choices for most conditions.

The column at the far right shows two different types of lures. The top two are twin spinners—a Danny's Old Reliable and a Nugget. At the bottom is Lindy's Wall-Eye Catcher—a new flat spinner design with extra vibration and kick.

These are only a handful of the many lures currently in use for Lake Erie's suspended walleyes. We suggest you pick up an assortment to experiment with.

EQUIPMENT

As with all methods of fishing, there are fine points of technique. The count down system involves more than just casting, counting and retrieving. Thus it's important to know the type of equipment that's needed and how to employ it.

Nearly any kind of freshwater rod and reel will work for the count down system. Baitcasting and spincasting both have their adherents, but probably the most popular is open-face spinning gear. The fixed-spool of a spinning reel allows the longest casts and gives the fisherman the ability to fire the lure into the wind.

Spinning rods should be 6-7 feet long, and should be designed for lures that weigh 1/4-1/2 ounce. A long rod helps increase your casting distance, set the hook better, and maintain tension while playing the fish. It also provides the leverage to sweep and pump your lure through the water.

The count down system is best accomplished with a slow retrieve. Thus a 3-1 gear ratio reel allows a more consistent lure retrieve. Some folks who use a 5-1 gear ratio reel have a difficult time disciplining themselves to "crank" slowly and steadily enough. If you are constantly casting, pumping and retrieving, a lightweight reel will help save your arms.

The accompanying photo shows several typical casting positions. Captain Tom Roginski of the Count Down occupies the back downwind corner at **A-1**, his son is fishing at A and Dave Csanda is fishing downwind from Position **B**. If there were more anglers aboard, they'd have to fill in at the less desirable "**C**" position.

Depending on where you are stationed in the boat and the force of the wind (and thus the consequent speed of drift), different weights are needed. The following chart shows our recommendations for a standard model weight-forward spinner.

WEIGHT SELECTION FOR FISH SHALLOWER THAN 17 FT.

WIND SPEED	LURE SIZE		
	POSITION A	POSITION B	POSITION C
calm to 7 mph	3/8 oz.	1/2 oz.	1/2 oz.
7 to 12 mph	3/8 oz.	1/2 oz.	5/8 oz.
12 to 18 mph	1/2 oz.	5/8 oz.	5/8 oz.
18 mph and over	5/8 oz.	5/8 oz. w/extra weight	5/8 oz. w/extra weight

NOTE: For depths over 17 ft., or during very strong winds, use 1/2 or 5/8 oz. spinners, either plain or with extra weight as needed.

FISH ACTIVITY

Two major factors usually combine to determine whether or not the fish will be active: water temperature and water clarity. The feeling among the experts is, "If they (walleyes) can't see it (the lure), they can't hit it." Turbidity still is and will continue to be a problem along the southwest shore of Lake Erie.

The vacillating winds, one moment dead calm—the next producing eight foot waves—drastically affect fishing. When a good northwestern wind comes

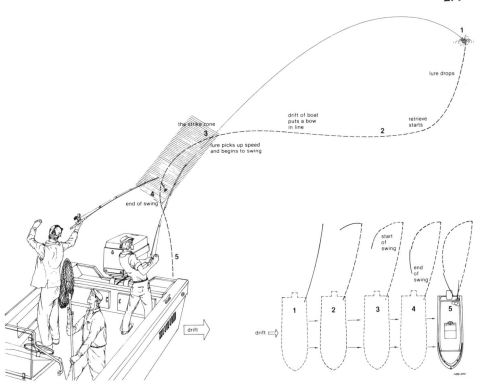

Playing The Swing

Because of the way the weight-forward spinner functions during the drift and retrieve, the lure changes speed and direction a number of times. Experience shows that many strikes are triggered when these changes occur. Indeed, there is even a probable strike zone along the lure's path.

Casting position within the boat makes a difference as to how this method of retrieve is executed. It's called "playing the swing," and works much the same as shown here.

Drift Position 1: *Cast the lure downwind and slightly to the side of the boat. The lure is allowed to sink until the retrieve is begun.*

Drift Position 2: *There is little tension on the line as the boat drifts toward the lure. The spinner just sort of swims along at a slight angle to the boat until the pull is almost perpendicular to the transom.*

Drift Position 3: *As soon as the lure draws even with the drifting boat, the slack disappears and the line suddenly tightens up. This action increases the speed and vibration of the lure. The drift is such that when this happens, a distinct turn in the lure's direction occurs, along with a "kick" and slight lift of the spinner itself. Apparently fish are triggered by this erratic movement. This is the beginning point of the "strike zone" where most strikes occur, and is commonly referred to as the start of the "swing."*

Drift Position 4: *Shortly after the line draws taut and the lure's circuit makes its first turn, another turn occurs. As the boat continues to drift and the line further straightens out, the lure kicks and lifts again. This point usually marks the end of the prime strike zone—the end of the "swing."*

Drift Position 5: *Although some fish can be caught anywhere from the last turn all the way back to the boat, they are generally few in number. Dropping the lure back so it falls momentarily and then giving it a lift or pump will help trigger a following fish.*

Naturally there are various modifications of "playing the swing." If you have a bad casting position, you must make whatever accommodations the situation calls for. Some old Lake Erie walleye hands constantly pump and drop the lure during the entire retrieve, while others use a more steady retrieve and only pump the lure every now and then. Others work the spinner in big sweeps. Regardless of how you fish the lure, however, you must constantly be on guard for a strike. If you get a tap and miss the fish, drop back on the lure and then slowly lift it again. You may reattract the fish for a "second whack."

in and stirs up the water along the south shore of the lake, the good fisherman heads *north* for clearer water.

Water temperatures, too, play a big part in walleye location. From spring to fall the water temperature in the western basin runs from a cool 55°F in May to a warm 75°F in August. Lake Erie, being "big water," has currents driven by seasonal prevailing winds. Thus these winds have an effect on both temperature and turbidity. In the beginning of the season the walleye schools will hang along the reefs along the south shore, but as the temperature starts to rise to the 60°F's and the water becomes murky, the fish move out farther and farther away from shore.

The section of Lake Erie you fish depends, of course, upon where your boat originally pulls out from. Packs of anglers can and do report good catches from many distant areas on any given day. Some anglers fish on the American side all the time. Others, particularly in late summer, fish the Canadian waters. Some alternate between both. While specific location on Lake Erie can be the subject of an entire book, most anglers can locate fish simply by asking questions at the various landings where they dock. It's as simple as that. Or, better yet, take a few trips with experienced charter captains to get the hang of things. It's a wise investment.

We think you'll agree there is a tremendous amount of information between the covers of this book. However, there's more to come! Fathering knowledge is a never-ending process, and we have many topics that could already be added to this book, if only there was enough space. We have conclusive evidence of how lunar periods affect big walleyes, and what effects pH has on walleye location. We didn't even touch the topic of ice fishing—something we have a lot of new concepts on that we'd like to share. Lakes—rivers—reservoirs—there are scads of subjects being further researched and refined on all these waters. *WALLEYE WISDOM* is only the beginning!

Some might feel that a book like this is what creates pressure on our fisheries. They're right! But suppression of knowledge is not the answer. We believe that knowledge, and the ability to catch fish, absolutely leads to responsible conservation, not the opposite. Always consider, "that with knowledge comes the responsibility to use that *knowledge wisely!*"

That's it, folks! If you study the information provided here and go out and catch more walleyes, then we've accomplished our purpose. Good fishing!

The Walleye Fisherman's
GLOSSARY

ADAPTATION: The process of getting used to or fitting into a particular set of environmental circumstances.

AGGREGATION: A group of gamefish or prey fish holding in an area, but not moving together in a school. See *school*.

ALGAE: Simple, one cell plants usually having the ability to photosynthesize sunlight into energy. Initial step in a food chain.

ALLEY: Parallel openings between patches of emergent weeds (usually bulrushes), or emergent weeds and the shoreline.

APPETITE MOODS: The three basic attitudes of fish toward feeding. See *positive, neutral and negative feeding moods.*

BACKTROLLING: A system of boat control, simultaneously moving a boat slowly in reverse and using lure or bait presentations (casting or trolling).

BASIC NATURE: A species' inherent makeup or tendencies which determines its niche in an environment.

BASIC NEEDS: The three basic survival requirements of any fish species; namely reproduction, suitable habitat and food. A favorable environment fulfills these needs.

BASIN ZONE: A lake zone. The area lying below the Deep Water Zone, beginning where hard bottom ends and soft bottom begins. This zone includes the deepest water areas.

BIOLOGY: The study of living things.

BITING: The feeding action of a hungry fish. See *striking.*

BOAT CONTROL: Boat use to aid bait or lure presentation. See *backtrolling, controlled drift, front trolling, speedtrolling.*

BOTTOM-BUMPER: A lure or rig which strikes the bottom (i.e. jig).

BOTTOM CONFIGURATION: A locational factor; the relative make-up (shape, size, depth, islands, etc.) of the bottom.

BOTTOM CONTENT: Bottom types in a body of water (rock, sand, gravel, silt, muck, submerged cribs, brush and/or trees, etc.).

BREAK: Any change in otherwise regular terrain.

BREAKLINE: That point in a body of water where there is a definite increase in depth—sudden or gradual—or a change in cover, like a weedline or brushline; edge of channel or hole; where two layers of water meet and differ in temperature, oxygen and/or turbidity; the limit of effective light penetration, etc.

BREAKLINE, SECONDARY: A second or auxilary point of change. For example, a second definite increase in depth after the first drop-off.

BRUSHLINE: The inside or outside edge of a line of brush.

CABBAGE: Any of the pondweeds (Potamogeton); usually attractive to gamefish.

CALENDAR, IN-FISHERMAN: A calendar based on ten identifiable periods of activity for various species of gamefish. These ten periods constitute a *fish cycle.*

CALENDAR PERIOD: Any of the ten periods of fish activity in the IN-FISHERMAN Calendar.

CLEAN BOTTOM: The bottom (usually hard bottom) of a body of water that is free of debris, etc.

CLIMATE: The average weather conditions for a region.

COLD FRONT: The line of impact when cold air forces the warm air upwards. As a cold front moves, cold air beneath is slowed down by contact with the ground, and piles up. This pile of cold air forces warm air up very rapidly, often causing storms. See *post-front.*

COLD WATER PERIOD: A period of the fish cycle which occurs twice—in early spring between the Frozen Water and Pre-spawn Periods, and in late fall between the Turnover and Frozen Water Periods. Most times applied to the fall season.

COMPETITIVE SPECIES: An aspect of *social condition* involving the relationship of species within a body of water, particularly in regard to available food and spawning areas.

CONTROLLED DRIFT: A system of *boat control* using an outboard, electric trolling motor or oars to keep a boat moving along a specific course.

COSMIC CLOCK: The sun's effect on water and local weather factors, such as barometric pressure, wind, cloud cover, seasonal change, etc.

CRANKBAIT: A lipped diving plug.

DEEP WATER ZONE: A lake zone. Hard bottom lying below the first major drop-off and below the open water zone. It ends where soft bottom begins.

DEPTH CONTROL: One of two primary factors in successful bait or lure presentation.

DISSOLVED OXYGEN: (DO). Oxygen chemically bound into water by forces such as wind and plants. It is utilized by fish.

DROP-OFF: A point where there is definite increase in depth.

ECOLOGY: The branch of biology dealing with relations between organisms and their environment.

ECOSYSTEM: A system formed by the interaction of a community of organisms and their surroundings.

ELECTROPHORESIS: A process that can determine the genetic make-up of fish.

EPILIMNION: The warmer layer of water above the *thermocline.*

EROSION: The process by which the surface of the earth is being constantly worn away. The most important elements responsible for erosion are rivers and streams, wind, waves and glaciers.

EUTROPHIC: A *lake classification* or lake type used to describe bodies of water characterized by high levels of nutrients in proportion to their total volume of water.

FANCAST: To make a series of casts systematically covering an area.

FISH CONTACT: Locating fish—usually by catching them. Includes visual observation.

FISH CYCLE: All ten Calendar Periods. See *Calendar,* IN-FISHERMAN.

FISHING PRESSURE: The number of anglers using a body of water.

FLAT: An area characterized by little or no change in depth.

FOOD CHAIN: A step-by-step representation of feeding relationships in a community. Food chains originate with the sun's energy and each link in the chain represents energy transfer. All the food chains in a community make up a food web.

FOOD PRODUCING AREA: Any area that seasonally produces forage for fish.

FRONT TROLLING: A system of *boat control* with the boat moving forward.

FROZEN WATER PERIOD: A period of the fish cycle when a body of water is mostly or completely covered by ice. In Southern waters, which rarely freeze, the sustained period of coldest water.

GEOLOGY: The science dealing with the earth's physical history.

HABITAT: The place where a plant or animal species lives.

HARD BOTTOM: Firm bottom areas (sand, clay, rock, gravel, etc.).

HIGH PROTEIN FORAGE: High-fat content, soft-rayed forage species such as ciscoes and whitefish.

HOLDING STATION: Any specific position regardless of depth where fish spend much of their time.

HYPOED LAKE: A body of water stocked with a species of fish to bolster its natural fishery.

HYPOLIMNION: The colder layer of water below the *thermocline.*

IMPOUNDMENT: A confined area where water accumulates, usually the result of damming a river. See *reservoir.*

INFILLING: The process by which higher surrounding terrain tends to fill in lower terrain.

INSIDE EDGE (OF WEEDS): A line of weeds between the shoreline and the weedline. See *outside edge* (of weeds).

JUNK WEEDS: Any type of weed usually not attractive to gamefish.

LAKE CLASSIFICATIONS: Broad categories of lake types; oligotrophic (infertile), mesotrophic (fertile), eutrophic (very fertile).

LAKE MODIFICATION FORCES: Forces such as ice action, wave action, erosion, etc., which change bodies of water.

LAKE TYPE: A group of bodies of water whose characteristics are similar enough to one another that they can be approached from an angling standpoint in much the same manner. See *lake classifications.*

LAKE ZONES: Four designated IN-FISHERMAN water zones: *shallow water, open water, deep water and basin zones.*

LIMNOLOGY: The study of the biological, chemical, geographical and physical features of bodies of water.

LITTORAL ZONE: Shallow water zone.

LOCAL WEATHER FACTORS: The prevailing weather conditions affecting the day-to-day locational patterns of a fish species.

LOCATIONAL PATTERN: Where, why and how a species positions itself to take advantage of its surroundings.

LOOSE ACTION PLUG: A lure whose side-to-side movements are wide and distinct.

MARL: Deposits of sand, clay and silt with a high concentration of shells (calcium carbonate).

MESOTROPHIC: *Lake classification* used to describe fertile bodies of water between the late-stage *oligotrophic* and early-stage *eutrophic* classifications.

MIGRATION: The movement of fish from one area to another. Migrations generally occur on a seasonal basis, from one set of distinct environmental conditions to another, such as from winter habitat toward spwaning areas. They would not be confused with *movements*.

MORAINE: A mass of rocks, sand, etc., deposited by a glacier.

MOVEMENT: The locational shift of fish from one area to another, generally on a daily or even hourly basis. Also can refer to fish changing from a neutral to a positive feeding mood, with fish shifting only a few feet from a resting to an advantageous feeding position. A *directional* movement is one which is made from one specific area to another specific area, usually at a fast rate of speed. A *random* movement is the slow milling activity made within a specific area.

NEGATIVE FEEDING MOOD: An *appetite mood* in which the attitude of fish is negative toward biting. Fish also are said to be inactive.

NEUTRAL FEEDING MOOD: An *appetite mood*. The attitude of fish which are not actively feeding but could be tempted through refined presentation. See *striking*.

NICHE: Based on a species' characteristics, and depending on competing species, an organism assumes a particular role and a set of physical surroundings within an ecosystem.

NURSERY AREA: Areas where fish species are reared to the fingerling stage.

OLIGOTROPHIC: *Lake classification* used to describe bodies of water characterized by low amounts of nutrients in proportion to their total volume of water. Infertile.

OPEN WATER ZONE: A lake zone. The upper water layer from the outside edge of the first major drop-off down to the deep water zone.

OUTSIDE EDGE (OF WEEDS): The *weedline*. The outside edge of a line of weeds.

PATTERN: Any consistently reoccurring locational/presentational situation.

PHOTOSYNTHESIS: Green plants have chlorophyll which allows them to synthesize organic compounds from water and carbon dioxide using the sun's energy. This is called photosynthesis, and produces oxygen.

POPULATION DENSITY: The number of individuals occupying a certain area. For example, the number of bass per acre.

POSITIVE FEEDING MOOD: An *appetite mood*. The attitude of fish which are actively feeding.

POST-FRONT: That period after a weather front. Usually used in reference to a cold front when the atmosphere becomes clear and bright, and is accompanied by strong winds and a significant drop in temperature.

POST-SPAWN PERIOD: The period immediately following spawning characterized by poor fishing because fish are recuperating and relocating.

POST-SUMMER PERIOD: A period of the fish cycle following the Summer Period. It can mean about a week or more of terrific fishing.

PRECAMBRIAN SHIELD: The Canadian Shield. A geological rock formation covering much of eastern and central Canada and some of the north central U.S.A.

PREDATOR: An organism which feeds on another.

PREDATOR/PREY RELATIONSHIP: An interrelationship between a species and an accessible and suitable forage.

PREFERRED FOOD: Food or forage best suited to a species' basic needs.

PRE-SPAWN PERIOD: The period of the fish cycle immediately before spawning when fish position themselves near their spawning grounds.

PRE-SUMMER PERIOD: The period of the fish cycle immediately following post-spawn. Fish mood is often positive, but fish establish a wide variety of patterns.

REEDS: Bulrushes or rushes.

RESERVOIR: Impoundment. A place where water is collected and stored.

RIG: A fishing boat; the hook, snell and other terminal tackle for live bait fishing; assembling tackle.

SADDLE: A site where a structural element narrows before widening again.

SCHOOL (OF FISH): A number of fish of the same or similar species grouped together and moving as a unit to benefit from the defensive and/or feeding advantages associated with coordinated activity.

SHALLOW WATER ZONE: *A lake zone.* The area out to the first major drop-off.

SHIELD WATER: Body of water located on the Precambrian or Canadian Shield. Specifically, a body of water in an area where the basin and surrounding terrain has had their nutrient-producing rock and sediment layers eroded away by glaciers.

SLICK: A sand or clay bar, point or drop-off devoid of weeds, brush, rock or boulders, etc.; a section of calm surface water in a river.

SOFT BOTTOM: Bottoms (silt, mud, muck, marl, etc.) which are not hard.

SOCIAL CONDITION: One of three elements helping to determine a species' locational pattern. It includes population density, food availability, and competitive species and how these interrelate.

SNAKETROLLING: A system of *boat control* in which a lure or bait is trolled in a weaving manner to cover a wide area and a range of depth levels.

SPAWN PERIOD: A brief period of the fish cycle directly linked to seasonal progression and a range of suitable temperatures. When a species reproduces.

SPECIES: A group of closely-related organisms which can produce offspring.

SPEED CONTROL: One of two primary factors in bait or lure presentation. The other is depth.

SPEEDTROLLING: A system of *boat control* in which a lure is trolled behind a boat moving at fast speed.

SPOOKING: Frightening or "turning off" one or more fish.

STRAGGLERS: Fish lingering apart from others of their species after a movement.

STRIKING: An involuntary reflex action prompted by a bait or lure. Fish are made to bite. See *biting.*

STRUCTURAL CONDITION: One of three elements helping to determine a species' locational patterns. It includes bottom configuration, bottom content, water characteristics, vegetation types and water exchange rate.

STRUCTURAL ELEMENT: Most any natural or man-made, physical features in a body of water. See *bottom configuration.*

SUMMER PERIOD: A period of the fish cycle when fish generally hold to patterns established during the last part of the Summer Peak Period.

SUMMER PEAK PERIOD: A short period of the fish cycle which begins after the first hot spell that remains for several days and nights. Fish begin establishing summer patterns at the latter portion of this period.

SUSPENDED FISH: Fish which are hovering considerably above the bottom in open water.

TAPER: An area that slopes toward deeper water.

THERMOCLINE: The center area of temperature stratification in a body of water. Specifically, the division between the epilimnion and hypolimnion. Temperature changes very quickly.

TIGHT ACTION PLUG: A lure whose side-to-side movements are short and distinct.

TOPWATER PLUG: A floating lure designed for use on the water's surface.

TOTAL ENVIRONMENT: The body of water a species lives in, and any outside stimuli influencing it.

TRANSITION (BOTTOM): The point where one type of bottom material changes to another.

TRIGGER: One of eight lures or bait characteristics designed to stimulate positive responses from fish (action, color, size, shape, scent, sound, vibration, texture). Triggers appeal to the sensory organs of a species.

TURNOVER PERIOD: A very brief period of the fish cycle when some lakes or reservoirs are in turmoil. A mixing or "turning over" of the water takes place as cold water on the surface settles and warmer water from below rises. This turnover homogenizes lakes that have thermoclined (layered according to water temperature) in summer and reoxygenates the water.

TWO-STORY LAKE: A body of water in which warm water species inhabit the upper portion while cold water species inhabit the deeper portion.

WATER CHARACTERISTICS: The characteristics of a body of water, usually referred to in terms of mineral content (soft, few minerals; medium, some minerals; hard, many minerals). The amount of minerals determines fertility.

WATER EXCHANGE RATE: The rate at which water enters or leaves a body of water.

WORKING METHOD: An aspect of presentation consisting of triggers, controls, gear selection and technique.